CINEMA ARTHURIANA

GARLAND REFERENCE LIBRARY
OF THE HUMANITIES
(VOL. 1426)

CINEMA ARTHURIANA
Essays on Arthurian Film

edited by
Kevin J. Harty

GARLAND PUBLISHING, INC. • NEW YORK & LONDON
1991

© 1991 Kevin J. Harty
All rights reserved

Library of Congress Cataloging-in-Publication Data

Cinema Arthuriana : essays on Arthurian film / edited by Kevin J.
Harty.
    p. cm. — (Garland reference library of the humanities ; vol.
1426)
  Includes bibliographical references and index.
  Filmography: p.
  ISBN 0-8153-0088-3
  1. Arthur, King, in motion pictures. 2. Arthurian romances in
motion pictures. 3. Arthurian romances—Adaptations—History and
criticism. I. Harty, Kevin J. II. Series.
PN1995.9.A75C5   1991
791.43'651—dc20   91-17238
                                                          CIP

Printed on acid-free, 250-year-life paper
Manufactured in the United States of America

In memory of Jamie and Richard

and for

Adam, Chuck and Jeff, Jim, John and Russell,
Matt and Charlie, Martin, Michael, and Yves
with thanks.

You may grow old and trembling in your anatomies, you may lie awake at night listening to the disorder of your veins, you may miss your only love, you may see the world about you devastated by evil lunacies, or know your honour trampled in the sewers of baser minds. There is only one thing for it then—to learn. Learn why the world wags and what wags it. That is the only thing which the mind can never exhaust, never alienate, never be tortured by, never fear or distrust, and never dream of regretting. Learning is the thing for you.

—T. H. White,
The Once and Future King

TABLE OF CONTENTS

Contributors ix

Preface xiii

Introduction xvii

1. The Arthurian Legends on Film: An Overview
   Kevin J. Harty 3

2. An Enemy in Our Midst: *The Black Knight* and the American Dream
   Alan Lupack 29

3. The Arthurian Legend in French Cinema: *Lancelot du Lac* and *Perceval le Gallois*
   Jeff Rider, Richard Hull, and Christopher Smith 41

4. Gawain on Film
   Robert J. Blanch and Julian N. Wasserman 57

5. Two Films That Sparkle: *The Sword in the Stone* and *Camelot*
   Alice Grellner 71

6. Monty Python and the Medieval Other
   David D. Day 83

7. The Ironic Tradition in Arthurian Films Since 1960
   Raymond H. Thompson 93

8. Camelot Twice Removed: *Knightriders* and the Film Versions of *A Connecticut Yankee in King Arthur's Court*
   Kevin J. Harty 105

9. Mythopoeia in *Excalibur*
   Norris J. Lacy 121

10. Fire, Water, Rock: Elements of Setting in *Excalibur*
    Muriel Whitaker 135

11. Morgan and the Problem of Incest
    Jacqueline de Weever 145

12. Blank, Syberberg, and the German Arthurian Tradition
    Ulrich Müller
    (translated by Julie Giffin) 157

13. Filming the Tristan Myth: From Text to Icon
    Meradith T. McMunn 169

14. Arms and Armor in Arthurian Film
    Helmut Nickel 181

15. A Bibliography on Arthurian Film
    Kevin J. Harty 203

Appendix: An Alphabetical Filmography
   Kevin J. Harty 245

Index 249

CONTRIBUTORS

Robert J. Blanch is Professor of English at Northeastern University in Boston. He is author of *Sir Gawain and the Green Knight: A Reference Guide* (1984), editor of *Sir Gawain and Pearl: Critical Essays* (1966), and coeditor of *Chaucer in the Eighties* (1986) and *Text and Matter: New Critical Perspectives on the Pearl Poet* (1990).

David D. Day is a graduate student in English at Rice University in Houston, where he is writing a dissertation on the influence of Anglo-Saxon legal concepts on *Beowulf*. Prior to entering the graduate program at Rice, he studied and practiced law in the Houston area.

Jacqueline de Weever is Professor of English at Brooklyn College of the City University of New York. She is author of *The Chaucer Name Dictionary* (1988), as well as articles on *Sir Gawain and the Green Knight* and the portraits of Candace in the Alexander Romances.

Julie Giffin holds a Bachelor of Arts degree from the University of Vermont and is currently studying German philology at the University of Salzburg.

Alice Grellner is Professor of English at Rhode Island College in Providence and has held a Fulbright Research Award at Cambridge University and a Fulbright Lectureship in Krakow, Poland. She has contributed articles on the use of the Arthurian legend in modern fiction and film to *The Arthurian Encyclopedia* (1986).

Kevin J. Harty is Associate Professor of English at La Salle University in Philadelphia. He has previously published essays on medieval drama, Chaucer, and film versions of the legend of King Arthur. He is coauthor of *Writing for Business and Industry* (1987) and editor of *Strategies for Business and Technical Writing* (3rd ed., 1989).

Richard Hull received his B.A. in Film Studies in 1990 from Wesleyan University in Middletown, Connecticut. Now an independent filmmaker living in Seattle, he is the director of an animated film, *Eat or Be Eaten*, which won the 1990 Frank Capra Prize.

Norris J. Lacy is Professor of French at Washington University in St. Louis and an Honorary President of the International Arthurian Society. He is the author or editor of thirteen books, including *The Craft of Chrétien de Troyes* (1980), *The Arthurian Encyclopedia* (1986), and *The Arthurian Handbook* (1988).

Alan Lupack is Curator of the Rossell Hope Robbins Library at the University of Rochester. He is the editor of *"Arthur the Greatest King": An Anthology of Modern Arthurian Poetry* (1989) and *Arthurian Drama: An Anthology* (1991). He also edits *The Round Table: A Journal of Poetry and Fiction.*

Meradith T. McMunn, Professor of English at Rhode Island College, is working on a book examining the relationship between visual and verbal narration in medieval romance. She is editor of a forthcoming edition of the dramatic records of the Scottish court for the University of Toronto Press's REED series and coeditor of *Beasts and Birds of the Middle Ages: The Bestiary and Its Legacy* (1989).

Ulrich Müller is Professor of Medieval German Literature at the University of Salzburg. His special field of interest is medievalism, a topic about which he has written and edited books and articles and organized conferences.

Helmut Nickel received his Ph.D. from the Free University of Berlin in 1958 with a thesis about the medieval equestrian shield in western Europe. In 1960, he joined the Department of Arms and Armor at New York's Metropolitan Museum of Art. He went on to head the department from 1968 until his retirement in 1989.

Jeff Rider is Assistant Professor of French and Medieval Studies at Wesleyan University in Middletown, Connecticut. He is the author of articles on various aspects of medieval literature and coeditor with Peter Allen of *Reflections in the Frame: New Perspectives on the Study of Medieval Literature* (1991).

Christopher Smith received his B.A. in Film Studies and French in 1990 from Wesleyan University in Middletown, Connecticut, where he currently is the Director of Telefund for the Wesleyan Annual Fund. His senior project was a film entitled *Two Sisters*.

Raymond H. Thompson is Professor of English at Acadia University in Wolfville, Nova Scotia. The author of *The Return from Avalon: A Study of the Arthurian Legend in Modern Fiction* (1985) and an Associate Editor of *The Arthurian Encyclopedia* (1986), he is preparing for publication a series of interviews with authors of contemporary Arthurian literature.

Julian N. Wasserman is Professor of English at Loyola University (New Orleans). He is coauthor of *The Poetics of Conversion* (1977) and *Thomas Hardy and the Tristan Legend* (1983) and coeditor of *Chaucer in the Eighties* (1986), *Sign, Sentence, Discourse, Language in Medieval Thought and Literature* (1989), and *Text and Matter: New Critical Perspectives on the Pearl Poet* (1990).

Muriel Whitaker is Professor of English at the University of Alberta in Edmonton. Her publications include *Arthur's Kingdom of Adventure: The World of Malory's Morte Darthur* (1984) and *The Legends of King Arthur in Art* (1990).

PREFACE

Few legends have been recast more often or in more forms than that of Arthur. From *dux bellorum* to immortal king, from medieval romance to Broadway stage, from Malory to Monty Python and Tennyson to television, Arthur has been familiar to many centuries and in numerous languages and media. The Arthurian tradition is rich and complex, with every generation, indeed every writer and artist, reinterpreting the material in light of contemporary conceptions of the King or current artistic, ideological, or even political views. In part, it is this "transposability" of the legend that explains, or at least permits, its popularity.

—Norris J. Lacy,
"Preface," *The Arthurian Encyclopedia* (1986).

The 1980s witnessed what was an almost cyclic rekindling of interest in the legend of King Arthur, an interest publishers have rushed to meet with a whole range of studies discussing the various forms that the legend of the Once and Future King has taken. This collection is the first devoted to the phenomenon of what I have called cinema Arthuriana, a growing body of more than forty film versions of the legend of King Arthur that dates from at least 1904, when Edison produced a film of Wagner's opera *Parsifal*.

The essays that follow are meant to suggest the wealth of the Arthurian cinematic tradition. They give further evidence of what Norris J. Lacy calls the essential "transposability" of the Arthurian legend. The essays are, with two exceptions, first published here. My initial overview of Arthurian film and the bibliography of secondary materials at the volume's end were previously published in *Arthurian Interpretations* but have been expanded and substantially revised. I am grateful to the editor of *Arthurian Interpretations*, Henry Hall Peyton III, for his encouragement of my work on Arthurian film and for permission to reprint here materials originally published in that journal.

In compiling this collection, I have benefited from the help of a great number of people. I wish first to thank all those who have contributed essays, especially Norris J. Lacy, for his encouragement and advice on this and other Arthurian projects, and Alan Lupack, who generously granted me access to his collection of Arthurian film stills and lobby cards. My own contributions to this volume were first presented in several versions as papers at various scholarly meetings in sessions chaired by Alice Grellner of Rhode Island College, Maureen Fries of New York SUC at Fredonia, Veronica M. S. Kennedy of St. John's University, and Anne Howland Schotter of Wagner College. I am grateful to them for providing me with a forum in which to air my ideas. I would also like to thank Mildred Leake Day, editor of *Quondam et Futurus*, for her continuing encouragement of my work on Arthurian film.

For help on matters filmographic and bibliographic, I am indebted to a succession of staff members in the Interlibrary Loan Department at La Salle University: Joy Collins, now at Drexel University; Don Root, now at the American School in Uxbridge, England; Nancy Tresnan; and Stephen Breedlove. Others who have provided assistance were Geraldine Duclow, Curator of the Theatre and Film Collection at the Free Library in Philadelphia; the staff of the Theatre and Film Collection of the New York Public Library at Lincoln Center; Madeline F. Matz, Reference Librarian in the Library of Congress's Motion Picture, Broadcasting, and Recorded Sound Division; Jackie Morris, Viewing Service Assistant at the British Film Institute's National Film Archive; Fiona O' Brien, Cataloguer at the British Film Institute's National Film Archive; Elias Savada, Research Associate, the National Center for Film and Video Preservation at the American Film Institute in Washington,

D.C.; Betty Newton, Manager of Records Management at the National Office of the Boy Scouts of America in Irving, Texas; Charlotte Savarese of the Danish Film Institute in Copenhagen; and J. Canfield of the Booking Department of FilmBank Distributors Limited in London.

My original research into the largely uncharted area of Arthurian film was supported by a grant for computer searches generously supplied by Brother James Muldoon, F.S.C., Dean of Arts and Sciences at La Salle University. Subsequently, the University's Committee on Leaves and Grants provided a grant to help underwrite the preparation of the manuscript for this book. I am especially grateful to the La Salle's former Provost and the Committee's former chair, Brother Emery Mollenhauer, F.S.C., for his enthusiastic support of this and other projects. Finally, I am happy to thank my editor, Gary Kuris, and his colleagues at Garland for their assistance, encouragement and careful attention to my manuscript, W. Scott Roberts for assistance with wordprocessing, and Steve Durfee for assistance with desktop publishing.

Kevin J. Harty
Philadelphia
October 1990

INTRODUCTION

There have been more than forty cinematic transpositions of the legend of King Arthur, and since at least 1904 the major names in the film industry both before and behind the camera have been associated with Arthurian film. The following essays detail the extent of that association. In the first essay, I offer a survey of Arthurian film, suggesting the range of approaches directors have taken in bringing the complex legend of the Once and Future King to the screen.

Alan Lupack follows with an analysis of Tay Garnett's *The Black Knight*, a film too often simply dismissed or grouped as a swashbuckler along with a number of other Arthurian films made during the 1950s and the 1960s. However, noting that the mood of the country and of much of Hollywood in the 1950s had a tremendous influence on the types of films made and the messages they contained, Lupack argues that *The Black Knight*, a film made in 1954, has more in common with such contemporary non-Arthurian films as *Invasion of the Body Snatchers* than it does with films like *Knights of the Round Table* or *Prince Valiant*. *The Black Knight* can be seen as an allegory of the triumph of American values at a time when those values were perceived to be under attack by forces within and outside the country.

Jeff Rider, Richard Hull, and Christopher Smith next discuss what many have considered the two most consciously medieval examples of Arthurian film, Robert Bresson's *Lancelot du Lac* and Eric Rohmer's *Perceval le Gallois*. They attempt to explain the fascination that the Arthurian legend held for Bresson and for Rohmer, a fascination rooted in the difference between an "Anglo-American" and a "French" response to that legend. Rider, Hull, and Smith further discuss the particularly "Bressonian" and "Rohmerian" touches in the two films and the relationship between the two films and their sources in medieval French literature.

Robert J. Blanch and Julian N. Wasserman then range slightly farther afield in a detailed discussion of one of the principal figures of Arthurian romance, Arthur's nephew Gawain. A rich literary tradition developed around the character of Gawain, an elegant, courteous knight, courageous and at times rash when on the battlefield and lusty and seductive when off. With this tradition as their background, Blanch and Wasserman then discuss the role Gawain plays in five films: *Prince Valiant, Gawain and the Green Knight, Monty Python and the Holy Grail, Excalibur,* and *Sword of the Valiant.* What they find is that, despite his appearance in these films, Gawain—"Camelot's flower of courtesy, valor, and love"—is long overdue for a comprehensive interpretation on film.

The most influential twentieth-century retelling of the Arthuriad has been T. H. White's *The Once and Future King*, a fictional tetralogy based on Malory. Parts of White's opus have come to the screen in unusual form. Disney's *The Sword and the Stone* is a full-length animated feature; *Camelot* is a reworking of the Broadway stage play. Both, Alice Grellner argues, do justice to their source while also downplaying the darker views of human nature found in White.

David D. Day examines *Monty Python and the Holy Grail* in further detail by laying bare the broad method to the film's madness. What is being sent up in *Monty Python* is not the medieval world itself but latter-day interpretations, cinematic and otherwise, of that world. As Day points out, "No sooner does the film evoke some definite idea about the Middle Ages than it juxtaposes against it modern preconceptions or motivations that gave it rise, almost always with hilarious results." As evidence for his reading of the film, Day uses the posters advertising the film as well as close readings of scenes from the film.

Raymond H. Thompson begins his discussion of the ironic tradition in recent Arthurian film with a nod to the past, noting that a tradition of irony has been a hallmark of Arthurian literature since medieval times. Thompson's essay then focuses on four films: *The*

Sword in the Stone, Monty Python and the Holy Grail, The Unidentified Flying Oddball, and NBC Television's 1989 film version of *A Connecticut Yankee in King Arthur's Court.* Monty Python, Thompson argues, remains closest to the tradition of Arthurian irony by using such techniques as the double reversal and the running joke to link episodes and by aiming wide in its goofiness to advance its story line through a succession of increasingly zany episodes designed to deflate heroic pretense.

In the nineteenth century, the best-known American example of Arthuriana was Mark Twain's *A Connecticut Yankee in King Arthur's Court.* In surveying films based on the novel, I uncover a pattern of cinematic exposition that emphasizes the book's comic touches but that fails to come to terms with Twain's dark view of humanity. In contrast, George Romero's *Knightriders,* the most "American" Arthurian film, depicts a society that successfully encounters humanity's dark side and that, in an affirmation of the validity and endurance of the American dream, reaffirms the role of a modern-day Arthur as Once and Future King.

Perhaps the Arthurian film that has attracted the most critical and popular attention has been John Boorman's *Excalibur.* Boorman claimed to be making a film version of Malory's *Morte Darthur,* but as Norris J. Lacy points out there are some marked differences between the film and its putative source. By carefully comparing Boorman's film with Malory's text, Lacy finds that the filmmaker is highly original in his conception but much less successful in his treatment of the legend of Arthur.

Muriel Whitaker continues the discussion of *Excalibur* with an essay focusing on Boorman's use of fire, water, and rock in the film as a way of reconciling romance with history in visualizing the Arthurian world for a contemporary audience. Whitaker argues for a greater range of sources for the film than Boorman may be willing to admit, sources that shaped the film's imaginative construct.

Women are central to the Arthurian legend. Jacqueline de Weever discusses the crucial role of Morgan le Fay in Arthurian romance and five films based at least in part on that romance tradition: *Knights of the Round Table, Camelot, Monty Python and the Holy Grail, Knightriders,* and *Excalibur.* In each film and the romance tradition they reflect, she finds a feminist subtext whose meaning readers and viewers might do well to ponder.

Even during the early Middle Ages, Arthur's popularity extended beyond the borders of England and across Western Europe. There is a strong German tradition of Arthuriana with the unique feature of focusing on one of Arthur's knights, Perceval, while almost ignoring Arthur himself. That tradition is, as Ulrich Müller argues, well reflected in two recent German films, Richard Blank's film of Wolfram von Eschenbach's *Parzival* and Hans-Jürgen Syberberg's monumental version of Richard Wagner's *Parsifal*.

In the late Middle Ages, the legend of Tristan was conflated with that of Arthur and the Knights of the Round Table. Meradith T. McMunn, in a discussion of *L'Éternel Retour, Tristan et Yseult, Lovespell*, and *Fire and Sword*, compares the ways in which medieval manuscripts and twentieth-century cinema face a common problem of "visual narration" in presenting the Tristan legend as its moves from words on the page to visual images.

Among the aspects of Arthurian film that deserve attention is its use of arms and armor. Helmut Nickel, writing from his perspective as Curator Emeritus of Arms and Armor at New York's Metropolitan Museum of Art, provides a wide-ranging and lively survey of costuming practices in Arthurian film.

While this volume represents the first full-length discussion of Arthurian film, there have been sustained interest in and critical discussion of individual films since Edison's *Parsifal* first appeared in 1904. The bibliography and filmography at the end of this volume provide information about these films and their critical reception, including citations of reviews, screenplays, and other materials.

Arthurian film, like the legend that inspired it, is a continuing phenomenon. As we go to press, the trade newspapers have been carrying notices of a new film, *The Fisher King*, from director Terry Gilliam in which a homeless visionary (Robin Williams) leads an arrogant deejay (Jeff Bridges) into a medieval fantasy world where they search for the Holy Grail and are redeemed. Doubtless, other directors will in the future continue to give us their cinematic versions of the legend of Arthur.

Cinema Arthuriana

1.

The Arthurian Legends on Film: An Overview

Kevin J. Harty

The term used in the title of this book, "cinema Arthuriana"—unlike "film noir," "western," or "cliffhanger"—does not define a film genre. Rather, it defines a twentieth-century medium for redefining and reinterpreting the legend of the Once and Future King.[1] Cinema Arthuriana had its beginnings in 1904, when Edwin Porter brought a version of Wagner's *Parsifal* to the screen for Edison. Perceval and the quest for the Grail entered the Arthurian canon around 1190 in Chrétien de Troyes's *Le Conte du Graal*. In Chrétien, the Grail was simply a mysterious vessel, but *Le Conte* was left unfinished, possibly because of the poet's death. The story of the Grail, however, held a continuing fascination for later writers, who, beginning with the Burgundian poet Robert de Boron in the early thirteenth century, identified the Grail with the sacred vessel that first held the wine at the Last Supper and subsequently caught the blood of Christ at the Deposition from the Cross. In Wagner's opera, the Grail was further transformed into the central symbol of an elaborate set of Christian rituals.

In bringing *Parsifal* to the screen for Edison, Porter attempted to capitalize upon the successful New York production of the opera in German and a planned touring production in English. *Parsifal* opened in New York at the Metropolitan Opera House on December 24, 1903. Despite protests from the Wagner Verein that a staging of the opera outside of Germany would amount to a sacrilege undermining the composer's intentions, New York audiences and critics alike acclaimed the production as the highlight of the opera season.[2] A second production in English opened at Boston's Tremont Theatre on October 17, 1904, and moved to Manhattan's New York Theatre on October 31 before going on tour.[3]

Porter's film, the most ambitious and costly he made while working for Edison (Niver 74), is over 600 feet long. It consists of eight episodes that vary in length from 20 to 382 feet: "Parsifal Ascends the Throne," "Ruins of Magic Garden," "Exterior of Klingsor's Castle," "Magic Garden," "Interior of the Temple," "Scene Outside the Temple," "Return of Parsifal," and "In the Woods." Porter positioned his camera so that all shots are from the audience's point of view. While the film features elaborate sets and some trick photography, the acting is highly exaggerated to suggest that the actors are singing as they stand or move about the set. Edison himself hoped to synchronize phonographic recordings of the music from the opera with the film, but the technology for such a venture did not yet exist (Bush 607-608). Adding to the film's problems, the run of *Parsifal* had to be cut short when the owner of the copyright successfully sued Edison for using the script of the opera without permission and thus forced the film to be withdrawn from circulation (Spears 336).

Directors returned to Wagner's operas in three other silent films. In 1909, Albert Capellani directed the well-received *Tristan et Yseult* for the French production company S.C.A.G.L.-Pathé, and in 1912 Mario Caserini directed screen versions of both Wagner's *Siegfried* and *Parsifal* for the Ambrosio Company of Turin. Caserini's *Parsifal* is much more detailed in its presentation than Porter's, but again the technology did not yet exist to combine camera and gramophone successfully.[4] Despite continuing problems with technology, other Italian directors brought versions of operas by Donizetti and by Verdi to the screen.

In 1920, the French director Maurice Mariaud attempted a version of *Tristan et Yseut* for Louis Nalpas. Mariaud's film consists of six songs, each 650 meters long.[5] In his outdoor settings, the cliffs of the Riveria stand in for those of Cornwall and Ireland. Mariaud's attempts at grandeur notwithstanding, the film fails to portray the desperation and the ardor of the two lovers. Less static than Porter's film, less involved than Caserini's, Mariaud's film reveals a director overwhelmed by the story he attempted to bring to the screen (Fescourt 193).

The hall of the Grail King in Porter's Parsifal. *(Courtesy of the Library of Congress.)*

Victorian poetry, rather than Wagnerian opera, provided the source for the second example of cinema Arthuriana, Vitagraph's 1909 production of *Launcelot and Elaine.* A free rendering of Tennyson's poem from *The Idylls of the King*, the film afforded its director, Charles Kent, several opportunities to display cinematic innovations while also doing justice to its poetic subject matter. The film includes shots inside a dark cave and close-ups of the tournament in which Launcelot fights to win the Queen's favor. Critics praised the film for successfully balancing action with narration and for using elaborate scenic displays to heighten its settings. A trade note for the film declared: "With the aid of a half dozen captions the entire story of King Arthur's most famous knight is told so simply to be within the mental grasp of the unthinking, while the rich poetic atmosphere of the poem is fully preserved for those to whom Tennyson is an open book."[6] To promote the film on the day of its release, November 13, 1909, Vitagraph ran an advertisement in *Moving Picture World* declaring that the film: "was a thoroughly artistic production of Sir Alfred Tennyson's most charming poem. The highest developments of photography, the vast resources of the producing plant and the very acme of pantomimic acting combine in this subject to establish a new standard" (13 Nov. 1909: 672). When the film was rereleased in January, 1914, an item in *Bioscope* noted it was "one of the finest productions, and greatest of successes, in poetical pictures" (15 Jan. 1914: suppl. xxxi).

In contrast to the wealth of information we have about *Launcelot and Elaine*, we know very little about New Agency's 1910 film *King Arthur, or The Knights of the Round Table* other than it boasted a cast of more than 100 actors in a well-mounted production.

Edison teamed up with the Boy Scouts of America in 1917 to produce a second Arthurian film, *The Knights of the Square Table*, or *The Grail*. The film reflects attempts by the founder of the Scouting movement, Robert Baden-Powell, to model the organization in part on the fellowship of the Round Table.[7] With screenplay by National Field Scout Commissioner James A. Wilder, who also plays the role of the Scoutmaster in the film, *Knights of the Square Table* skillfully tells parallel stories of two groups of boys, one a gang of delinquents, whose leader's prize possession is a book recounting the quest for the Holy Grail, and the other a group of Scouts. Thanks to a series of misadventures, the leader of the delinquents is seriously wounded during a robbery in which he is forced to participate. The Grail Knight appears to him and cures him, after which he and his gang join up with the Scouts.

The most promising Arthurian film project of the decade turned out, unfortunately, to be one that was never completed. In 1916, D. W. Griffith announced plans for a spectacle, *The Quest of the Holy Grail*, based on the famous Grail frieze by Edwin Austin Abbey that decorates the second floor Delivery Room of the Boston Public Library. After obtaining the rights from Abbey's widow, Griffith, for reasons never explained, abandoned the project.

Cinema Arthuriana took a comic turn with Emmett J. Flynn's 1920 production for Fox of *A Connecticut Yankee at King Arthur's Court*, the first of several screen adaptations of Twain's novel. Twain himself might not have recognized the film as an adaptation of his novel. Where Twain presented his readers with Hank Morgan, the quintessential self-reliant New Englander ("a Yankee of the Yankees"), the film gives viewers Martin Cavendish, a wealthy young man whose mother wants him to marry Lady Grey Gordon. Cavendish in turn wants to marry his mother's secretary, Betty. One night, while reading about the Age of Chivalry, Cavendish is knocked unconscious by a burglar. In a dream, Cavendish finds himself in sixth-century England at Arthur's court. Thereafter, the film's plot follows the general outlines of Twain's novel until Cavendish reawakens from his dream and elopes with Betty.[8]

Despite its infelicities to its source, Flynn's film garnered much critical praise. Burns Mantle dubbed the film the second-best screen comedy of the year, counting Chaplin's *The Kid* as the first (51), while Frances Taylor Patterson saw the film as proof of the screen's potential for intelligent comedy rather than simply for slapstick (143-144). In adapting Twain's novel, those responsible for the film missed no opportunity to add touches of contemporaneity to the screenplay. References abound to the Volstead Act, Tin Lizzies, and the Battle of Argonne. Further, the subtitles rely heavily upon American slang and colloquialisms, and the army of rescuing knights arrives on motorcycles rather than on bicycles as they did in the novel. Finally, Flynn's film has a photographic and cinematic dignity that make it important as a film: "The Middle Ages are given pictorial eloquence in a manner that would have made Sir Walter Scott jealous" (Review, *Exceptional Photoplays* 2).

The success of Flynn's silent version of Twain's novel doubtless contributed to Fox's decision to make a talking version directed by David Butler and released in 1931 as *A Connecticut Yankee*. Butler's production, like Flynn's, takes some license with the details of Twain's plot. Here Hank Martin, played by Will Rogers, is knocked unconscious by an armored figure while trying to repair a radio for a slightly crazed customer who believes he is listening in on discussions from Arthur's Round Table. In a dream, Martin finds himself in England in the year 528. Where Twain's Hank had amazed Arthur's court and confounded Merlin by striking a match to produce fire "magically," Hank Martin uses a cigarette lighter. Motorcycles once again replace bicycles when the knights come to the rescue, but Martin's attacking forces also use a fleet of automobiles, machine guns, sawed-off shotguns, and several tanks and airplanes. The always practical Martin even installs a service station in Camelot where knights can get their armor washed, oiled, and polished. The film, which also features Myrna Loy as Morgan le Fay and Maureen O'Sullivan as Alisande, proved such a critical and commercial success that it was rereleased in 1936.

In the 1940s, cinema Arthuriana took a number of curious turns. Comedy combined with the British war effort in Marcel Varnel's

1942 film *King Arthur Was a Gentleman*. Friends present the film's hero, a Chaplinesque sad sack named Arthur King, with a sword he imagines to be Excalibur. When King is ordered to the front, imagination gives way to a belief in the sword as a talisman. No longer meek, King performs a series of heroic acts only to have his faith in magic, and his courage, shattered when his friends convince him that the sword is not Excalibur. While the film does contain some funny scenes and good songs, it is overly long and consistently misses "opportunities to indulge in fantasy" in an effective way (Quinlan 223).

The Second World War influenced another example of cinema Arthuriana, *L'Éternel Retour*, Jean Cocteau's 1943 modernized version of the Tristan story directed by Jean Delannoy. Here, however, the war's influence is disturbing. Made during the Occupation, the film is at times less than subtle in its racism. In his screenplay, Cocteau adds to the Tristan story a sinister, if not pathological, family, the Frossins: Gertrude, Marc's sister-in-law; her mad husband, Amédée; and their adult dwarf son, Achille. These three join forces with Marc to subvert at every turn the uncontrollable love that Patrice (Tristan) and Nathalie (Iseult) have for each other. Unfortunately, "the hero and the heroine in their blond supremacy may represent the Teutonic herrenvolk, whilst the Frossins are the degenerate products of the lower Romance races, the offal of a culture the Teutons should destroy, the Aryan burden" (Review, *Monthly Film Bulletin* 22). Properly the first Arthurian "art film," *L'Éternel Retour* streamlines the Tristan story while suggesting, almost Nietzsche-like, that legends live on—hence the significance of the film's title—reborn without the knowledge of their heroes or heroines. Indeed, as the film's final credits appear, Cocteau notes for the audience: "And so begins their real life..." (Cocteau 99). The main incidents of the legend are all present in updated form in the film, although the presence of Achille drew mixed responses from critics. Some saw him as one of the film's outstanding features, "a concentrated symbol of the world's evil and conventional hypocrisy," while others saw him as "just plain ghastly" and a major flaw.[9]

Twain's *A Connecticut Yankee in King Arthur's Court* returned to the screen in 1949 in Tay Garnett's production for Paramount starring Bing Crosby in the title role. Truer to the plot of Twain's novel than either the 1921 or the 1931 versions, this third film version is, nonetheless, in many ways the least successful. Crosby fans may well applaud his amply displayed musical talents, but Garnett makes

Susan Ashley (Evelyn Dall) and Arthur King (Arthur Askey) examining "Excalibur" in King Arthur Was a Gentleman.

little use of the cinematic possibilities of his source. The directorial method used throughout the film calls for the plot to advance not by dramatic interaction but rather by song mixed with silly dialogue. The film suffers from a lack of anything approaching Twain's comic genius, although at least one critic has read the film as an example of the archetype of the time-travel romance (Wachhorst 340-359).

In 1949, the Hollywood serial also weighed in with an Arthurian cliffhanger, Columbia's *Adventures of Sir Galahad*. True to its genre, this fifteen-part serial[10] presents a convoluted plot indebted to bits and pieces of the legend. Galahad must retrieve the missing Excalibur as the Saxons invade England. Merlin's role is ambivalent. Modred, disguised as the Black Knight, is clearly the villain, but Merlin at first uses his magic to harass Galahad, and Morgan le Fay helps him counter Merlin's magic and defeat the Saxons. Once the Saxons unite with Modred to kidnap Guinevere, Merlin joins forces with Galahad to retrieve Excalibur from the Lady of the Lake and to rescue the Queen. As reward for his bravery, Galahad is then made a Knight of the Round Table.

While the medieval setting for *Sir Galahad* allowed for some variation from the stock scenes typical of cliffhangers, this serial set, with one exception,[11] a pattern for Arthurian films made in the 1950s and the early 1960s. Despite the armor and the swordplay, the characters are really nothing more than cowboys chasing each other across medieval versions of the Great Plains of the Old West. The tradition of the movie western in fact combined with the technical possibilities afforded by CinemaScope to produce the next three examples of cinema Arthuriana: MGM's *The Knights of the Round Table* (1953), Twentieth Century Fox's *Prince Valiant*, and Warwick and Columbia's *The Black Knight* (both released in 1954). Although MGM claimed that its researchers in Hollywood and in England stuck "close to the facts," basing their script on Malory's "studious work,"[12] the film presents a curious jumble of Arthuriana.

Arthur's claim to the throne is disputed by his stepsister, Morgan le Fay, and her husband, Modred. Arthur wins the initial dispute, but Morgan and Modred continue to harass him. Lancelot, riding to a council called to settle the disputed succession, rescues Elaine, here Percival's sister, and joins Arthur in routing a group of knights sent by Modred to ambush the King. Arthur's subsequent pardon of Modred causes Lancelot to leave court in anger, whereupon he defeats a sinister Green Knight who has been holding a beautiful lady prisoner. The lady turns out to be Guinevere, whom Lancelot escorts safely back to court.

While it is clear in *Knights* that Lancelot and Guinevere are infatuated with each other, the film shows them exchanging only longing glances and one brief kiss, which Modred and Morgan happen to witness. Modred then accuses the Queen of treason. She is spared from the stake, but Lancelot is banished from the kingdom. In a rapid series of events, Modred then leads a rebellion against Arthur, whom he kills, and Lancelot casts Excalibur into the sea, kills Modred, pays a last visit to a now-cloistered Guinevere, and pledges his life and that of his son Galahad to reestablishing peace throughout England.

In its general outline, some details of the plot of *Knights* do bear a resemblance to earlier versions of the legend of King Arthur. But performances in the film are, as the review in the *New York Times* points out, on the level of "'Sir Lancelot went thataway'" and "'The rest of you knights follow me'" (17). What *Knights* presents is a sort

Guinevere (Ava Gardner) and Lancelot (Robert Taylor) in Knights of the Round Table.

of *Classics Illustrated* version of the legend of Arthur, in which the good guys wear white armor and the bad wear black.[13] The film is more notable for its use of CinemaScope—charging armies, clashing swords, and colorful pageantry in full wide-screen spectacle—than for its use of Arthurian materials.

With *Prince Valiant*, Hollywood turned from the *Classics Illustrated* to the comics, as Henry Hathaway filmed a version of Hal Foster's long-running strip.[14] Again, CinemaScope provided moviegoers with spectacular interior and exterior views, including a giant fire that engulfs a castle and serves as the film's climax. The plot, however, is fairly wooden.

As in the comic strip, Valiant is a Viking prince driven into exile. In a series of battles, he fights his former countrymen under the leadership of the traitorous Sir Brack both to regain his own throne and to help Arthur secure his. Valiant is successful in both endeavors and rewarded by Arthur for his deeds with knighthood. But *Prince Valiant*, like *Knights*, reflects Hollywood's continued fascination with medieval themes, even though directors there have often been unable to do justice to a period of history so obviously rich in cinematic possibilities. Hathaway, whose credits included the direction of more than sixty films, later disavowed the film, recalling that he had made the film "as a personal favor to Daryl [Zanuck]. I didn't particularly care one way or the other and the picture looked it" (Eyman 11).

The Black Knight is slightly more successful in its attempt to translate the story of Arthur to the screen. The Black Knight is the hero, a blacksmith named John, rather than the stock villain, whose character the *New York Times* compared to that of Hopalong Cassidy (Review 27). The film's plot is totally contrived—to overthrow Arthur, King Mark is in league with a band of Saracens who have turned Stonehenge into a temple for human sacrifice—although it does owe a small debt to several more orthodox Arthurian tales, especially in the character of John, who goes from commoner to knight and savior of the Round Table. It is possible to see in John's characterization an analogue to those of the young Perceval who bungles his way into knighthood and of the so-called "Fair Unknown" who, though young and inexperienced, eventually succeeds in deeds of derring-do.[15]

In 1963, four Arthurian films were released. The first, independent filmmaker Bruce Baillie's *To Parsifal*, is a meditation on the role of myth in contemporary life. Inspired by T. S. Eliot's *The*

Lancelot (Cornel Wilde) and Guinevere (Jean Wallace) in The Sword of Lancelot.

Waste Land as much as by Wagner's opera, *To Parsifal* is set in and around modern-day San Francisco. The director described the work as being about the legendary Parsifal (who does not appear in the film): "It is a tribute . . . to the hero and to the opera, although it is not an attempt to reproduce or 'cover' the opera itself" (Polt 51).

The Sword of Lancelot, released in Great Britain under the title *Lancelot and Guinevere*, retains some of the influence of the movie western that can be seen in Arthurian movies made in the 1950s. CinemaScope once again afforded ample opportunity for spectacle. However, in making the film, Cornel Wilde, who also starred in the title role, chose to concentrate less on swordplay and chase and more on the love between Lancelot and Guinevere and its tragic consequences. Indeed, Wilde was disappointed in the way the film was released by the studio. *Sword* won the Gold Prize in an Italian film festival and was critically well received in both England and the United States, but the publicity surrounding the film's release treated it like a swashbuckler (Coen 57-58).

Loosely based on Malory's *Morte Darthur*, Wilde's film is the first to deal unhesitatingly with the adultery between Lancelot and Guinevere. The film's Arthur, however, is much older than his counterpart in Malory. He is in fact an old man married to a much younger woman, so the film cannot fairly balance the conflict among the principals in the love triangle. Central to this conflict is the tension between love and loyalty, between marriage and friendship. While loyalty is a central theme in many of Wilde's films (Kaminsky 23), *The Sword of Lancelot* so clearly favors the two lovers that "this Lancelot and Guinevere deserved a happy ending" (Review, *Films and Filming* 24). Instead, Wilde has Lancelot first win Guinevere from Modred for Arthur, then later rescue her from the stake, only finally to lose her to the convent.

In Nathan Juran's *Siege of the Saxons*,[16] Arthur is ailing as the Saxons eagerly await his death in hopes of overrunning England unopposed. Arthur foolishly entrusts his safety to a former champion, Edmund of Cornwall, who is in league with the Saxons. Edmund's first attempt to murder Arthur and his daughter, Katherine, fails thanks to the efforts of an outlaw, Robert Marshall. Edmund's second attempt on Arthur's life is successful, but Robert is able to rescue Katherine. She then refuses an offer of marriage from Edmund, who lays claim to the throne, as Robert and Katherine seek out Merlin. Edmund's coronation is interrupted by the wizard, who challenges the pretender to pull Excalibur from its scabbard. Edmund fails, Katherine succeeds, civil war ensues, Katherine and Robert are victorious, and, with order once more restored in the kingdom, Katherine and Robert marry and rule England.

Siege of the Saxons has, of course, no basis in previous versions of the Arthurian legend. The influence of the movie western on this British-made film is apparent,[17] as is its debt to the legend of a later medieval hero, Robin Hood. Robert Marshall does not steal from the rich and give to the poor, but his status as an outlaw nonetheless loyal to the true king echoes the legendary loyalty of Robin Hood to the absent Richard I, often chronicled on film and television.

The stories of the Sword in the Stone and of Arthur's early childhood provide the plot of the first full-length animated version of the legend of Arthur, Disney's *The Sword in the Stone*, also made in 1963. Loosely based on the first book of *The Once and Future King*, T. H. White's tetralogy, the Disney film recounts the education of Arthur, better known as Wart, a young boy intent on learning to be a squire to his loutish foster brother, Kay. Wart's education takes an unexpected turn when he meets Merlin and his talking owl, Archimedes. Merlin soon takes charge of Wart's education, turning him in quick succession into a fish, a squirrel, and a sparrow so that he may learn a series of valuable lessons about life.[18]

Merlin's nemesis is Mad Madame Mim, an evil witch whom Merlin eventually defeats in a magical battle of wits. Wart, meanwhile, still a would-be squire, forgets Kay's sword and pulls Excalibur from the stone for Kay to use in a tournament. At first, no one believes Wart's feat, but when he repeats the deed, he is proclaimed king. The film is unique in its portrayal of Arthur's childhood, a topic always murky in medieval versions of the legend of Arthur. Its treatment of the topic is limited to some degree by its genre, but as a cartoon *Sword* is vintage Disney.[19]

White's *The Once and Future King* was also the source for the next example of cinema Arthuriana, Joshua Logan's 1967 film version of the Broadway musical *Camelot*. Both the play and the film are in a way generic oddities. They are musical tragedies, not musical comedies.[20] The film explores a wide range of ideas: the frailty of romantic love, marital infidelity, the betrayal of friendship, the destruction of ideals, and the triumph of right over might. As in the musical play, the downfall of Camelot is clearly caused by the tension created in Arthur's court by the Arthur-Guinevere-Lancelot triangle.

While admitting to some dissatisfaction with the Broadway play, Logan in no way deepened the story he transferred to the screen. His *Camelot* simply presents, rather than examines or explains, the issues it raises. To his credit, Logan rejected the usual gloomy Hollywood backlots for the spectacle afforded by location shots in Spain. But, following White's lead, Logan also tinkered with inherited tradition. While White had made Lancelot ugly—"He looked like an African ape" (317)—Logan, thanks to his casting and direction of Franco Nero in the role, created a Lancelot who is an overly pristine, sanctimonious cad and who, within minutes of raising a knight he has just killed from the dead, beds Guinevere.[21] For screen audiences, Cornel Wilde's earlier *Sword of Lancelot* brought the adultery of Lancelot and Guinevere out into the open; Logan's film continues to focus on that love and its tragic consequences, but on a one-dimensional level.

In the 1970s, no fewer than nine films were made about aspects of the legend of Arthur. In 1972, the French director Yvan Lagrange went to Iceland to film an operatic version of the story of Tristan.

Tristan et Iseult adds nothing new to the legend of the doomed lovers; the director's intent was otherwise. Lagrange subtitled his film "Opera en scope-couleurs" to signal his interest in harmonizing the conflicting artistic demands and in exploring the conflicting artistic subtleties afforded by working simultaneously in several media. Such a multimedia approach focuses the viewer's attention on the conflict between love and war that Lagrange sees at the heart of the legend (Cornand 103-104). While not always successful, the film is nonetheless an interesting attempt to tell an old tale in a new way.

Less successful is Stephen Weeks's *Gawain and the Green Knight*, released in 1973. Anyone even vaguely familiar with the anonymous fourteenth-century poem *Sir Gawain and the Green Knight*, the finest Arthurian romance in Middle English, will find little to recognize in this film. Those more widely read in Arthuriana will find in the film a mindless pastiche of elements drawn from medieval tales of Yvain, Gawain, Perceval, and others. In dealing with medieval themes, Weeks, like many of his Hollywood counterparts, is unable to tell a straight story and instead tries to conflate many unrelated storylines into one whose whole is greater than the sum of its parts. The result is either ludicrous or ponderous, depending upon the viewer's background and point of view. Weeks himself blamed United Artists for the film's final messy state (Berry 7), but in a bigger budgeted remake ten years later, *Sword of the Valiant*, Weeks again presented a film with little relationship to the poem that was his source and again proved himself a director incapable of dealing with the complexities of one of the masterpieces of medieval literature.

Much more successful, and indeed one of the best examples of cinema Arthuriana, is Robert Bresson's 1974 film *Lancelot du Lac*. For the general outlines of its plot, Bresson's film owes much to the *Mort Artu*, the final section of the great thirteenth-century prose retelling of the legend of Arthur known as the Vulgate Cycle.[22] Bresson's interests include, however, more than simply charting the demise of Arthur's court. Originally entitled *The Grail*, the film is an apocalyptic meditation on the downfall of the Middle Ages because of the era's loss of a sense of the spiritual, which the Grail—intentionally absent from the film (Williams 10-13)—symbolizes.

Bresson turns the traditional Arthurian triangle into a square. Gawain's love of Guinevere, Lancelot, and Arthur suggests a pattern of conflicting loyalties. The film opens with Lancelot's unsuccessful return from the quest for the Grail. His failure to learn from the quest the value of the spiritual over the secular sets into motion a pattern of events that bring about the downfall of Camelot. But the film is at times—thanks to Bresson's conscious use of anachronisms (Estève 102-108)—strikingly modern in its concerns. No one, the film seems to say, finds salvation, not Arthur, not his court, especially not Lancelot who dies in battle staring heavenward but murmuring Guinevere's name.

In light of Bresson's film, *Monty Python and the Holy Grail*, made in 1975, might seem a movement from the sublime to the ridiculous. There is, though, more to the Python film than slapstick. What is being lampooned in *Monty Python* is not the legend of Arthur, but rather earlier film treatments of that legend. Against carefully chosen authentic backdrops of castles and their ruins, the film presents what may at first only appear to be the broad satire and farce that have become the Python trademark: holy hand grenades, killer rabbits, a castle of maidens wishing X-rated punishment for their sin of lighting a Grail-shaped beacon in the tower, and so forth.[23] But there is a method to the madness here. (Terry Jones, the film's codirector, knows what he is about: he is the author of a scholarly study of the character of the knight in medieval literature.[24]) The film abounds in conventions from and threads of the legend of Arthur, as well as in Hollywoodesque swashbuckling adventures, spectacles, and fights to the death—and just a note or two of Bresson's gloom and doom sent up, of course, comically.

King Arthur, the Young Warlord, also made in 1975, seems not to have been released commercially, although it does exist as a ninety-minute videotape directed by Sidney Hayers, Patrick Jackson, and Peter Sasdy. The film presents Arthur, as the narrator solemnly announces, "a Celtic warrior in a time of tribal dissension and battle whose legend surpassed his deeds." Arthur's possible historicity has its basis in the Celtic attempts in the fifth century to repel successive waves of Saxon invaders. This film pits Arthur, here brother to Kai and son to Llud, against Saxons, Picts, and Jutes, as well as against Mark of Cornwall, in his attempt to save his people. At the film's conclusion, Arthur has had only limited success in this attempt. In literary treatments, Arthur is successful not only in saving his people but also in uniting all of England and eventually in extending his rule across much of western Europe.

Clearly, the most authentically medieval example of cinema Arthuriana is Eric Rohmer's 1978 *Perceval le Gallois*. Rohmer consciously set out to make a new kind of film on a medieval theme. Rejecting earlier attempts by Bresson, Olivier (in *Henry V*), and Hollywood in general as unrealistic in their portrayals of the Middle Ages, he sought to "rediscover the vision of the Medieval period as it saw itself" (Tesich-Savage 51-52). Unlike previous examples of cinema Arthuriana, Rohmer's film carefully follows a medieval text, Chrétien de Troyes's twelfth-century poem *Le Conte du Graal*, for his treatment of the story of Perceval. *Perceval Le Gallois* is not a film of Wagner's opera, but a film that unfolds narratively in the manner of a medieval romance.[25]

Rohmer cuts from Chrétien's unfinished text the final adventures of Gawain in order to focus on Perceval. Then, where Chrétien concludes his narrative about Perceval with a comment that Perceval simply learned how Christ was crucified on Good Friday, Rohmer has his Perceval take the central role in a version of a medieval passion play, where the hero's spiritual rebirth is shown as a true union with Christ. Where Bresson had shown the spiritual bankruptcy of the Middle Ages, Rohmer finds the soul of the period and in it a lesson for the present day.

Twain's *Connecticut Yankee* returned to the screen in 1979 in a film released by Disney as *The Spaceman and King Arthur* in Great Britain and as *The Unidentified Flying Oddball* in the United States. In the film, a NASA malfunction hurls Tom Trimble, an astronaut in full space suit, and his robot companion and look-alike, Hermes, back to the sixth century, where Trimble must save not only himself but also Arthur. Trimble has two nemeses, Merlin, who is out to undo him, and Mordred, who is out to undo Arthur. With some slight variation, the film retains one of the funniest scenes from Twain's novel in a comic subplot involving Trimble, Hermes, and Alisande, who goes about with a goose whom she claims is her bewitched father in tow. In Twain, Hank had to endure the continued company of a herd of swine whom Sandy was convinced were bewitched maidens (Chapter 20). If not the most successful of film adaptations of Twain's novel, *Oddball* may be the funniest.

The Legend of King Arthur takes a slightly more traditional approach to Arthurian materials. A coproduction of the BBC, Time-Life Television, and the Australian Broadcasting Commission, this program, a series of eight thirty-minute episodes, was originally shown on BBC in October and November, 1979. More recently, it has been aired in the United States on the Arts and Entertainment Cable Network. *Legend* straightforwardly tells of the rise and fall

The Arthurian Legends on Film

of the Round Table by focusing on the continuing jealousy of Morgan le Fay and the continuing passion of Lancelot and Guinevere.

In contrast, another 1979 film, *Tristan and Isolt*—released on videotape as *Lovespell*—strays very far from any recognizable source, medieval or otherwise. Directed by Tom Donovan for Clar Productions, the film starred Richard Burton as King Mark, one of a series of roles Burton took at the time in an effort to earn money at the expense of his reputation as a serious actor.

In the 1980s, the tradition of cinema Arthuriana continued, with some of the most notable films coming from German directors. In 1980, Richard Blank directed a ninety-minute version of *Parzival* for West German television. Blank's film differs from earlier screen versions of the story of the Grail in two ways. First, Blank used Wolfram von Eschenbach's *Parzival*, written sometime after the year 1200, for his source. Wolfram's poem, which runs to nearly 25,000 lines in rhymed couplets, is the acknowledged masterpiece of German literature of the High Middle Ages. Wolfram obviously knew Rohmer's source, Chrétien's uncompleted French poem, which Wolfram dismissed as doing injustice to the story of the Grail. In Wolfram's version, the court of Arthur and the Grail legend are clearly linked in the character of Parzival, who is related to Arthur through his father and to the Grail society through his mother. Second, Blank's approach to the legend of the Grail, which abounds with references to the modern world, provides a more straightforward and accessible reading of that legend than previous examples of cinema Arthuriana were able to bring to the screen.[26]

In 1981, a second German director, Veith von Fürstenberg, made his debut with a film of the Tristan story, *Feuer und Schwert—Die Legende von Tristan und Isolde*. Von Fürstenberg's source is not the version of the legend handed down through opera but rather the much distilled medieval tale of the fated lovers. To his medieval sources, themselves often a jumble of conflicting details, von Fürstenberg adds some personal touches. In the film, Isolde knowingly gives Tristan the love potion to drink. Isolde bears Tristan a child, and Tristan, once rejected by Isolde, who hopes to end the civil war in Cornwall between forces loyal to her husband and forces loyal to her lover, turns marauder pillaging the countryside. While not a commercial success, the film does offer a reading of the legend notable for the poetry of its visual images.[27]

More successful, and much more controversial, is Hans-Jürgen Syberberg's film version of Wagner's *Parsifal* (1982)—*the* opera movie of all times according to Jack Kroll (49). Running a total of 255 minutes, Syberberg's film presents the opera in a claustrophobic labyrinth that is constructed out of the cracks and crevices of an enormous model of Wagner's death mask. The final scene takes place before a double cave eventually revealed to be the nostrils of that mask. While inadequate technology had hindered earlier efforts to bring Wagner's opera successfully to the screen, Syberberg's production succeeds by using elaborate sets—some oversized, some miniature—puppets, expert dubbing, and the daring twist of having the title character played alternately by a man and a woman. Parsifal, the savior, is, as Thomas Elsaesser points out, "male *and* female, and his saving grace [is] the recognition of both as parts of the same self" (138).[28]

Equally controversial is John Boorman's 1981 film *Excalibur*. Critical reaction to the film was sharply divided. Pauline Kael dismissed the film's dialogue as "near-atrocious" (146), while Michel Ciment, in a long survey of Boorman's career, saw the film as the culmination of Boorman's own cinematic quest (179-201). Boorman himself indicated that he was determined "to tell the whole story of the *Morte D'Arthur*," although he saw Malory as "the first hack writer" (Kennedy 33). His comments not withstanding, *Excalibur* is not a cinematic translation of Malory. Boorman has, instead, been free with his sources, conflating materials as is directorial practice, to suit his needs. Arthur is the Grail King, but the Grail is stripped of any Christian associations. In a film where the king and the land are one, the Grail is the central symbol of a murkily defined pagan fertility ritual. Boorman's vision of the Grail owes more to Jessie Weston than it does to Malory.[29] The central character in the film is Merlin, who links the past and the future, and events in the film revolve around a trinity of women, Igrayne, Guinevere, and Morgana (Boorman's conflation of the traditionally separate characters of Morgawse, Nimue, and Morgan le Fay), and their complex relations with Arthur, Lancelot, and Merlin.

George Romero's *Knightriders* (1981) offers a different vision of the quest, a quest not for the Grail but for the American dream. Set in western Pennsylvania, *Knightriders* examines the values of Arthurian society as they are practiced by a group of motorcycle stunt riders. Romero's film presents the usual cast of Arthurian characters—though Morgan here is a combination of Morgan le Fay and

Modred, along with a Friar Tuck and an assortment of stock heavies and bad guys. Romero's surface debt is to the film western by way of its subgenre the biker film, but Romero's deeper debt is, as he indicated in an interview, to the long tradition that sees Arthur as Once and Future King: "The motorcycle culture seemed to fit the Arthurian story. The bikers are a romanticized image, at least in this country. They have their own culture and attitude of this is us, and the rest of the world is you. That made sense on a pure story level, and as allegory" (Burke-Block 25). In the final analysis, *Knightriders* presents a utopic quest, a meditation on the possibility of recreating the Arthurian ideal in a troubled modern-day America.

Two Arthurian films were made in 1982. Dorian Cowland's *Excalibur, the Raising of the Sword*, which premiered at the Welsh International Film Festival in 1983, tells the story of a youthful Merlin's search for Excalibur, and Clive Donner filmed a three-hour version of the legend of Arthur entitled *Arthur the King* for CBS. The network, however, promptly shelved the completed product until it was finally shown on television on April 26, 1985. In Donner's version, an Alice-like tourist falls into a hole at Stonehenge and lands in the company of Merlin and his lover, Niniane. Together, they ploddingly rehearse the story of Arthur and the Knights of the Round Table.

More garbled than plodding is Stephen Weeks's already-mentioned remake of his earlier film of *Sir Gawain and the Green Knight*. The remake, entitled *Sword of the Valiant*, was released in 1983. It differs from its predecessor only in terms of budget—Weeks spent much more money on this version with little to show for the increased investment—and of cast. Sean Connery plays an iridescent Green Knight, while Trevor Howard is cast as a very tired and much too old King Arthur.

Much more interesting, if not always successful, was a BBC "silent version" of Malory, aired in 1984 as *The Morte D'Arthur*. Part drama, part mime, the film stars the Royal Shakespeare Company's John Barton as the knight-prisoner Sir Thomas Malory, who narrates the events of the last two books of the *Morte*. As Barton speaks, Malory's narrative comes to life in a series of choreographed scenes enacting the collapse of the Arthurian ideal.

A Russian Arthurian film, *Novye Prikluchenia Janke pri Dvore Kovola Artura (The New Adventures of a Connecticut Yankee at King Arthur's Court)*, began production in 1987 under the direction of Viktor Gres. Dovzhenko Studios released the film the following year. Despite its title, the film is not just a version of Twain's novel but a fantasy based on all his works.

Twain's *Connecticut Yankee* returned to the screen in a telemovie that NBC aired on December 18, 1989, a year that coincidentally marked the hundredth anniversary of the novel's publication. Primarily a vehicle for two popular television performers, this film cast Keshia Knight Pulliam from *The Cosby Show* as the Yankee, Karen Jones, and Michael Gross from *Family Ties* as Arthur. The Yankee introduces Camelot to, among other things, karate, aerobics, Polaroid cameras, Walkmans, and tape recorders. While the general outline of Twain's novel remains intact, those responsible for this silly telemovie were scrupulous in avoiding any of the substantive or controversial issues raised by the novel.

Arthurian film proved it could be both traditional and modern in Jytte Rex's 1989 film *Isolde*. In Rex's retelling, the standard triangle is played out among Isolde and two characters simply identified as the Warrior and the Husband in a film that successfully balances action with metaphysical speculation.[30] Finally, 1989 witnessed the distribution of an Arthurian blockbuster, *Indiana Jones and the Last Crusade*, the third film in Steven Spielberg's Jones trilogy.[31] The film chronicles a modern-day quest for the Holy Grail—here, with its traditional identification as the cup Christ used at the Last Supper, a guarantor of the final triumph of good over evil.

Few legends have been told as often or in as many forms as that of Arthur, King of the Britains. For more than eighty years, directors and screenwriters have found in that legend a ready source for their films: some good, some bad, some serious, some more light-handed. As Norris J. Lacy points out in his preface to *The Arthurian Encyclopedia*, Arthur is "a timeless ideal, born in the Middle Ages but living anywhere, at any time" (vii). The films discussed here further attest Arthur's survival as the Once and Future King.

NOTES

[1] For the purposes of this discussion, cinema Arthuriana includes films that directly treat the story of Arthur and the Knights of the Round Table, the story of the Grail, and the story of Tristan and Isolde. Excluded from the category are two types of films. The first includes films such as *Seven Faces of Dr. Lao* (1964), which treat Arthurian characters only in passing. (Here, one of the title character's faces is that of Merlin.) The second includes films such as the 1984 film version of Bernard Malamud's *The Natural*, which treat Arthurian themes only indirectly or analagously. (In

The Arthurian Legends on Film

The Warrior (Kim Jansson) and Isolde (Pia Vieth) in Jytte Rex's Isolde. *(Courtesy of the Danish Film Institute.)*

this case, a Perceval-like Roy Hobbs joins the Knights, a baseball team managed by a "wounded" Pop Fisher.)

[2] On the controversy surrounding the New York production, its critical reception, and the touring production in English, see *New York Times* 27 Dec. 1903: 12; 28 Aug. 1904: 13; 14 Sept. 1904: 9; 18 Oct. 1904: 6; 23 Oct. 1904: 4. 6; and 30 Oct. 1904: 4. 3.

[3] An advertisement for Edison's film (*New York Clipper* 12 Nov. 1904: 895) mentions both New York productions of the opera and announces that a "complete illustrated lecture is furnished with each film."

[4] For a summary of the film's plot, see *Moving Picture World* 28 Dec. 1912: 1307-1308.

[5] I have not seen this film, and my source for information concerning it—Richard Abel, *French Cinema: The First Wave, 1915-1929* (Princeton: Princeton University Press, 1984)—presents contradictory information, listing the film's title twice as *Tristan et Yseut* and once as *Tristan et Yseult* and dating the film twice as 1921 and once as 1920 (17, 162, and 655).

[6] For reviews of the film, see *Moving Picture World* 27 Nov. 1909: 759; and *New York Dramatic Mirror* 20 Nov. 1909: 16. (The former review is reprinted in *Selected Film Criticism, 1896-1911*, ed. Anthony Slide. [Metuchen, N.J.: Scarecrow, 1982], p. 58.) The trade note appears in *Moving Picture World* 23 Oct. 1909: 565.

[7] Michael Rosenthal traces Baden-Powell's successive statements, beginning in 1904, linking the Scouting movement with the legend of Arthur. See *The Character Factory: Baden-Powell and the Origin of the Boy Scout Movement* (New York: Pantheon, 1986).

[8] For a complete synopsis of the film's plot, see Scott O'Dell, *Representative Photoplays Analyzed* (Hollywood, Calif.: Palmer Institute of Authorship, 1924), pp. 248-249.

[9] Compare, for instance, the review in *Variety* 17 Dec. 1947: 8, 22, and that in the *New York Times* 5 Jan. 1948: 15. The film also got into trouble with the Catholic church. The Legion of Decency banned *L'Éternel Retour* by placing it in its Class C, or Condemned, category because the film "presents a glorification of immoral actions" and "contains suggestive sequences" ("Legion Bans French Film," *New York Times* 29 Mar. 1948: 18).

[10] The fifteen episodes were "Stolen Sword," "Galahad's Daring," "Prisoners of Ulric," "Attack on Camelot," "Galahad to the Rescue," "Passage of Peril," "Unknown Betrayer," "Perilous Adventure," "Treacherous Magic," "The Sorcerer's Spell," "Valley of No Return," "Castle Perilous," "The Wizard's Vengeance," "Quest for the Queen," and "Galahad's Triumph." See Alan G. Barbour, *The Serials of Columbia* (Kew Gardens, N.Y.: Screen Facts Press, 1967), [p. 47].

[11] The one exception was a 1953 Spanish film version of the opera *Parsifal* directed by Daniel Mangrane. For a review of this not widely distributed film, see *Film français* 488 (13 Nov. 1953): 20.

[12] MGM documents the extensive research that supposedly made *Knights* possible in an unpaginated souvenir booklet distributed when the film was released, *Knights of the Round Table* (New York: Al Greenstone, 1954).

[13] For further discussion of *Knights* as the *Classics Illustrated* version of the legend of Arthur, see the review of the film when it was rereleased in 1963 in *Films and Filming* 5 (June 1963): 37.

[14] The strip first appeared on February 13, 1937. See Wilhelm J. Fuchs, "Prinz Eisenherz," *Jugend, Film, Fernsehen* 19. 3 (1975): 183-184.

[15] The story of the Fair Unknown can be found in medieval French, Italian, German, and English literature. It was first told in a verse romance, *Le Bel Inconnu*, written in the late twelfth century by Renaut de Beaujeu.

[16] The film was released in the United States as *Siege of the Saxons* and in England as *King Arthur and the Siege of the Saxons*.

[17] Interestingly, *Siege* even shares some stock footage with *The Black Knight* for scenes of battles and castle panoramas.

[18] In White's novel, Arthur is turned into a fish, an ant, a wild goose, and a badger.

[19] This view of the film was not shared by all critics when *Sword* was released in 1963. See the excerpts from reviews reprinted in *Film Facts* 6 (Dec. 1963): 286-287.

[20] White himself made this point in reacting with considerable annoyance to negative reviews of the play from critics who wanted something more akin to *My Fair Lady*. See "What It's Like to Be Translated into 'Camelot,'" *Vogue* 15 Feb. 1961: 117. In general, the film received bad notices. For an exception, see *Variety* 25 Oct. 1967: 6.

[21] Logan discusses the film and its making in *Movie Stars, Real People, and Me* (New York: Delacorte, 1978), pp. 194-213.

[22] Jane Sloan presents a detailed synopsis of the film's screenplay in *Robert Bresson: A Guide to References and Resources* (Boston: Hall, 1983), pp. 83-88; however, Sloan wrongly identifies the film's source as *Le Chevalier de la Charette* by Chrétien de Troyes.

[23] For the screenplay and a number of production-related documents, see *Monty Python and the Holy Grail (Book)*. (New York: Methuen, 1977).

[24] Chaucer's Knight: *The Portrait of the Medieval Mercenary* (1980; rpt. New York: Methuen, 1985).

[25] The "medievalism" of the film's narrative technique is discussed by Lucy Fisher in "Roots: The Medieval Tale as Modernist Cinema," *Field of*

Vision 9-10 (Spring 1980): 21-25, 33. For Rohmer's screenplay, see *L'Avant-scene cinéma* 221 (1 Feb. 1979): 9-64.

[26]Showings of Blank's film have been limited to German television. My sources for information about the film are *The Arthurian Encyclopedia*, ed. Norris J. Lacy et al. (New York: Garland, 1986), p. 49; and Ulrich Müller, "Parzival 1980—Auf der Bühne, im Fernsehen und im Film," in *Mittelalter-Rezeption II*, ed. Jürgen Kühnel et al. (Göppingen: Kümmerle, 1982), pp. 623-640.

[27]Von Fürstenberg's film was shown at Cannes on May 20, 1981. See the review in *Variety* 1 June 1981: 18, and the brief entry in *The Arthurian Encyclopedia*, p. 606.

[28]The most insightful comments on *Parsifal* remain the director's. See Syberberg's *Parsifal: Ein Filmessay* (Munich: Heyne, 1982).

[29]For a detailed discussion of this point, see Martin B. Shichtman's "Hollywood's New Weston: The Grail Myth in Francis Ford Coppola's *Apocalypse Now* and John Boorman's *Excalibur*," *Post Script* 4 (Autumn 1984): 35-48.

[30]Of tangential interest is a second Scandinavian film, Hrafn Gunnlaugsson's *I Skugga Hrafnsina* (*In the Shadow of the Raven*), released in 1988, which uses the names of Isolde and Trausti (Icelandic for Tristan) for the principal characters and includes a love potion, but which is otherwise a swashbuckling film about a blood feud in the tradition of the Icelandic sagas.

[31]While *Last Crusade* was the third film in the trilogy to be made, it is the first chronologically in its recounting of the hero's life and adventures.

WORKS CITED

Berry, Dave. "Stephen Weeks." *Film* 37 (May 1976): 6-7.

Burke-Block, Candace. "The *Film Journal* Interviews . . . George Romero on 'Knightriders.'" *Film Journal* 84 (4 May 1981): 25.

Bush, W. Stephen. "Possibilities of Synchronization." *Motion Picture World* 2 Sept. 1911: 607-608.

Ciment, Michel. *John Boorman*, trans. Gilbert Adair. London: Faber, 1986.

Cocteau, Jean. *Three Screenplays*, trans. Carol Martin-Sperry. New York: Grossman, 1972.

Coen, John. "Producer/Director: Cornel Wilde." *Film Comment* 6 (Spring 1970): 52-61.

Cornand, André. Review of *Tristan et Iseult*. *Image et son* 284 (May 1974): 103-104.

The Arthurian Legends on Film

Elsaesser, Thomas. Review of *Parsifal. Monthly Film Bulletin* 50 (May 1983): 137-138.

Estève, Michel. *Robert Bresson.* Rev. ed. Paris: Éditions Seghers, 1974.

Eyman, Scott. "'. . . I Made Movies . . .': An Interview with Henry Hathaway." *Take One* 5 (Feb. 1976): 6-12.

Fescourt, Henri. *Le Foi et les montaignes.* Paris: Montel, 1959.

Kael, Pauline. "Boorman's Plunge." *New Yorker* 57 (20 Apr. 1981): 146-151.

Kaminsky, Stuart. "Getting Back to Basics with Cornel Wilde." *Take One* 5 (Oct. 1976): 22-24.

Kennedy, Harlan. "The World of King Arthur According to John Boorman." *American Film* 6 (Mar. 1981): 30-37.

Kroll, Jack. Review of *Parsifal. Newsweek* 101 (31 Jan. 1983): 49.

Lacy, Norris J., et al., eds. *The Arthurian Encyclopedia.* New York: Garland, 1986.

Mantle, Burns. Review of *A Connecticut Yankee at King Arthur's Court. Photoplay* 20 (June 1921): 51.

Niver, Kemp R. *The First Twenty Years: A Segment of Film History.* Los Angeles: Locare Research Group, 1968.

Patterson, Frances Taylor. *Cinema Craftsmanship.* New York: Harcourt, 1921.

Polt, Harriett. "The Films of Bruce Baillie." *Film Comment* 2 (Fall 1964): 50-53.

Quinlan, David. *British Sound Films: The Studio Years 1928-1959.* Totowa, N.J.: Barnes and Noble, 1984.

Review of *The Black Knight. New York Times* 29 Oct. 1954: 27.

Review of *A Connecticut Yankee in* [sic] *King Arthur's Court. Exceptional Photoplays* 4 (Mar. 1921): 2.

Review of *Knights of the Round Table. New York Times* 8 Jan. 1954: 17.

Review of *Lancelot and Guinevere. Films and Filming* 9 (July 1963): 24.

Review of *L'Éternel Retour. Monthly Film Bulletin* 13 (28 Feb. 1946): 22-23.

Spears, Jack. "Edwin S. Porter." *Films in Review* 21 (June-July 1970): 327-354.

Tesich-Savage, Nadja. "Rehearsing the Middle Ages." *Film Comment* 14 (Sept.-Oct. 1978): 50-56.

Wachhorst, Wyn. "Time-Travel Romance on Film: Archetypes and Structures." *Extrapolation* 25 (Winter 1984): 340-359.

White, T. H. *The Once and Future King*. 1958. New York: Berkley, 1966.

Williams, Alan. "On the Absence of the Grail." *Movietone News* 47 (Jan. 1976): 10-13.

2.
An Enemy in Our Midst
The Black Knight and the American Dream

Alan Lupack

Of the many film versions of the matter of Britain, one of the most unusual is the 1954 production *The Black Knight*. Other Arthurian movies generally have a firm foundation in traditional stories, even when they alter and reshape those stories fairly radically. *Lancelot and Guinevere*, for instance, deals with the love affair that Malory and others make central to the downfall of Arthur's kingdom, even though the movie allows itself cinematic license in the treatment of that love. *Sword of the Valiant* is a modern retelling of *Sir Gawain and the Green Knight*, though it takes its hero into realms of which the medieval author did not conceive. *Camelot* is consciously based on T. H. White's *The Once and Future King*. Rohmer's *Perceval* takes its inspiration from Chrétien de Troyes. And the 1949 version of *A Connecticut Yankee in King Arthur's Court*, directed by Tay Garnett, who also directed *The Black Knight*, is obviously rooted in Twain's novel, even if Bing Crosby as Hank Morgan is more crooner than crusader.

While these films contain elements or episodes that are unknown to medieval legend, all of them appear familiar to anyone versed in Arthurian tradition. Garnett's *The Black Knight*, however, hardly seems cut from the same cloth. Though in this film Arthur and his knights reside at Camelot and gather around the Round Table and some familiar characters appear, there is little else that is traditional.

Certainly, there is no medieval or modern version of the story that one could point to as a source or even an analogue. As the review in the *Monthly Film Bulletin* observed, "The film is gleefully disrespectful of history and tradition..." (147).

Even the hero of *The Black Knight* is unlike the usual hero of Arthurian romance. The film is the story of John, a blacksmith in the service of the Earl of Yeonil. John loves the earl's daughter Linet but is told by the earl that no relationship can develop between him and Linet because of the difference in their stations. The threat to John's personal happiness is paralleled by a threat to Camelot. John learns that Palamides and his Saracens, who are in league with King Mark's Cornishmen in a plot to take over Arthur's kingdom, have been masquerading as Viking raiders to create panic and instability in Britain. In order to prove his accusation of treason against Palamides, John must acquire the skills of a knight and adopt a secret identity as the Black Knight. Ultimately, through his ability and with a sword he made with his own hands, John saves both the woman he loves and the kingdom from the foreign threat; and as a result he is knighted and is granted the hand of Lady Linet in marriage.

Arthurian romance, and medieval romance in general, abounds with examples of men and women who are performing menial tasks but who turn out in the end to be noble. However, these characters, like Malory's Sir Gareth, who works in Kay's kitchen, are noble by birth, and the normal pattern of a romance is a revelation of that nobility rather than an actual change in station. (The only example of a commoner's rising to knighthood that comes to mind is in the non-Arthurian poem *Rauf Coilyear*, in which a collier gives shelter to Charlemagne on a cruelly stormy night and is later rewarded with knighthood.)

The unprecedented plot of *The Black Knight* is clearly something other than the kind of spectacular cinematic adaptation of Arthurian material that took place a year before its release in *Knights of the Round Table*. Though there is no dearth of spectacle in *The Black Knight*, it is very strange spectacle indeed in an Arthurian context. A routing of pagans about to sacrifice Christians at Stonehenge, the defeat of Saracens attacking Camelot—what have these to do with Arthur? Or even with each other? As the *New York Times* review noted, "One wonders how Saracens happened to be in England when ritual sacrifices were being made at Stonehenge or at Camelot, for that matter" (27). The reviewer for *Commonweal* made a similar observation: "I could never quite figure out what the Saracens were doing in olde England; but there are many other odd things in this movie including a wild bacchanal at Stonehenge that had me baffled" (188). Either such unusual elements as these and the rise of a blacksmith to knighthood and nobility must be considered a hodgepodge of absurdities, or some justification or at least explanation must be offered for linking them in an Arthurian movie. The explanation seems to be that director Tay Garnett was creating a thoroughly Americanized version of the Arthurian legends, a version that reflects perennial American values and ideals as well as specific American concerns of the 1950s.

Though *The Black Knight* was produced by Warwick, a British company, Garnett, the director, and Alec Coppel, the screenwriter, were both Americans, as was the star, Alan Ladd. The basic story they combine to create has been common in American literature ever since Benjamin Franklin wrote about his rise from poverty to power. Having arrived in Philadelphia with almost no money, Franklin tells us in his *Autobiography*, he reached a point, through industry and ingenuity, where he met with kings and even sat down to dinner with one. This was and still is for many the American Dream.

In *The Black Knight*, that dream is realized by John the blacksmith. In fact, from beginning to end, its plot focuses the viewer's attention on his rise. Even the opening sequence wherein a minstrel sings a song to a ballad tune defines the protagonist's task. The words of the song do not tell the traditional ballad tale of death or tragic love. Rather, they are about a brave young man who must earn the right to be a knight and win his lady.

The question of John's station is central throughout the movie. When he tells Linet, played by Patricia Medina, that their love is impossible because "You're the earl's daughter," she responds, "That doesn't make me any better than you are. A birthright's an accident, nothing more." Of course, the plot demands an obstacle to their love. The earl, who does not share his daughter's democratic views, dismisses the blacksmith from his service.

Thus far, the plot is fairly standard stuff, but what follows is far less predictable. John is comforted by the earl's friend Sir Ontzlake, who says to him, "You made spurs here; apply them to yourself. You have ambition; fashion it like a suit of armor." While the earl's reaction is just what might be expected in a hierarchic society, Sir Ontzlake's could only come from someone who believes that ability and hard work are more important than inherited titles or the trappings of knighthood. And the notion that ambition can become the "armor" that John needs to prove himself worthy of a noblewoman is reminiscent of another American author who saw knighthood as something symbolic rather than as a literal condition of birth or wealth. In *The Story of King Arthur and His Knights*, Howard Pyle, after telling of Arthur's drawing the sword from the stone, writes, "Thus Arthur achieved the adventure of the sword that day and entered into his birthright of royalty. Wherefore, may God grant His Grace unto you all that ye too may likewise succeed in your undertakings. For any man may be a king in that life in which he is placed if so be he may draw forth the sword of success from out of the iron of circumstance" (35).

I am not suggesting a borrowing from Pyle, but it does seem clear that *The Black Knight*, with its armor of ambition, is in the same tradition as Pyle's sword of success. The symbolic nature of the knight's equipment extends even further in Garnett's film. After the minstrel's song, which precedes the opening credits, and a brief scene showing a column of knights riding to a castle, the setting shifts to the blacksmith's forge where John is fashioning a sword that he intends to give as a present to the Earl of Yeonil. The viewer sees in quick succession various stages in the production of the sword until, at last, a fine weapon is raised with pride by its fashioner.

This emphasis on the making of the sword seems strange at first. Should not an Arthurian tale tell how a sword is used rather than how it is made? But in actuality the way John obtains his sword is as important as the way Arthur receives his in more traditional versions of the matter of Britain. Because of his dismissal from the earl's service, the gift is never given to the one for whom it is intended. But Sir Ontzlake, who has seen a demonstration of the quality and keenness of the sword, tells John, "You made it with your own hands. Now let it make you." The sword wrought by John's industry and skill becomes symbolic of those qualities. The fact that he made it himself indicates that he will be a self-made man. As Ontzlake advises him, "Knighthood is a flower to be plucked." While such a statement could not have been made when knighthood was in flower, it is a clear indication that the Arthurian legend has been translated into a different mythical realm. This is no sword destined for a hero by a fairy power; it is one the hero must hammer and temper and sweat over. As he shapes the sword, he shapes his own destiny.

Ontzlake's training of John is depicted in a series of short scenes showing the two practicing with lance, sword, knife, and then lance again. The collage effect parallels that of the scenes of the making of the sword and once again suggests the industry and hard work of the future knight. The viewer sees how, with practice, the foolish mistakes of the beginner are corrected and ultimately the skill of the accomplished knight is acquired.

Sir Ontzlake himself is important to the thematic statement of the movie. He not only becomes an adviser and a teacher for John but is also an example of what can be achieved. Though now a knight of the Round Table, he was, as he tells John, "not always a knight. Some are born to it; I was not." After teaching John about the possibilities of life, he helps him learn how to use a sword to save Arthur's kingdom.

The choice of Ontzlake's name may be an intentional allusion to Malory. In Caxton's edition of Malory (but not in the Winchester manuscript, where the name is Outlake or some variation thereof), Ontzlake is the name of the knight in the Arthur and Accolon episode whose patrimony has been taken from him by his brother Damas. Though the character of Ontzlake and his role are very different in the *Morte Darthur*, the name does seem appropriate to the person who teaches John to use the sword fashioned with his own hands. Damas will give him none of his inheritance except what "Ontzlake kepeth thorow prowesse of his handes" (Malory I:127). But whereas Ontzlake achieves justice only when Arthur defeats Damas's champion, Accolon, and gives Ontzlake his due, in *The Black Knight* Arthur's lands must be saved for him by John with Ontzlake's assistance.

If this analysis is correct, John embodies the American Dream. Perhaps this explains the lack of any attempt to make him act like a British knight. Though many of the cast members are British and speak with decidedly British accents, Ladd does not even try to sound as if he comes from anywhere outside the United States. The reviewer for *Time* comments, "Nor kann this knight e'en parler ye Englysshe langue, bot muttereth mayhappe in Frensshe, as, 'Yagottalissena me. Englans gonnabeen vaded'" (110).

A striking visual image that marks John as the American hero is the heraldic device he wears: an eagle with wings spread wide, or "displayed," to use the heraldic term. This is the same position in which the American eagle is portrayed, as on the dollar bill. It is not, of course, the American eagle; but it might well pass for a medievalized version of that symbol. And, interestingly, John wears the eagle, in the form of a medallion, even before he adopts the identity of the Black Knight. The symbolic suggestion is therefore

Alan Ladd in the title role in The Black Knight.

that those qualities that make John a worthy knight were inherent in him before he received training from Sir Ontzlake. As in the popular notion of the American Dream, his native ability rather than any advantage of birth leads to his success.

In the end, John does achieve what he desires when he is rewarded for his service with knighthood and Lady Linet. Thus, he completes the rags-to-riches pattern. That this is not a fanciful interpretation is confirmed by a statement made by the director in his autobiography: "Fundamentally, the plot was one of those bootblack-to-President things. Alan, as a kid, worked in a blacksmith's shop, hammering out armor. With diligence, courage, and lots of help from Coppel's script, he worked his way up to a fiery sword" (Garnett 286).

But more is going on in *The Black Knight* than a simple rags-to-riches or "bootblack-to-President" story. If John is symbolically representative of American values, there is a threat to those values, indeed to the stability of Arthur's kingdom. The danger comes from a foreign invader, from treason within, and from an attack on Christianity. Given this combination and the mood of America in the fifties, it seems plausible that the threat to Camelot may be seen as a thinly disguised allegory of what was perceived at the time as the Communist threat.

Though not directly relevant to my thesis, it is interesting that on the same page of the November 27, 1954 edition of *America* on which a brief review of *The Black Knight* appears, there is also an advertisement for a book called *America Faces World Communism* (259). The advertisement quotes a general who says the book "Presents . . . the methods of the greatest conspiracy against mankind that history records." Another endorsement in the advertisement says that the author "sees clearly the Communist threat and helps his readers to see its magnitude."

Ironically, it is Palamides in the film who says, "Certainly there is an enemy in our midst." Actually, there are two. Palamides himself is the representative of the foreign power, the Saracens, who are in league with one of Arthur's own subjects, King Mark. The danger is all the greater because those who would defend Arthur's kingdom are "looking across the sea."

John is the first to recognize the nature of the threat. When the Earl of Yeonil's castle is sacked and burned, he follows one of the pillagers, Palamides' servant Bernard, to Camelot. But since the raiders were disguised as Vikings, he is not believed and is under sentence of death unless he can prove his accusation. Ontzlake later recognizes the magnitude of the danger and tells John that "there is treason all about us and it must be stamped out before all of us—you and I and King Arthur himself— are overwhelmed."

Perhaps most prominent in this context is the threat to Christianity. In fact, much of the movie is devoted to documenting this threat. As Nora Sayre has pointed out in her book on the cold-war films of the fifties, Churchill defined Communism as a "peril to Christian civilization" and many clergymen preached that "the Communists were going to destroy Christianity and morality" (10-11).

The Black Knight depicts the forces seeking to undermine Arthur's rule as such a threat to Christian civilization. There is none of the religious ambiguity about Arthur's realm that is sometimes found in Arthurian story. The kingdom is undoubtedly Christian. Early in the movie, when Sir Hal is being knighted, he must vow to be in all things a Christian gentleman. John, like his father before him, proves himself a supporter of the church. His father had made a cross of peace, formed from the weapons thrown down by defeated invaders. John gives the cross to the local abbot, who tells him that he, like his father, is a good Christian.

In contrast, the hostile forces are intent on destroying Christianity. When the raiders masquerading as Vikings attack and burn the abbey, one of them rips a cross from around the neck of a monk, looks at it scornfully, then spits on it before hurling it to the ground. Coming shortly after John has given the cross to the abbot, this scene puts John in opposition to these pagans. After setting fire to the abbey, Mark and Palamides' minions line up many of the monks to be executed, as Palamides asks with a wry smile, "Are Christians invincible against arrows?"

Mark, the other enemy within, is worse than his accomplice. He is, as we are told, "a baptized Christian king." But this is only "to deceive Arthur." Actually, he believes that "there's danger in this Christianity," a statement that almost parallels Marx's well-known statement that "religion is the opiate of the masses." In this context, it would be difficult to present a character who espouses atheism, but Mark is an advocate of what is depicted as a particularly debauched style of paganism. He wants the high priest at Stonehenge to be the religious leader of Britain.

Just what that would mean is demonstrated by a fascinating scene set among Stonehenge's megaliths. The abbot and some of his monks have been brought to Stonehenge along with Lady Linet, all of whom are to be sacrificed to the sun god in a pagan ritual. There is heavy drinking and much of what passed in the fifties for sensuous dancing. Of course, the Black Knight arrives just in time to save Linet from the descending sacrificial sword and to free the monks from the cages in which they are suspended and under which fires have been lit. He is followed by Arthur and his knights, who disperse the pagans and, at the King's command, topple the megaliths as a sign of "heaven's wrath against the evil practiced here."

The cliché of the last-minute rescue of the damsel in distress is repeated when Linet is saved from the other enemy within. She has been taken to Palamides' castle so that she can be questioned about the Black Knight. The Saracen turns her over to his servant Bernard so he can "persuade her to talk." In this scene, the servant clearly represents a foreign threat. Bare-chested and dark-featured, he is willing, even delighted, to torture the heroine.

Aside from the features of Bernard and Palamides, also dark and foreign-looking, there are other striking visual representations of the Saracens' foreignness and of the danger they embody. In the room in Palamides' castle where Linet is held captive and then rescued, there is a mural in the background depicting a Satanic figure, a sort of demonic hell-mouth, which marks the villains as more than believers in a different religion; it shows them to be agents of the devil.

Given the importance of the sword in the symbolic framework of the movie, it seems quite significant that Palamides does not have a broadsword of the type forged by John. Rather, he wields a scimitar. The alien sword marks him as a character at odds with the good and true knights of Arthur's court. But even without such a marker, Palamides must be looked on with some suspicion. He is traditionally Tristan's rival in love for Isolde. Never quite able to win her or to best Tristan in any way, he has moments of weakness but generally remains noble and, in Malory, is converted in the end. The treacherous, scheming, deceitful, and haughty Palamides of *The Black Knight* is quite a different person. And his failings are emphasized by being divorced from the courtly-love context of medieval romance. The best of knights can be driven to temporary insanity by unrequited love, but without his passion for Isolde (a character who does not appear in the film) to mitigate or at least explain his actions, Palamides appears to practice evil for its own sake. He becomes a figure as satanic as the mural in his castle suggests.

One other visual symbol has unavoidable significance in this scheme. In the mass assault by the Saracens at the end of the movie, all of the attackers wear red tunics, making them almost literally a "red horde." Since John's intelligence-gathering has resulted in the nullification of the Cornish threat, the attackers are left without their allies. This allows for a fairly easy victory by the forces from Camelot and leads to John's knighting because he has saved the kingdom.

The mood of the country and of much of Hollywood in particular in the fifties had a tremendous influence on the types of films made. It has become a commonplace of film criticism that movies like *Invasion of the Body Snatchers* (made just two years after *The Black Knight*) and other science-fiction films that describe a threat to humanity are allegories for the dangers of Communism. As Peter Biskind has observed, "It has long been evident, in fact from the moment the first blob oozed its way across the screen, that the little green men from Mars stood in the popular imagination for the clever red men from Moscow. The media portrayed Russians in such lurid fashion that the connection was inevitable, even if unintended by writers and directors" (185).

A similar dynamic seems to be at work in *The Black Knight*. The threat is not from an alien planet but from an alien nation and an alien philosophy. There is surely the kind of "Us/Them" framework that Biskind defines, in which "that which threatened consensus was simply derogated as 'Other.'" And, as he goes on to say, "The Other was indeed communism" (186). The dark and treacherous Saracens and the pagan religion of the Cornishmen are as great a danger to Western civilization as the pods of *Invasion of the Body Snatchers*.

When *The Black Knight* is seen as an allegory for the triumph of American values over a Communist threat, the strange and untraditional elements make perfect sense. Forming a familiar pattern, they mark *The Black Knight* as a work in the tradition of Lowell's *Vision of Sir Launfal* and Twain's *A Connecticut Yankee in King Arthur's Court*. Like them, it departs radically from standard Arthurian story in order to create a tale that is thoroughly a product of its time and thoroughly American.

WORKS CITED

Biskind, Peter. "Pods, Blobs, and Ideology in American Films of the Fifties." *Invasion of the Body Snatchers*, ed. Al LaValley. New Brunswick, N.J.: Rutgers University Press, 1989. 185-197.

Garnett, Tay, and Fredda Dudley Balling. *Light Your Torches and Pull Up Your Tights*. New Rochelle, N.Y.: Arlington House, 1973.

"The Jones Girl and the Alan Lad." *Commonweal* 61 (19 Nov. 1954): 188-189.

Malory, Sir Thomas. *Le Morte Darthur: The Original Edition of William Caxton*, ed. H. Oskar Sommer. 4 vols. London: Nutt, 1889.

Pyle, Howard. *The Story of King Arthur and His Knights*. New York: Scribner, 1905.

Review of *The Black Knight*. *Monthly Film Bulletin* 21 (Oct. 1954): 147.

Review of *The Black Knight*. *Time* 64 (8 Nov. 1954): 110.

Sayre, Nora. *Running Time: Films of the Cold War*. New York: Dial, 1982.

W., A. "'The Black Knight' Wins His Spurs at Globe." *New York Times* 29 Oct. 1954: 27.

3.

The Arthurian Legend in French Cinema
Lancelot du Lac and *Perceval le Gallois*

Jeff Rider, Richard Hull, and Christopher Smith

This essay seeks first to explain the common significance of the Arthurian legend for Robert Bresson and Eric Rohmer and second to situate the films *Lancelot du Lac* (1974) and *Perceval le Gallois* (1978) within their bodies of work. We begin by considering the place of the Arthurian legend in modern French culture and go on to discuss the legend's appeal to these directors. The second part of the essay identifies the uniquely "Bressonian" and "Rohmerian" elements of the two films. The third part explores the directors' reasons for adapting two literary models, the *Mort Artu* (or *Mort le Roi Artu*)[1] and Chrétien de Troyes's *Conte du Graal*,[2] and suggests why they widely diverged from these models in the conclusions to their films.

The Arthurian legend fascinated both Bresson and Rohmer. Bresson had already drawn up a detailed outline for *Lancelot* in 1956 (Esteve 75; A[mengual] 55; Prédal 6). Rohmer, who had taught Chrétien de Troyes's *Conte du Graal* while a high school teacher, adapted the story for television in 1964. He filmed illustrations from "thirteenth-, fourteenth-, and fifteenth-century manuscripts, and then add[ed] a commentary which explained the story." Dissatisfied with the result, he began planning the film version of the romance, which he realized fourteen years later (Tesich-Savage 51; Magny and Rabourdin 10). Both films were thus long-term projects conceived years before the films were made and were kept alive until the directors were able to raise the money to make them.

Bresson and Rohmer were attracted to these Arthurian projects by the strangeness of the Arthurian world for modern audiences, especially for modern French audiences, and by the role and associations of the Arthurian legend in French culture.[3] For contemporary audiences, the world of the Arthurian legend is strange historically, materially, and culturally. Its denizens dress, talk, act, and think differently. But for the French, the legend is also *cinematically* strange, having appeared only rarely in French-language films. In 1979, Jacques Durand published a list of fifty-seven chivalric films made between 1910 and 1978 (39); only four of these were French.[4] Of the thirty-four films that Kevin J. Harty (119-137) lists in his filmography and bibliography of Arthurian films made between 1904 and 1984, only five are French.[5] No chivalric or Arthurian films were made in French between Jean Delannoy's *L'Éternel Retour* and Bernard de la Tour's *Du Guesclin* in the 1940s and the films made in the 1970s by Yvan Lagrange, Bresson, Frank Cassenti, and Rohmer, a gap of almost twenty-five years. Rohmer, at least, was clearly aware of this hiatus (see his remarks cited in Magny and Rabourdin 15).

This cultural and cinematic strangeness was seductive to directors as creative, independent, and artistic as Bresson and Rohmer. As Jacques Fieschi notes, a "process of distancing . . . lies at the foundation of all [Rohmer's] cinema" (5), and Rohmer himself acknowledges that "making *Perceval* was . . . a means of getting off certain well-trodden paths" (Adair 231). His much-discussed fidelity to Chrétien's text, his use of medieval music for the sound track, and his imitation of the visual style of medieval manuscript illuminations in an effort "to rediscover the vision of the medieval period as it saw itself" (Tesich-Savage 51) may all be seen as efforts to take full advantage of his subject's potential strangeness. The strangeness of Bresson's *Lancelot du Lac* lies more in the camera than in front of it, and his film has impressed French critics as "a most singular work" (Vitoux 73), whose "composition . . . is uniquely, totally specific" (G[uignet] 29). In this film, notes Capdenac, Bresson takes us into a "'strange/foreign [*étrange*] country' . . . inhabited by the armed phantoms of anxiety and the unconscious" (59).

The two directors were also intrigued by the role and associations of the Arthurian legend in contemporary France. In Anglo-American culture, the Arthurian legend has served as a means of quasi-historical reflection since the early Middle Ages. For a modern English-speaking audience, every treatment of the Arthurian legend, in whatever medium and however patently fictitious or inaccurate, refers to a dim, mythological past, and is thus a statement about the way things were or the way they might have been, or should have been—and is also, therefore, a statement about the way present-day Anglo-American culture is, might be, or should be.

The Arthurian legend plays an altogether different role in France. The past to which modern French treatments of the legend refer is not shadowy and mythological but datable and literary. The principal referent is not a pseudo-historical recollection of archaic military glory and political ascendancy but some of the greatest works of medieval literature: above all, the twelfth-century verse romances of Chrétien de Troyes, like the *Conte du Graal*, and the thirteenth-century prose romances of the Vulgate (or Lancelot-Grail) Cycle, for instance, the *Mort Artu*.[6] A French audience today associates the Arthurian legend with artistic greatness rather than with the thwarted imperial destiny of a pseudo-historical king.

The different expectations with which French- and English-speaking audiences approach modern treatments of the Arthurian legend, and the different contexts in which they interpret and judge them, are neatly emblematized in the initial reactions of reviewers to Rohmer's casting of Fabrice Luchini in the role of Perceval. In an interview recorded while he was still at work on *Perceval*, Rohmer states that he chose Luchini for the role before he wrote the script, that he wrote the script with Luchini in mind, and that there was only one way, Luchini's, to play the role. Luchini's interpretation of the role, in other words, embodied his directorial intentions perfectly (Tesich-Savage 54-55).

In general, French reviewers applauded his choice. Mireille Amiel wrote that the character Perceval "cannot be disassociated from the actor (Fabrice Luchini) playing the role (and this [brilliant bit of casting] is not the least of the *auteur's* merits)" (7). Danièle Dubroux thought that the casting, along with everything else in the film, was suitable to the text of Chrétien de Troyes, that the actors played their roles "perfectly"; she further noted that Luchini's "hallucinatory stare [regard] ... reproduces the stare of a child who has been quieted by reality" and attributed the film's "oneiric dimension" to this "illuminated stare, of a waking dreamer or a sleepwalker," which "guides the vision [regard] of the spectator, making him or her discover the world of chivalry at the same time as [Perceval]" (43). Max Tessier observed that "the dumbfounded air of Fabrice

Luchini/Perceval is not the least surprising element of this unusual work, and, through him, more than through any other [element], Rohmer plays on a distancing humor that is constantly present" (72).

English and American reviewers generally had a different reaction. Stanley Kauffman thought that Luchini was "goofy" (31). Andrew Sarris said that Luchini's Perceval reminded him of the "bemused ultra-Catholic bourgeois played by Jean-Louis Trintignant in [Rohmer's] *My Night at Maud's* (1969), but without Trintignant's charm" (76). Gerald Clarke wrote that "Luchini is more a suggestion of a knight than a knight himself. With a receding chin, concave chest, and dangling, half-open mouth, he looks as if he would be afraid to kill a mouse with a trap, much less joust with a man in armor" (104). Marsha McCreadie observed that, as Perceval, Luchini was the "dopiest looking of all [the 'silly looking' characters] . . . we're meant to chuckle, perhaps at the *naif*, but here the hero has clearly been chosen to look ludicrous and baffled" (54).

The French appreciation and the Anglo-American depreciation of Luchini—reactions that echo critics' response to the film in general—can be attributed to essentially different attitudes toward the Arthurian legend. The English and American critics, viewing the film as a treatment of a mythological past, as a pseudo-historical reflection, compared Luchini to their concept of a "real" (i.e., mythological) knight and find him ludicrous. For French critics, viewing the film as an artistic adaptation of a work of medieval literature, Luchini's conformity to a modern concept of "authentic" knighthood was unimportant: they were more interested in what the casting revealed about the *auteur's* understanding of his material.[7]

The literary associations of the Arthurian legend in French culture made it an attractive point of departure for Bresson and Rohmer. Compare their choice and treatment of their narrative models with those of, say, John Boorman. Linguistic limitations, considerations of target audiences, and cultural chauvinism all undoubtedly played a part in Bresson's decision to base his film on the *Mort Artu* and Rohmer's to base his on Chrétien, just as they did in Boorman's choice of Malory's *Morte Darthur* as a source—albeit a loose one—in making his *Excalibur*.[8] Boorman's invocation of the *Morte Darthur*, however, was also shaped by the Anglo-American associations of the Arthurian legend: he was interested in the mythological impact of the entire legend, and this led him to invoke a comprehensive literary model that relates Arthur's entire career.[9] Bresson and Rohmer chose literary models of far more limited narrative scope, which possess greater unity of action, time, and place.

The same biases are evident in the directors' differing degrees of fidelity to their literary models. Rohmer is the most faithful, Boorman the least. Rohmer and Bresson abridge their model narratives, but, except at the very end of the films, neither invents or rearranges narrative elements; Boorman does both freely. The French directors' greater respect for their sources derives from the fact that these stories *are* the inspirations for their films: the films are an important manifestation of the reception of medieval French literature in modern French culture.[10] The inspiration for Boorman's film, on the other hand, is not Malory's narrative, not a literary past. Ultimately, because his film stands in the same relation to that mythological past as the medieval literary work—they are both treatments of a common legend, reflections on the same moment of the pseudo-past—Boorman felt less obliged to follow his model.[11]

The Arthurian legend, in sum, offered Bresson and Rohmer an aura of "strangeness" coupled with an atmosphere of "great literary art." Such a combination was irresistible and immensely valuable to such doggedly original arch-*auteurs*. It gave them the opportunity and the freedom to create two highly personal visions of the Middle Ages, and it explains their enduring desires to make films based on parts of that legend.

Lancelot du Lac is a thickly constructed film whose narrative is propelled by a number of formal devices. To begin with, many of the sound effects have an unnatural quality, yet Bresson uses them in ways that pretend to evoke a naturalistic ambience. This technique gives the illusion of a natural setting: the audience hears horses whinny and gallop, hears the knights' armor clanking as they walk, hears an earthenware vessel being emptied. Some of these sounds are anchored visually; others are not. The sounds have been so elaborately constructed and enriched, however, that they take on a life and a significance of their own when the audience hears them, bold and alone, on the sound track. The whinnies that one hears off-screen, for example, are not intended to make one believe in the presence of off-screen horses. They are hyperreal intrusions that create a sense of anxiety and hidden meaning, both because one cannot attach them to anything in the frame and because their peculiar quality undermines their credibility. The clanking cacophony of armor similarly serves to enhance this impression.

Guinevere (Laura Duke Condimas) in Lancelot du Lac.

From left to right, Gauvain (Patrick Bernard), Lancelot (Luc Simon), and Arthur (Vladimir Antolek) in Lancelot du Lac.

The Arthurian Legend in French Cinema 47

Perceval (Fabrice Luchini) and Blanchefleur (Arielle Dombasie) in Perceval.

The battle between Anguingueron (Sylvain Levignac, left) and Perceval (Fabrice Luchini) in Perceval.

The lighting in *Lancelot* is likewise simultaneously naturalistic and significant. It is generally low-key (dim and subdued) and diffused. The only high-key scenes in the film (scenes with bright, even lighting) are those in the tournament sequence, and this contrast makes these rounds of civil violence in the sun the visual opposite of the dark forest in which the knights meet their fated end.

The earth, to which everything will eventually fall, is the visual leitmotif of the film. Shots and scenes often begin and end with the camera pointing at the ground, and the audience sees a great many feet and hooves. Bresson uses the black, green, and brown colors of the earth to set off, and to contrast with, the white, grey, and silver shades of human constructions. This concentration on the earth thematizes the film's vertical dimension and knighthood's descent through it. In the opening scenes, the mounted knights cut a swathe of destruction through the dark forest, and their collective death is predicted by an old woman hunched on the ground. At the end of the film, one sees the same knights, ambushed by archers hiding in the trees above them, falling into a pile of armor on the same dark forest floor.

Bresson's objective visual presentation of his material prevents the audience from identifying strongly with any of the characters. The shots from horseback at the tournament, again, are the only exceptions to this objectivity, and even these are too steady to be point-of-view shots that might communicate the inner experience of the characters. Bresson's habitual casting of nonactors in the starring roles likewise prevents the audience from identifying with them on the basis of experience. The audience thus has no reason to empathize with Lancelot, for example, when he is injured in the tournament. They have not had enough screen time with the hero at this point to feel any particular sympathy for him, and his injury seems inevitable in the context of the general fate of knighthood in the film. Guinevere, too, is cold—her lighted bedroom window is more inviting than her face—and the unindividuated destroyers of the film's opening scenes are reflected in the heap of anonymous armor with which the film closes. The knight are as constrained by the thematization of the space they occupy and by the formal devices used to portray them as they are by their armor, which none of them ever completely removes.

Visually, *Perceval le Gallois* is theatrical and distant. No effort is made to create a sense of filmed history, an impression that one is watching something that really happened or that could have happened. Rohmer establishes this distance between film and audience in several ways. The props and set are stagelike and highly stylized. Modeled on illuminations found in medieval manuscripts, the set consists principally of reflective silver trees and uniformly beige castles. The actors' gestures also derive from these illuminations and seem stiff and artificial. All of the sound is anchored visually: everything one hears originates from something on the screen. The script (Chrétien's text, edited and modernized by Rohmer),[12] the period music, the sung narration, and the visibility of the chorus and musicians, also contribute a stagelike feel. Rohmer increases, or at least does nothing to soften, the theatricality of what he has assembled in front of his camera by making that camera as invisible as possible: the camera movements, when they occur, are practical and functional, the shots are long, the cuts straightforward and unobtrusive. This invisible camera allows the director to focus the audience's attention on other things.

Rohmer thus takes great pains to emphasize the theatricality of the film, its production, the mechanics of "performing" the story. In Chrétien's romance, this performance is divided between the narrator, who addresses the audience and describes what the characters feel and think as well as what happens, and the characters, who think aloud or speak to one another. Rohmer, interestingly, does not assign the role of narrator to a single voice, character, or set of characters, such as the chorus, but divides this role between the chorus and the characters. Perceval, for example, may narrate his own thought and actions in the third person as well as speak his "lines." The distinction between narrator and character is further effaced when the members of the chorus leave their conventionally removed space and participate in the action as speaking characters. The disintegration or dispersion of the narrative voice prevents the audience from identifying with the characters or even focusing exclusively on them. It invites the audience instead to concentrate on the manner in which the tale is told.

Rohmer thus takes an already culturally distant story and removes it farther from his audience through staging, camera work, and an unconventional redistribution of the narration. His presentation of Chrétien's text encourages the audience to focus on the cinematic renarration, both visual and aural, of the tale, a renarration that is ultimately the film's major theme.

The situation of the Arthurian legend in French culture offered common advantages to Bresson and Rohmer and permitted them to create perhaps the most formally "Bressonian" and "Rohmerian" of all their films. The Arthurian legend, and the particular narrative that each director used as a model, however, also offered them advantages and opportunities related to their individual styles and themes.

"In the sparse, medieval world of Camelot where everything from battle to bath to bed takes on the air of a formal ritual," as Fred Barron observes, "Bresson is in his element. His cinematic style and the content of the story are in perfect harmony . . . " (34). Jean Delmas and Vitoux point out that Bresson's trademark antipsychologism, antitheatricalism, and depersonalization of the actors are made less remarkable and less disconcerting by the archaic strangeness of the legendary material (Delmas 21; Vitoux 73). "By picking out such a well-known tale as the legend of Camelot," Barron further notes, "Bresson has freed himself totally from the narrative: a liberation he has long sought" (34). This tale—especially the love of Lancelot and Guinevere, which, Bresson states, "give[s] the film its movement: ("*Lancelot du Lac*: Un film de Robert Bresson" 48)—also offers Bresson the advantage of a ready-made emotional response in his audience, with, and against, which he can play. The tension between the passionate emotion associated with this love in the minds of the audience and the utter dispassion of the actors is perhaps the primary source of the audience's impression that the film has a metaphorical or metaphysical dimension.

The *Conte du Graal*, too, offered Rohmer particular advantages and continuities with his earlier work. Most of the film is spoken in a narratorial voice that, even if it is divided among the various actors, recalls the narrators of Rohmer's earlier series of six films, the *Contes Moraux*. *Perceval* also contains, as Fieschi notes, "an adolescent eroticism" reminiscent of these earlier films (5). There is moreover a substantial thematic continuity between the *Contes Moraux* and *Perceval*. Perceval, as both Tom Milne and George Morris point out, is a typically Rohmerian hero (Milne 193-194; Morris 10), and Lucy Fischer observes that "the themes of the romance are relevant to the sensibility of the director's six . . . 'Moral Tales' . . . a romance like Chrétien's *Perceval and the Grail* contains the ideological roots of Rohmer's world-view" (21). Crisp (84) and Amiel (7) likewise remark on the continuity of "the underlying moral values" (Crisp) of *Perceval* and the *Contes Moraux*, and Rohmer says that he was intrigued "less by the magic [of the *Conte du Graal*] than by the moral, less by the esoteric tale than by the *roman d'apprentissage*" (Rohmer 7); he may have left out some of

The Arthurian Legend in French Cinema 51

the "fantastic and magical aspects" of the text, he says, but he "kept everything having to do with the moral theme: the simultaneously moral and amorous apprenticeship of Perceval" (Magny and Rabourdin 16).

Having followed their medieval narrative models faithfully for most of their films, however, Bresson and Rohmer break cleanly away from these models at the end in order to draw their own starkly moral conclusions. The ultimate attraction of the *Mort Artu* and the *Conte du Graal* for Bresson and Rohmer seems indeed to have been the authority these works would confer by association on the directors' inventions. The subject of *Lancelot du Lac*, in Capdenac's terms, is "the collapse of a world in fury and ferocity," "the end of a world and a legend sinking in the horror and cruelty of a general disaster" (57, 59). In the *Mort Artu*, Bresson found what is arguably the greatest representation of such a disaster in Western literature, one that also possesses what Delmas calls a "fecund uncertainty that permits [one] to make a metaphor of it" (21). The two things that drew him to the *Mort Artu*, Bresson tells us, were a desire "to draw it from what is our mythology," to make it accessible to a modern audience, or, in other words, to make a metaphor of it, and "a situation, that of the knights who return to Arthur's castle without the Grail. The Grail, which is to say the absolute, God . . ." ("*Lancelot du Lac*: Un film de Robert Bresson" 48). The film is thus the metaphorical representation of the collapse of a godless world.

The one problem with the *Mort Artu*, from Bresson's point of view, is that it is insufficiently grim and pessimistic: the collapse is gradual and never total. Arthur, Lucan the Butler, and Girflet all survive the battle against Mordred on Salisbury Plain, and although we later discover Arthur's tomb in the Black Chapel and may presume that he has died of his wounds, we are never sure: we last see him alive in Morgan's boat and care, his death is not described, and we never see the body. Guinevere enters a convent after the battle and dies there a short time later: "but never," the medieval author tells us, "had a high-born lady had a finer and more repentant end to her life, or more tenderly begged Our Lord for forgiveness." Lancelot and his kinsmen Bors, Lionel, and Hector are not even present at the final battle. They return to England only after they have heard of Arthur's death and defeat and kill Mordred's sons in a subsequent conflict. Lionel dies in this battle, but Hector, Bors, and Lancelot all end their days as hermits. The Archbishop of Canterbury, one of Lancelot's two companions in his final days, is sleeping and dreaming at the moment of Lancelot's death, and in his dream he sees "a great company of angels . . . carrying to heaven the soul of our brother Lancelot." The body is returned to the castle of Joyeuse Garde, where it is placed in a magnificent tomb in the main church (Cable 191-235).

This ending was far too cheerful and hopeful for Bresson, so he changed it and had Arthur, Lancelot, and all their knights die together on the scrap heap of godless passion and ambition. What *Lancelot du Lac* shows us is not cinema in the service of medieval literature, but medieval literature transformed into a cinematic mask for twentieth-century alienation.

The conclusion to *Perceval le Gallois* departs more sharply still from its narrative model. The Passion play is simply not in Chrétien's romance, which leaves Perceval taking communion with his hermit uncle on Easter morning, goes on at some length to relate the further adventures of Gawain, and breaks off in the middle of one of these adventures. It is in fact this lack of satisfactory conclusions to both Perceval's and Gawain's adventures that makes the romance so enigmatic and has attracted such critical attention. Rohmer's departure from his model at this point is all the more surprising because of his scrupulous fidelity to it up to this point. The Passion play moreover represents a "tearing rupture," as Fieschi puts it, not only with the preceding portions of this film, but with all of Rohmer's preceding films: here, "for the first time in his work," writes Fieschi, "the filmmaker attains a direct pathos" (6). Rohmer adduces three reasons for this ending. First, "I wanted a brilliant ending . . .," a "surprise ending . . . [that would] bring out strong emotions . . . the audience should be carried away by it." Second, "if I represented the Passion, it's also because it is an important motif for the Middle Ages and very tempting for a cinéaste." "But the essential reason," third, "is that it is in the logic of Perceval's search": "Perceval, in the beginning, believes that God is a warrior, and in the end he realizes that God is a victim, a man humiliated, beaten"; "it very much seems that the text is centered on the Christian, Christly, idea that God is Christ. I did nothing more," concludes Rohmer, "than be faithful to Chrétien de Troyes" (Magny and Rabourdin 16-17; Tesich-Savage 55-56). The notions that Chrétien's text is centered on a "Christly idea" and that the Passion was "in the logic" of Perceval's search are highly debatable. It is undoubtedly true, however, that the Passion was a temptation to both the Catholic moralist and the filmmaker in Rohmer, and it is very much "in the logic" of his reading and adaptation of the romance. What Rohmer has filmed, in other words, is not Chrétien's romance, but his, Rohmer's, profoundly Catholic, highly moralized interpretation of Chrétien's romance. The Passion is not a particularly apt and likely conclusion to the medieval romance, but it is an apt and likely conclusion to Rohmer's interpretation of the romance.

The conclusions to both films, then, are less "in the logic" of their medieval narrative models than they are "in the logic" of Bresson's and Rohmer's reading and interpretations of those narratives as moralistic, Catholic, French filmmakers. In both cases, the medieval narrative served as a means of grasping and expressing an individual's thoroughly contemporary concerns. And is it not in this way, and for this purpose, that these works, the Arthurian legend, indeed the entire Middle Ages, remain a viable part of modern-day culture?

NOTES

We would like to thank Professors John Frazer, Kevin J. Harty, and Norris J. Lacy for their helpful comments on this essay. We would also like to thank Steven Lebergott and Connie Fraser of the Olin Library Interlibrary Loan Office for their extensive help in acquiring secondary materials. We are likewise grateful for a grant from the Office of Academic Affairs of Wesleyan University, which permitted us to screen these two films while preparing the essay.

All translations are ours unless otherwise noted.

[1] *La Mort le Roi Artu,* ed. Jean Frappier (Geneva: Droz, 1964); trans. James Cable, *The Death of King Arthur* (Harmondsworth: Penguin, 1971).

[2] Chrétien de Troyes, *Le Roman de Perceval ou le Conte du Graal,* ed. William Roach (Geneva: Droz, 1959); trans. D.D.R. Owen, *Arthurian Romances* (London: Dent, 1987), pp. 374-495.

[3] We use the words "French," "English," "American," and "Anglo-American" in this essay to refer to cultural traditions rather than to political or geographical formations.

[4] The four films are *Du Guesclin* (dir. Bernard de la Tour, 1948), *Lancelot du Lac, La Chanson de Roland* (dir. Frank Cassenti, 1978), and *Perceval le Gallois.*

[5] The five films are: *Tristan et Yseut* (dir. Maurice Mariaud, 1920), *L'Éternal Retour* (dir. Jean Delannoy, 1943), *Tristan et Iseult* (dir. Yvan Lagrange, 1972), *Lancelot du Lac,* and *Perceval le Gallois.*

⁶The most easily accessible introduction to the twelfth- and thirteenth-century Arthurian romances is still to be found in R.S. Loomis, ed., *Arthurian Literature in the Middle Ages* (Oxford: Clarendon, 1959).

⁷The difference between the Arthurian legend's associations and situation in the two cultures—mythic, historical, and popular in Anglo-American culture, literary, scholarly, and elite in French culture—is also evident (1) in the numbers of chivalric and Arthurian films made in French and in English (see notes 4-5 above), (2) in the fact that at least six of the seven French films listed in notes 4 and 5 are based on distinct, famous literary models (three are based on the legend of Tristan and Iseult, one on the *Mort Artu*, one on the *Chanson de Roland*, and one on the *Conte du Graal*), and (3) in the difficulty Bresson and Rohmer encountered in raising the money they needed to make their films (Crisp 85; Hanlon 187; Magny, *Eric Rohmer*, 156).

⁸When Rohmer was asked if he might consider making a film based on a work of English literature, for example, he replied that it was unlikely because "there is the problem of language . . . . Unfortunately, I have no knowledge of English at all" (Adair 234).

⁹"I think of the story, the history," says Boorman, "as a myth. The film has to do with *mythical* truth, not historical truth . . . ." He goes on to add that he "was determined...to tell the whole story of the *Morte D'Arthur* . . . " (cited in Kennedy 31, 33).

¹⁰Jean-Pierre Lefebvre writes that "*Lancelot du Lac* does not belong to objective history but instead to the heroic and chivalric (and mystical) literature of the twelfth century" (34), and Dubroux notes similarly that "*Perceval le Gallois* . . . is based in large measure on the scholastic memories of our [French] childhood" (42); Fabrice Luchini called *Perceval* "a scholarly project" (*Cinématographe* 44 [Feb. 1979], 15 cited in Crisp 86). On the literary and scholastic associations of the two films for a French audience, see also Adair 230-231; Amiel 7-8; Armes 82; Magny, "Eric Rohmer ou la quête du graal," 26; Magny and Rabourdin 10; Prédal 8; Rohmer 6-7; Tesich-Savage 51.

¹¹Boorman says that he told "the actors that they are not reenacting a legend. They are creating it . . . " He felt free, for example, "to have Uther Pendragon, Arthur's real father and the 'primogenitor' of the whole saga, if you like, drive the sword into the stone, rather than Merlin, as in Malory." "The thing about myths," he remarks, "is that they're a body of stories completely homogeneous and interrelated, yet also completely flexible. You can rearrange or extend or elide the order of events quite liberally without destroying the meaning" (Kennedy 33-34).

¹²Rohmer's script has been printed in *L'Avant-scène cinéma* 221 (1 Feb. 1979): 9-64.

WORKS CITED

A[mengual], B[arthélemy]. Review of *Lancelot du Lac*. *Positif* 162 (Oct. 1974): 55-56.

Adair, Gilbert. "Rohmer's *Perceval*." *Sight and Sound* 47 (Autumn 1977): 230-234.

Amiel, Mireille. "*Perceval le Gallois*: Des arts, des armes et des lois. . . ." *Cinéma* 242 (Feb. 1979): 7-9.

Armes, Roy. *The Ambiguous Image: Narrative Style in Modern European Cinema*. Bloomington: Indiana University Press, 1976.

Barron, Fred. "Robert Bresson's *Lancelot du Lac*: That Hollow Ring." *Take One* 7 (Dec. 1974): 34.

Cable, James, trans. *The Death of King Arthur*. Harmondsworth: Penguin, 1971.

Capdenac, Michel. Review of *Lancelot du Lac*. *Ecran* 29 (Oct. 1974): 57-59.

Clarke, Gerald. "Knight Errant." *Time* 114 (20 Nov. 1978): 104.

Crisp, C. G. *Eric Rohmer: Realist and Moralist*. Bloomington: Indiana University Press, 1988.

Delmas, Jean. "Robert Bresson et ses armures." *Jeune cinéma* 82 (Nov. 1974): 19-24.

Dubroux, Danièle. "Le Rêve pédagogique." *Cahiers du cinéma* 299 (Apr. 1979): 42-43.

Durand, Jacques. "La Chevalerie à l'écran." *L'Avant-scène cinéma* 221 (1 Feb. 1979): 29-40.

Estève, Michel. *Robert Bresson: La passion du cinématographe*. Paris: Albatros, 1983.

Fieschi, Jacques. "Une Innocence mortelle." *L'Avant-scène cinéma* 221 (1 Feb. 1979): 4-6.

Fischer, Lucy. "Roots: The Medieval Tale as Modernist Cinema." *Field of Vision* 9-10 (Winter-Spring 1980): 21-25, 33.

G[uiguet], J[ean]-C[laude]. Review of *Lancelot du Lac*. *Image et son* 285 (June-July 1974): 29.

Hanlon, Lindley. *Fragments: Bresson's Film Style*. Cranbury, N.J.: Fairleigh Dickinson University Press, 1986.

Harty, Kevin J. "Cinema Arthuriana: A Bibliography of Selected Secondary Materials." *Arthurian Interpretations* 3 (Spring 1989): 119-137.

Kauffman, Stanley. Review of *Perceval le Gallois*. *New Republic* 179 (21 Oct. 1978): 30-31.

Kennedy, Harlan. "The World of King Arthur According to John Boorman." *American Film* 6 (Mar. 1981): 30-47.

"*Lancelot du Lac*: Un film de Robert Bresson." *L'Avant-scène cinéma* 155 (1 Feb. 1975): 47-49.

Lefebvre, Jean-Pierre. "Le Cinéma de derrière l'emulsion." *Cinéma Québec* 4 (May 1975): 34-36.

McCreadie, Marsha. Review of *Perceval le Gallois*. *Films in Review* 76 (Jan. 1979): 53-54.

Magny, Joël. *Eric Rohmer*. Paris: Rivages, 1986.

_____. "Eric Rohmer ou la quête du graal." *Cinéma* 242 (Feb. 1979), 19-31.

_____, and Dominique Rabourdin. "Entretien avec Eric Rohmer." *Cinéma* 242 (Feb. 1979): 10-18.

Milne, Tom. "Rohmer's Siege Perilous." *Sight and Sound* 50 (Summer 1981): 192-195.

Morris, George. Review of *Perceval le Gallois*. *Take One* 7 (Jan. 1979): 10.

Prédal, René. "Bresson et son temps." *Cinéma* 294 (June 1974): 4-11.

Rohmer, Eric. "Note sur la traduction et sur la mise en scène de *Perceval*." *L'Avant-scène cinéma* 221 (1 Feb. 1979): 6-7.

Sarris, Andrew. Review of *Perceval le Gallois*. *Village Voice* 23 Oct. 1978: 75-76.

Tesich-Savage, Nadja. "Rehearsing the Middle Ages." *Film Comment* 14 (Sept.-Oct. 1978): 50-56.

Tessier, Max. Review of *Perceval le Gallois*. *Ecran* 76 (15 Jan. 1979): 71-72.

Vitoux, Frédéric. "L'Armure sied à Bresson." *Positif* 163 (Nov. 1974): 72-73.

4.

Gawain on Film

Robert J. Blanch and Julian N. Wasserman

Gawain, the son of King Lot of Lothian and of King Arthur's sister ("Anna" in Geoffrey of Monmouth, "Morgawse" in Malory), is a key figure in Arthurian legend. Frequently portrayed as the knight *par excellence*, especially in early tales, Gawain attempts to gain self-knowledge through the instrument of *aventures*. Such realistic adventures or quests in which Gawain is engaged often highlight elements of magic and the world of fantasy. In this essay, we shall explore, first, the conventional depiction of Gawain in the medieval chronicle and romance traditions, and second, the characterization of Gawain in five theatrical films: *Prince Valiant, Gawain and the Green Knight, Monty Python and the Holy Grail, Excalibur,* and *Sword of the Valiant*.

Gawain's initial appearance as a significant literary figure may be traced to his delineation in Geoffrey of Monmouth's *History of the Kings of Britain* (ca. 1136), a charming fusion of political and ecclesiastical history and fiction. Frequently described as Arthur's nephew (241, 248, 258), the youthful Gawain is sent by his father "to serve in the household of Pope Sulpicius, who had dubbed him a knight" (223).[1] Other sections of Geoffrey's chronicle, however, depict Gawain's loyalty, especially to Arthur, and his martial prowess in the Gallic expeditions against Lucius Hiberius, a fictional Roman emperor or procurator (241-242, 248). Although Gawain displays true valor by rallying the scattered troops of the Britons and by fueling their active pursuit of the enemy (253), one central flaw in his character, rash behavior, is revealed when he decapitates the emperor's nephew (241).

In the *Roman de Brut*, a French verse translation (ca. 1155) of Geoffrey's *History*, the Anglo-Norman Wace calls attention to Gawain as a courteous knight: "This Gawain was a courteous champion, circumspect in word and deed, having no pride nor blemish in him" (Wace and Layamon 57). Gawain's prudence is somewhat suspect, however, for "that very frank and gentle knight" (64) acts impetuously when the Britons' honor is besmirched (87-90). While the remainder of Gawain's portrait underscores both his valor and virility in battle (106) and his loyal service to Arthur (57), one new aspect of Gawain's character is revealed: his concern with "ladies' love" after the rigors of war have passed.[2] The second chronicle successor to Geoffrey's *History*, Layamon's *Brut* (ca. 1190), provides a free rendition in English alliterative long lines of the material from Wace. Like Wace, Layamon emphasizes Gawain's martial boldness (Wace and Layamon 213, 219). Unlike Wace, however, Layamon depicts Gawain as the "dearest of men" to Arthur (221) and as a linguistically skilled counselor to the King (242).

In the French Arthurian tradition, especially in the twelfth-century courtly romances of Chrétien de Troyes, Gawain represents an ideal knight, renowned for his courtesy, urbane manners, and prowess in arms.[3] Arthur extols Gawain's courteous speech in the *Graal* (*Story of the Grail* 93), and Keu praises Gawain's refined diction: "Well do you [Gawain] know how to sell your words, which are very fair and polished" (92). But Gawain's knightly qualities of courtesy and elegance are frequently viewed by Chrétien as mere symbols of pride and worldliness, for Gawain is inordinately concerned with his chivalric reputation and glory. This preoccupation with honor and self-esteem is revealed in such episodes as those involving the knight Guinganbresil (*Story of the Grail* 100) and the wounded knight under the oak tree (*Grail* 137-140). Similarly, in Chrétien's *Lancelot*, Gawain's failure to mount the dwarf's cart (92-93) and to rescue Guinevere (137-139) reveals his spiritual paralysis, his entanglement in pride and chivalric reputation. As Busby notes (395-396), Gawain seems incapable of perceiving the significant link between love and chivalry, and thus he fails as a great knight.

Some French romances composed after Chrétien's works, including *La Mule sans Frein* ("The Mule Without a Bridle," ca. 1200), emphasize Gawain's courtesy, boldness, and loyal adherence to promises (Brewer 28-42). Other romances, however, delineate Gawain as a Lothario, a man who effortlessly creates and is lured into romantic liaisons. Although French writers usually do not portray Gawain as an adulterous lover, they view him as a casual wooer of available single women and as a master designer of one-night stands.[4] In *Le Chevalier à l'Épée* ("The Knight of the Sword," ca. 1200), the host of a castle commands his daughter and Gawain to sleep naked in the same bed. Just as Gawain attempts to make love to her, the girl warns him of a magic sword, a sword safeguarding her chastity, that hangs above their bed. Fearful that his reputation as a lover will be compromised, Gawain then edges closer to the lady. After the sword twice leaps down and wounds him, Gawain's amorous desires remain unfulfilled, and his fame as a sexual ensnarer is punctured. Since the host perceives Gawain as the best knight in the world, the daughter is allowed to marry him. The romance concludes, however, with a series of incidents revealing the girl's deceitfulness and with Gawain's ultimate rejection of her (Brewer 59-74).[5]

In *Hunbaut*, another aspect of Gawain's role as passionate lover is revealed, for Gawain's amorous and knightly reputation marks him as an instant love object for women who meet him for the first time (Brewer 54-58). Although the host of a castle begs his beautiful daughter to give Gawain one kiss, Gawain kisses her four times, thereby angering her father. Later that night, the lady creeps into Gawain's bed, "and so they lay all that night together" (58), with Gawain leaving the castle hurriedly at dawn.

Some English romances, offshoots of the chronicle tradition, usually gloss over Gawain's reputation as a lover. The author of the Alliterative *Morte Arthure* (ca. 1400), for example, portrays Gawain as a proud knight noted for courage and for reckless disregard for personal danger. In the Gawain-Priamus encounter, Gawain displays both martial prowess and frivolity as he "goes forth all alone, / As one stalwart and sturdy in search of adventure" (Krishna 66). Gawain's final battle intensifies the picture of him as a chivalric warrior, for even the villainous Mordred praises him: "He was Gawain the good, most gracious of men, / And the greatest of knights who lived under God, / The man boldest of hand, most blessed in battle, / And the humblest in hall under all the wide heavens" (101). Finally, Arthur identifies Gawain's death on the battlefield with the end of Camelot's splendor (103).

Other Middle English romances, notably those that do not reflect the conventions of the chronicles, trace a more complete portrait of Gawain's essential qualities. The author of *Sir Gawain and the Carl of Carlisle* (ca. 1400) calls attention to Gawain's valor and chivalric standards: "a man who was true and strong and brave in his deeds ... and yet so bold in every fight" (Brewer 92). While Gawain's courteous speech (94) and magnanimous conduct (97) are also noted, the dramatic centerpiece of this romance is Gawain's behavior in love. Since Gawain is enamored of the Carl's wife, the Carl allows her to join Gawain in bed for a night of lovemaking. Just as Gawain is on the verge of intercourse with the woman, the Carl suddenly halts the sexual activity and invites his daughter to sleep with Gawain for the remainder of the night (97-98). On the following morning, however, the Carl praises Gawain's loyal obedience to his rules (99). The tale then concludes with Gawain's marriage to the Carl's beautiful daughter (101).

Although *Sir Gawain and the Carl of Carlisle* provides a full delineation of Gawain's character traits, *Sir Gawain and the Green Knight*[6] adds a few more twists, for Gawain's mettle is tested in multiple ways. After Gawain accepts the Green Knight's challenge and decapitates him (Borroff 8-10), thereby displaying courage and upholding the integrity of Camelot, he must set forth on a quest, an adventure governed by a system of play-rules. In particular, the rules of the game demand that Gawain locate the Green Chapel and there, a year and a day[7] later, receive his blow of the axe from the Green Knight (9-10). On the way, however, Gawain stops at Castle Hautdesert, the fairylike setting for Gawain's entrapment (16-18). Soon after meeting the lord of the castle, Bercilak, and his wife (18-21), Gawain enters into an agreement with his host, an exchange of winnings (23-24). The spoils of the lord's hunt (outdoor games) will be exchanged for Gawain's bedroom winnings (the Lady's indoor games of amorous play). Then, by reversing courtly love conventions and by exploding the traditional conception of Gawain, the poet portrays the Lady as an aggressive lover attempting to ensnare the cowering Gawain, her passive "beloved," in a series of three temptations (24-41). Although Gawain preserves his chastity, he is guilty of duplicity, for he conceals the Lady's gift, ostensibly a lifesaving green and gold girdle, from Bercilak (38-41).

Finally, after Gawain arrives at the Green Chapel (45), he receives three blows from the Green Knight (47-48). Although the first two strokes of the Knight's axe are feints, Gawain displays cowardice by flinching from the first axe-thrust. The Knight then reveals his true identity as Bercilak de Hautdesert and proceeds to link Gawain's behavior in the three temptation scenes with the three strokes of the axe (49-51). Once Gawain recognizes his imperfection, his violation of the covenant with Bercilak, he acknowledges his faults—pride, cowardice, faithlessness, and covetousness—to the Green Knight. *Sir Gawain and the Green Knight* concludes with Gawain's resolve to wear the girdle, a token of his fault, upon his shameful return to Camelot (52). Although Gawain is mortified by his unchivalric conduct, the rest of Arthur's court view the adventure much differently, for they playfully agree to wear a baldric, a sash of bright green, as a sign of his essential honor and integrity (53).

With this background established, it is now possible to focus on the conception of Gawain in five films.

In *Prince Valiant* (1954), directed by Henry Hathaway,[8] Gawain's reputation as a lover is satirized.[9] Gawain (Sterling Hayden) is depicted as a big clumsy oaf in love and as the foil of Prince Valiant (Robert Wagner), Gawain's squire. Since Gawain adores Valiant's sweetheart, Princess Aleta of Ord (Janet Leigh), he mistakenly believes that she will return his love. To make matters worse, Valiant cannot bear to inform Gawain that both men are attracted to the same woman.

The next film, *Gawain and the Green Knight* (1973), directed by Stephen Weeks,[10] is a loose adaptation of the fourteenth-century English romance. Although it reproduces faithfully some elements of the original poem—the use of a narrator, gamelike atmosphere, and play rules—Weeks's version reflects too strongly the influence of Jessie L. Weston's *From Ritual to Romance*. In particular, Weeks pays homage to Weston's vision of a pagan vegetation or nature god who yearly rises to fullness and then dies (34-64); the old year thus passes away so that a new year and god can be born.

The ritualistic note of Weeks's film is sounded in the narrator's initial commentary: "This is when pagan gods haunted the world, and good men longed for miracles." Soon after the Green Knight interrupts Arthur's Yuletide festivities, the seasonal aspects of the movie flare into prominence. Wearing green hair and armor, suggestive of youth, freshness, and the rebirth of life in nature, the Knight (Nigel Green) holds merely a staff, but no holly bob, in his hand. This staff, an emblem of the life force, is then twirled by the Knight until the fertile sapling is metamorphosed into an axe. Once the boyish Gawain (Murray Head) agrees to participate in the

Knight's "beheading game," he is given a year, not the legalistic "year and a day," to find the Green Chapel—because he is young. Such an emphasis on vigor and immaturity continues with Gawain's departure from Camelot, as the narrator intones, "He left a green youth determined to return a man." The last important example of seasonal symbolism appears in the closing frames of the film. As the Green Knight ages before melting into the ground, he reiterates the movie's underlying fertility myth: "The full cycle of the year is turned. As every green shoot of spring returns to the earth, so return I."

Apart from his extravagant use of Weston's vegetation theories, Weeks inserts an unorthodox love interest into his film and omits the crucial temptation scenes of the Middle English poem.[12] In Chrétien's *Yvain*, ostensibly the source of the romantic episode in Weeks's movie, Sir Yvain leaves Arthur's court and eventually arrives at a magic spring adjacent to a mysterious stone (14). When Yvain pours water over the stone, resulting in the creation of a violent cyclone, a belligerent knight (the Black Knight of the movie) appears suddenly (14). After engaging in combat, the mortally wounded knight retreats to his castle with Yvain in pursuit (15-16). In his haste to capture the knight, Yvain becomes trapped by suddenly lowered portcullises (16-17). Yvain remains imprisoned in a sealed room until he is visited by the beautiful Lunete, a maidservant of the slain knight's lady (17). Lunete offers Yvain a magical ring that makes him invisible, allowing him to escape from an angry mob within the castle (18-19). Eventually, through the crafty assistance of Lunete, Yvain wins the heart of the dead knight's wife, Lady Laudine, and marries her (20-37).

In addition to this interpolation from Chrétien, Weeks adds several new elements. First of all, although in *Yvain* Gawain is an important supporting character, one who is excessively devoted to chivalric exploits, Weeks's film conflates the traditional Gawain figure with the character of Yvain in order to shape a new Gawain. Second, while Yvain loves Lady Laudine in Chrétien's narrative, the Gawain-Yvain personality in the movie is attracted to Linet (Lunete), Laudine's matchmaker.

Monty Python and the Holy Grail (1975), directed by Terry Gilliam and Terry Jones, sharply differentiates the aura of chivalric tradition from the "mud, squalor, and death" (Byron and Weis 247-248) of actual life in the Middle Ages.[13] The film skewers the Arthurian legend, including the quest of the Grail, as well as cinematic depictions of the age of knighthood.[14] Gawain's conventional role as a paragon of chivalric valor is, of course, not safe from ridicule. In one brief but memorable scene, Tim the Wizard points out to King Arthur and his band a mysterious cave, "a cave where a vital clue to the grail's whereabouts is located" (Schickel 58). Soon afterward, the small white bunny guarding the cave's entrance is transformed into a killer rabbit, which slays Gawain, its reluctant challenger. Since the rabbit suggests a medieval emblem of lechery and fertility,[15] Gawain's literary reputation as a lover is lampooned in this cinematic battle.

Unlike *Prince Valiant* and *Monty Python*, movies that unintentionally or intentionally send up aspects of the Arthurian legend, John Boorman's *Excalibur* (1981) is a serious film effort to recapture the epic scope of Arthur's life from birth to death (Ciment, "Deux Entretiens" 20; Ciment, *Boorman* 188) and to unfold, not to reenact, the mythic world of the Arthurian age (Kennedy 31, 33-34). Although Boorman attempts to portray "the whole story of . . . [Malory's] *Morte Darthur*" (Kennedy 33), the Grail quest section of the movie, at least, is rooted in Weston's *From Ritual to Romance* (Shichtman 41; Ciment, "Deux Entretiens" 19; Ciment, *Boorman* 185).

Boorman expands the cinematic treatment of Gawain's character. After King Arthur convokes a banquet-meeting of the Round Table, a drunken Gawain (Liam Neeson) rashly discloses Lancelot's worth and Guinevere's amorous longings for Lancelot. Although Guinevere forgives Gawain's "hasty words" and implores him to drink wine from Lancelot's cup, thereby cementing once again the bond of friendship between the two knights, Gawain hurls the goblet on the floor. Infuriated by his accusation, Arthur wishes to fight Gawain. What is not noted in this film, however, is Gawain's special relationship with Arthur, a relationship springing from blood ties, fealty, and mutual admiration. Two days after the fateful banquet, Lancelot, "championing the Queen" so as to prove her innocence, challenges Gawain in the lists. Although Gawain displays his traditional prowess in arms by deftly parrying Lancelot's blows, he is defeated and, begging for mercy, declares the Queen's innocence.

The final scene in *Excalibur* involving Gawain focuses on the search for the Grail, the source of redemption both for the land and for the Round Table.[16] Although Gawain boldly asserts, "We will find the Grail or die!" his end is imminent. Perceval soon sees a horse riding with a dead man strapped to it. Perceval recognizes the

The Green Knight (Sean Connery) and Sir Gawain (Miles O'Keeffe) in Sword of the Valiant.

rider and laments Gawain's death at the hands of the villainous Mordred.

Sword of the Valiant (1984) was Stephen Weeks's second adaptation of *Sir Gawain and the Green Knight*. Unlike his earlier *Sir Gawain and the Green Knight*, a crude work emphasizing Weston's fertility myth theories, *Sword of the Valiant* includes a relatively mature cinematic vision and sophisticated special effects.[17] It is, however, a mediocre film, fancifully blending the narratives of *Sir Gawain* and Chrétien's *Yvain* with a London version of Hollywood Arthuriana.

As the film opens, King Arthur's Yuletide feast is interrupted by the appearance of the Green Knight (Sean Connery), holding a huge axe (not the traditional holly sprig, an emblem of peace). Proposing a game, a challenge to the Camelot brotherhood, the Knight demands that his head be hacked off his shoulders. Although the Green Knight contends that he will not flinch or defend himself when one blow is delivered, he suggests that another stroke will be given within a year:

"A cut for a cut! Who's the jolly gambler to play my game and put his courage on the line of my neck?" After an aged Arthur (Trevor Howard) berates the court for its silence and cowardice, he prepares to take up the challenge. Then Gawain (Miles O'Keeffe) intervenes and decapitates the Green Knight. Mysteriously, in both of Weeks's films, Gawain, only a humble squire, quickly must be dubbed a knight by Arthur before responding to the Green Knight's challenge.

Gawain is again offered twelve months, not the traditional "year and day," to repay his debt (a blow for a blow). The Green Knight also proposes a four-line riddle that Gawain must solve by the Green Chapel meeting. Such a verbal puzzle, not appearing in Weeks's earlier film, contains the deathless line, "When life is gladness, emptiness," formulated by some English scriptwriter. After the Knight departs from Camelot, Arthur praises Gawain for restoring honor to the court, and the Christmas feast then begins in earnest. But Gawain grumbles, "I don't think I'm hungry."[18]

As the quest begins with Gawain riding off through mist into a wild forest, Weeks departs from his Middle English source and shifts to the narrative of Chrétien's *Yvain*. The dialogue becomes silly and the plot fanciful. For example, as his journey starts, Gawain asks his guide and faithful companion, Squire Humphrey (a newly invented character in both Gawain films), how he will relieve himself in "this tin suit."[19] Gawain and his guide then veer west because, as Humphrey claims, "the wind blows west." Throughout the quest, Gawain is preoccupied with earthly things—beds, food, and wine—items that should be "stolen, hunted, or requisitioned."

The remainder of the film, a fantastic mixture of disparate elements, appears to mock Arthurian romances generally and Gawain specifically. While jousting with the knight-guardian of Lyonesse, Gawain learns that his armor, given to him by Arthur, is only *ceremonial*, for the King has not fought in years. He is knocked off his horse, and the combatants engage in hand-to-hand battle. Gawain is, however, victorious. While this episode clearly toys with the medieval tradition of knightly challenge, Gawain's reputation as a valorous warrior, although punctured by this less-than-heroic treatment, stays relatively intact.

Other distinguishing characteristics of the traditional Gawain appear in *Sword of the Valiant*. At Lyonesse, for instance, Gawain falls in love with the beautiful Linet (Lunete of Chrétien's romance), a woman who offers a magical ring in order to preserve Gawain's life. In other episodes, especially those involving the friars or the battle with Baron Fortinbras's son, Gawain displays wit; yet the cumbersome dialogue of the film, a trendy fusion of medieval and modern diction, occasionally gets in the way. In the battle scenes, Gawain demonstrates skill in fighting with a sword, and in Fortinbras's dungeon, Gawain is stalwart as he readies himself for torture on the rack, a scene not depicted in Weeks's earlier film.

Despite this relatively faithful reflection of Gawain's traditional roles—lover, verbal manipulator, and warrior—the legendary picture of Gawain's courtesy and elegance is defaced occasionally in *Sword of the Valiant*. At one point, an unkempt Gawain wears tattered clothes as he attempts to enter a castle. When rebuffed by the castle's porter, Gawain affirms his chivalric reputation and then boldly asserts, "If you don't let me in, you'll be whipped for your insolence."

In summary, the conventional portrait of Gawain in medieval romances, the elegant, courteous knight who fights courageously, if not rashly, and who seduces or woos ladies lustily, is frequently missing in recent Arthurian films. Apart from his treatment in Weeks's two movies, both of which are severely flawed renditions of a Middle English romance, Gawain appears to be viewed by filmmakers as a mere appendage to Camelot's Round Table. Although Hollywood's versions of Arthurian legends ring hollow at times, still the movies recognize the essential glory and tragic demise of King Arthur. What is long overdue, then, is a faithful and comprehensive film interpretation of Gawain, Camelot's flower of courtesy, valor, and love.

NOTES

[1]Gawain's chivalric service to Sulpicius may represent the source of the knight's reputation as an exemplar of courtesy. In the *Brut*, another English chronicle based upon Geoffrey of Monmouth, Layamon points out Gawain's assistance to the pope and then traces the knight's chivalric virtues: "Walwain [Gawain] was full noble-minded, in each virtue he was good; he was liberal, and knight with the best" (Wace and Layamon 214).

[2]In a speech directed to Earl Cador, Gawain notes the link between chivalry and love: "Peace is very grateful after war .... Merry tales, and songs, and ladies' love are delectable to youth. By reason of the bright eyes and the worship of his friend, the bachelor [aspirant to knighthood] becomes knight and learns chivalry" (73). Although Wace describes this speech as a "jest," Gawain's comments may have given impetus to his conventional medieval reputation as a lover.

[3]Busby contends (386-387) that Gawain appears in French romances as "an impersonal, ideal knight" and as a static staple of romances, especially in terms of courtesy, chivalry, and physical prowess.

[4]Busby claims (394) that Gawain represents a "depersonalized lover," for "Gawain's relationships with women are almost without exception superficial and physical. . . . He also seems to be well-known for his amorous activities."

[5]In both medieval English and French romances, Gawain is linked frequently with an antifeminist tradition (Gawain as the reviler of women). See Dove 20-26.

Although this essay will not focus in detail on later, thirteenth-century French texts, it should be noted that Lancelot supplants Gawain as the central heroic figure in the French prose romances of the Vulgate Cycle; in such romances Gawain is severely flawed. The author of the *Mort*, for example, portrays Gawain as a ruthless avenger (Cable 123ff.), the knight who precipitates the fall of Arthur's kingdom, and as a ladykiller (41-44, 50-51).

[6]The standard scholarly edition of *Sir Gawain* is Tolkien-Gordon-Davis. An excellent poetic translation is Borroff; subsequent page references to this translation will appear parenthetically in our text.

[7]"Year and day," rooted in Germanic court procedure and in English common law, represents a legal "court day." For information on this legal tradition and on its role in *Gawain*, see Blanch 347-352.

[8]Hathaway later disavowed the film; as he stated to Scott Eyman (11), "I don't really care to talk about it. . . . I did it [*Valiant*] as a personal favor to Darryl [Zanuck]. I didn't particularly care one way or the other, and the picture looked it."

[9]Although the *Time* critique of this film does not note this point (106), the reviewer claims that Hathaway and the film's producer (Robert L. Jacks) have captured the "inner mood of stilted boyhood reverie" of the comic strip on which this movie is based and have produced an entertaining story ("all a small boy could ask for").

[10]In his *Gawain and the Green Knight*, "an allegory of life where the goal is death" (Berry 7), Weeks attempted to recreate the romantic aura of a pre-Raphaelite painting. According to Weeks, however, once United Artists reshaped the movie into "Walt Disney, a Prince Valiant-type of kids picture," the resultant film was completely different from what Weeks had envisioned.

[11]According to one reviewer, at least, ". . . admirers of the poem in its Tolkien edition will have to wait for a film which captures even a fraction of the original's cryptic complexity" (Baxter 169).

[12]In this respect, Weeks's perspective reveals a misinterpretation of the original text. His cinematic alterations, however, may reflect his awareness

of the evolution of medieval romance from an adventure involving knights-errant to a love quest.

[13] Schickel contends (58) that *Monty Python* "pats down the entire chivalric tradition for bloody and dangerous residual ideas," especially "the gory stupidity of ancient but still potent fancy." Furthermore, according to Schickel, the movie attacks the human penchant for violence.

[14] In his initial review of *Python* (34), Canby claims that the film pokes fun at "the legend, courtly love, fidelity, bravery, costume movies, movie violence and ornithology." Similarly, Canby notes that *Python* parodies "the sound of knighthood," particularly in film treatments of the Arthurian legend ("clanking armor, horses' hoofs").

Later, in his "Film View" on "New Comedies" (2: 15), Canby interprets the battle scene at the end of *Python* as "a how-to guide for filmmakers who want to shoot a spectacular battle scene without missing any cliches, the sort that have been made obligatory through the years by 'Ivanhoe,' 'El Cid' and dozens of other solemn epics."

[15] Technically, in the Middle Ages, the hare was an emblem. For an explanation of this animal symbolism, see Ferguson 20. For a reference to the symbolic hare in medieval literature, see the Monk's portrait in Chaucer's *General Prologue* to the *Canterbury Tales*: " . . of huntyng for the hare/Was al his lust" (I. 191-192), as well as the note for 1. 191 (Chaucer 807).

[16] Rooted in Weston's fertility myth theories, the Grail quest of *Excalibur* includes a knight who "must undergo an ordeal of loyalty and patriotism in order to redeem Arthur and the land" (Shichtman 43).

Viewing the medieval period as an age identified with a comprehension of nature and with a reverence for the land (Ciment, "Deux Entretiens" 20), Boorman claims that twentieth-century people explore the Grail legend because "it speaks to us of a period when nature was unsullied and man in harmony with it" (Ciment, *Boorman* 186).

[17] Kim Newman, a reviewer of *Sword*, contends (164), however, that this confusing film is not "an improvement over [Weeks's] earlier, purer film."

[18] "In order to broaden the appeal of the material, Weeks has opted for a kind of ghastly jokiness . . . that turns the film into an unsatisfactory crossbreed of Robin Hood and Monty Python" (Newman 165).

[19] Such an emphasis on excretion, nor manifested in Weeks's earlier film, is somewhat reminiscent of Cervantes's *Don Quixote*.

WORKS CITED

Baxter, John. Review of *Gawain and the Green Knight*. *Monthly Film Bulletin* 40 (Apr. 1973): 168-169.

Berry, Dave. "Stephen Weeks." *Film* 37 (May 1976): 6-7.

Blanch, Robert J. "The Legal Framework of 'A twelmonyth and a day' in *Sir Gawain and the Green Knight.*" *Neuphilologische Mitteilungen* 84 (1983): 347-352.

Borroff, Marie, trans. *Sir Gawain and the Green Knight: A New Verse Translation.* New York: Norton, 1967.

Brewer, Elisabeth, trans. *From Cuchulainn to Gawain.* Cambridge, England: Brewer, 1973.

Busby, Keith. *Gauvain in Old French Literature.* Amsterdam: Rodopi, 1980.

Byron, Stuart, and Elisabeth Weis, eds. *The National Society of Film Critics on Movie Comedy.* New York: Grossman, 1977.

Cable, James, trans. *The Death of King Arthur.* Harmondsworth: Penguin, 1971.

Canby, Vincent. "Film View: New Comedies—Serious, Farcical, Slapstick." *New York Times* 1 June 1975: 2. 15.

_____. Review of *Monty Python and the Holy Grail*. *New York Times* 28 Apr. 1975: 34.

Chaucer, Geoffrey. *The Riverside Chaucer*, ed. Larry D. Benson et al. 3rd ed. Boston: Houghton Mifflin, 1987.

Chrétien de Troyes. *Lancelot, or the Knight of the Cart*, trans. William W. Kibler. In *The Romance of Arthur*, ed. James J. Wilhelm and Laila Zamuelis Gross. New York: Garland, 1984.

_____. *The Story of the Grail [Perceval]*, trans. Robert White Linker. 2nd ed. Chapel Hill: University of North Carolina Press, 1960.

_____. *Ywain: The Knight of the Lion*, trans. Robert W. Ackerman and Frederick W. Locke. New York: Ungar, 1957.

Ciment, Michel. "Deux Entretiens avec John Boorman." *Positif* 242 (May 1981): 18-31.

_____. *John Boorman*, trans. Gilbert Adair. London: Faber, 1986.

Dove, Mary. "Gawain and the *Blasme des Femmes* Tradition." *Medium Ævum* 41 (1972): 20-26.

Eyman, Scott. " '... I Made Movies....' " *Take One* 5 (Feb. 1976): 6-12.

Ferguson, George. *Signs and Symbols in Christian Art.* New York: Oxford University Press, 1966.

Geoffrey of Monmouth. *The History of the Kings of Britain*, trans. Lewis Thorpe. Harmondsworth: Penguin, 1966.

Kennedy, Harlan. "The World of King Arthur According to John Boorman." *American Film* 6 (Mar. 1981): 30-37.

Krishna, Valerie, trans. *The Alliterative Morte Arthure: A New Verse Translation*. Lanham, Md.: University Press of America, 1983.

Newman, Kim. Review of *Sword of the Valiant*. *Monthly Film Bulletin* 52 (May 1985): 164-165.

Review of *Prince Valiant*. *Time* 63 (12 Apr. 1954): 106.

Schickel, Richard. "Legendary Lunacy." *Time* 105 (26 May 1975): 58-59.

Shichtman, Martin B. "Hollywood's New Weston: The Grail Myth in Francis Ford Coppola's *Apocalypse Now* and John Boorman's *Excalibur*." *Post Script* 4 (Autumn 1984): 35-48.

Tolkien, J. R. R., and E. V. Gordon, eds. *Sir Gawain and the Green Knight*. 2nd ed. rev. Norman Davis. Oxford: Clarendon, 1967.

Wace and Layamon. *Arthurian Chronicles*, trans. Eugene Mason. New York: Dutton, 1962.

Weston, Jessie L. *From Ritual to Romance*. 1920. Garden City, N.Y.: Doubleday, 1957.

5.

Two Films That Sparkle:
The Sword in the Stone and *Camelot*

Alice Grellner

Two musical films, totally different in content, tone, and targeted audience, have drawn their subject matter and inspiration from T. H. White's tetralogy *The Once and Future King*, the one book more responsible than any other for the twentieth-century revival of the popularity of the legend. Each remains true to at least one aspect or dimension of White's vision, while eliminating or downplaying much of the novel's mulitfaceted, ambivalent, misogynistic, often contradictory, and darkly pessimistic view of human nature. The Disney animated film *The Sword in the Stone*, based on White's first Arthurian book, is lively, amusing, fanciful, and wholly optimistic in tone, with wonderfully evocative music by George Bruns. The opening scenes are charming. The pages of an illuminated manuscript are turned while a voice sings a ballad recounting the background of the story. Illuminations shift to illustrations, and when the sword appears on an anvil on top of a stone in the square before the church, a voice takes up the story to describe the Dark Age that fell on England after Uther's death, "without law and without order, when the strong preyed on the weak." The scene shifts to a forest, where wolves and eagles are preying on the weak, and finally zeroes in on Merlin, a blundering old codger, living in a clearing in the forest conversing with his owl, Archimedes, and waiting for Wart to drop in. Wart, the young Arthur, is at the moment tagging along after Kay, who is trying to kill a deer. Wart climbs out on a limb to see better.

When the limb breaks, alerting the deer and causing the arrow to shoot far into the forest, Wart sets out to retrieve it, while Kay stomps off home.

This is one of the many minor changes Bill Peet, the cartoon's story writer, makes in White's tale, in the interest of simplicity and visual humor. In White's story, Wart goes after a hawk that Kay had lost through improper handling, and before he meets Merlin in the clearing he has a brief encounter with King Pellinore, foreshadowing the crucial role that Pellinore and his sons will play in subsequent books. In the film, however, Wart simply goes after the arrow, quite unaware that a wolf is dogging his heels, and in a scene reminiscent of a Jacques Tati film innocently thwarts this symbol of evil, until, in trying to pull the arrow from a tree, he quite literally "drops in" through the thatched roof of Merlin's cottage. Merlin presents himself as a soothsayer and prognosticator, a wizard who knows the future because he is living backward and has already been there. Peet preserves and expands on Merlin's magic home, with dishes that not only wash themselves but pack themselves with the books into a small bag for the trip back to the castle. But Merlin warns Wart not to "get any idea that magic will solve all your problems."

Sir Ector is drawn as a portly, red-haired country squire who gives Wart demerits that he must redeem by doing kitchen duty. He readily hires Merlin as a tutor and houses him in a leaking ruin of a tower. When Pellinore turns up in a rainstorm, Merlin sends Archimedes down to spy on them and bring back the news: that a tournament will be held and the winner will receive the crown. Wart is told he can go as Kay's squire and becomes more energetic than Kay in practicing the arts of chivalry. Meanwhile, Wart's "education" continues under Merlin's unorthodox tutelage. Merlin teaches Wart the important lessons of life he will need when he is king: how to use his imagination; how to use his intellect to outwit the strong who "will try to conquer you." Other lessons are "Always look before you leap," "Love is a powerful thing," and "Get an education" by learning to read. He teaches these lessons by turning Wart into a fish, a squirrel, and a bird, and Wart's adventures as these animals parallel Kay's training as a knight. Some of the most delightful artwork in the film is found in these sequences, with the vivid primary colors of Wart's orange jerkin and Merlin's blue magician's cloak preserved in the animal colors, set against the subtle blues, greens, greys, and browns of the moat. When Wart as a squirrel is pursued by a girl squirrel, Merlin tells him, "You're on your own, lad. I'm afraid magic can't solve this." But Merlin's gentle misogynist laughter at Wart quickly backfires when he himself becomes the object of unrequited love. Later, the cook complains that the kitchen is bewitched when the dishes wash themselves to music that swings, in a sequence that uses the magic of animation to create a nightclub chorus line out of dishes and tableware.

One of the charms of the film is the way it plays off of fairy-tale allusions: the wicked wolf pursuing Wart in the woods, the Cinderella image of Wart doing dishes and being told he cannot go to the tournament after all, Wart's falling into the clutches, à la Hansel and Gretel, of Mim, the wicked witch in the woods. This shapeshifter, part Morgan le Fay and part Nimue, changes sizes like Alice in Wonderland, has a temper like the Red Queen, and competes with Merlin in a battle of wits and sexes, in a long sequence, for which there is no source in White, that allows the animators full scope to indulge in their favorite techniques of rapid movement, impossible situations, astonishing reverses, and the animated-cartoon equivalent of the car chase. Though not my favorite sequence in the film, it is very likely a favorite with children, and the moral Merlin draws from it, one of the several gems scattered throughout the "lessons" of the film, is "It was worth it, if you learned something. Knowledge and wisdom is the real power."

Wart does finally get to go as Kay's squire to London, as we knew all along he would, since it was his fate to draw the sword from the stone. "Let the tournament games begin," the announcer cries out in an anticipatory echo of the opening of the twentieth-century Olympics, just as Wart realizes he has forgotten Kay's sword. Although White put the blame for this on Kay, as he did earlier in losing the hawk, the film writer has made Wart a gawky, slightly clumsy teenager who would be likely to forget things and get into trouble with his elders. It is Archimedes who points out the sword in the churchyard, and when Wart gives it to Kay, it is Kay, portrayed throughout as a big country lout, who tries to take the credit. When they return to the churchyard for a second try, church music swells as Wart draws it out again. Everyone laughs, but Pellinore declares, "It's a miracle," and the solemn voice from the opening scenes announces, "So at last the miracle had come to pass."

A final scene by way of epilogue has Wart sitting alone on a throne wearing a huge crown. He tries to run away, but at every door he tries he meets cries of "Long live the King." In desperation, he calls on Merlin, who had disappeared suddenly just before the trip

Merlin and the boy Arthur in The Sword in the Stone.

to London after exclaiming, "Well, blow me to Bermuda." Now he returns wearing Bermuda shorts and a loud touristy-looking modern shirt. But he consoles Wart and tells him that "they'll be writing books and even make a motion picture about you—something like television, without commercials," a wonderful and completely accurate bit of hindsight prophesying.

The movie *Camelot* (1967), starring Richard Harris, Vanessa Redgrave, and Franco Nero, is based on the 1960 stage musical of the same name by Alan Jay Lerner and Frederick Loewe. Like *The Sword in the Stone*, *Camelot* took its inspiration from T. H. White, but primarily from Books III and IV, *The Ill-Made Knight* and *Candle in the Wind*. But there are also references in the dialogue and story to material from the earlier books and to Tennyson's *Idylls of the King*. The musical play was only moderately well received on Broadway. However, by the time the film came out, four years after John F. Kennedy's death, its mystique and lyrics had come to be identified with that "one brief, shining moment," and the public was

Madame Mim in The Sword in the Stone

ready to accept the ideology and the romance, the humor, the satire, and the fantasy of the movie as an escape from the disillusionment of Vietnam, the bitterness and disenchantment of the antiwar demonstrations, and the grim reality of the war on the evening television news.

Americans at home wanted desperately to believe that their involvement in Vietnam was a use of might *for* right, and they were doomed, like Arthur in the play, to ask, "What went wrong?" The movie-going public was also apparently willing to accept the conventional masculine fantasy that all beautiful women secretly dream of being abducted, ravished, tied to a tree, in short raped. Guinevere is insulted when Arthur assures her that he has no intention of doing these things and petulantly asks him, "Why not?" The movie came out on the eve of the woman's liberation movement. It is hard to imagine that this exchange would have been in the film had it been made five years later. It has no basis in the book, and it has nothing to do with subsequent events, except to indicate that Guinevere, like most women, is a wanton, who will ultimately succumb to her penchant for illicit adventure. This impression is reinforced later in the film when Vanessa Redgrave and her maidens, wearing filmy garments and dancing with the abandon of Isadora Duncan, sing of the lusty month of May, "when everyone goes blissfully astray." The song foreshadows her infidelity, though her initial reaction to Franco Nero's priggish Lancelot is to try to bring him down from his narcissistic pedestal. The attempt is doomed from the start, for it is an attempt to deny, to herself and to him, their mutual attraction. It too has no basis in White, who depicts her as being kind to Lancelot because Arthur asks her to, and as being hurt by *his* cruelty and indifference. White's "ill-made knight," whose cruelty to Guinevere turns to love when he sees the hurt in her eyes, becomes in Lerner's version, a comically self-adulating perfectionist. Lerner's Arthur, however, is closer to White's original conception than either Lancelot or Guinevere. A dreamer, a pacifist, somewhat shy, fearful, and unsure of himself in love, because it is the one thing Merlin never taught him anything about, he suffers a Hamlet-like paralysis at the thought of confronting the lovers. This conception of Arthur appears to stem from White's own psyche. Sylvia Townsend Warner in her prologue to *The Book of Merlyn* (1977) says that, throughout his life, White suffered from fears, which he fought with "courage, levity, sardonic wit, and industry" (ix). Lerner captures this perfectly when he has Arthur say, the night before his wedding, "I know what my people are thinking tonight," and answers himself in song: "I wonder what the king is doing tonight? He's scared! He's wishing he were in Scotland fishing tonight!" Arthur is afraid of women, afraid of his own sexuality, and afraid of hurting others. His training by Merlin to think himself into the minds of others is at once his strength and his weakness. Each of these characterizations, whether radically changed or dramatically simplified from its source, works in the film to create an Eden-like Camelot, where "the rain may never fall till after sundown," and where the inhabitants *almost* achieve earthly perfection.

Our first view of Lancelot, standing on a parapet of a fairy-tale castle, clutching the parchment calling knights to the Round Table, and singing, "C'est Moi," reinforces this impression. "Had I been made a partner of Eve, we'd be in Eden still." Even the illicit love is almost hallowed, as long as it is not admitted, because the lovers love Arthur and he loves them and forgives them even as they sin, because Lancelot wins Guinevere's love by working a miracle, and because time seems to stand still. Because the lovers do not grow older, as they do in the novel, they can still hope, and can be symbols of hope. Arthur becomes almost godlike, even as his old plan of using might for right, and then replacing might with civil law, begins to fall apart. For there is a serpent in the garden, and his name is Mordred, the offspring of a brief, incestuous union between Arthur and his half-sister Morgause long before, a son-nephew whom Arthur must love and accept because he is good, and because he has now rejected might even for right. Mordred insists, with the ruthless honesty of the truly wicked, that Arthur must absent himself from the castle overnight, so that the lovers can fall into his trap. He insists, in White's own summary of Malory's *Morte Darthur*, "on blowing the gaff on Launcelot and Guinevere's affair, which Arthur was content to overlook, as long as it was not put into words" (Warner xi). From this point on, the action moves with the inevitability of a Greek drama. White himself likened the story to the Orestian trilogy, with the sins of the father not only visited on but replicated by the son. Lerner, however, stops short of having Arthur engage in warfare with Mordred, possibly because it would have complicated the clean romance story line. So the final scene, with Arthur knighting young Tom of Warwick and ordering him to return to Warwick to tell the tales of Camelot, takes place in the predawn preparations for a battle with Lancelot, a scene filled with mist, as vague and confusing as Arthur's anguished efforts to find an explanation for what went wrong with his dream. Lancelot and Guinevere come to ask his forgiveness and to say goodbye. Guinevere has cut her glorious golden hair and is in the care of the "holy sisters," though earlier in the film there were hints, in the May song and the mockery of Lancelot's fanatical religiosity, that she symbolized the earlier pagan religion. Now Guinevere the wanton has become penitent.

Arthur sadly explains that he cannot call off the battle because "they've forgotten justice, they want revenge." There is nothing to be done. They must leave decisions to God. The sense of fatality and doom is enhanced by the music. The dark gloomy tones of the cinematography and costumes are in strong contrast to the virginal white-on-white of Guinevere's first appearance, the soft greens and golds of the tight shots of Guinevere and Arthur or Guinevere and Lancelot singing their loves and their dreams, or the pastel profusion of the May Day dance. The music changes from the lilting, mildly mocking rhythms of the early songs "C'est Moi," "I Wonder What the Common Folk Are Doing Tonight," "Where Are the Simple Joys of Maidenhood?" and "How to Handle a Woman." It becomes slow, sentimental, almost solemn, and helps to seduce the audience into accepting the unlikely premise that wrongdoing becomes wrong only when it is publicly disclosed. The stunning cinematography, along with the catchy lyrics, plays no small part in compressing the action and suggesting the epic sweep of the story. The opening scene is shot in the mist, with Arthur asking Merlin, present only in his imagination and in the camera's eye, how he blundered into this absurdity, a question many Americans were beginning to ask by the end of the sixties, and a question T. H. White tried to grapple with at the end of the thirties. The voice of Merlin tells him to think back, and Arthur recreates himself as Wart, first meeting Merlin. Not that far back, Merlin tells him, but "The day you met Guinevere." The audience is magically transported twice through time, making a quick cinematic allusion to Arthur's boyhood, which is referred to later in the dialogue, when Arthur tells Guinevere how Merlin taught him to think by turning him into animals, "well, by making me believe he turned me into animals."

After a charming but unorthodox wooing scene, the camera shifts to the castle, a long shot of Guinevere riding a white horse led by Arthur, their procession to the altar against a background of lighted candles, and a shot of Arthur slipping a ring on Guinevere's finger. The scene shifts to a map of England, with Arthur's voice explaining to Guinevere in ponderous logic that it is better to be alive than dead. His monologue continues while he goes behind a curtain and is wheeled out in a bathtub, as he outline his plan to use might *for* right instead of holding that might *is* right, and to build a table with no head, for knights to talk across. It continues over a montage of shots, giving a flavor of Hollywood's conception of life in this anachronistic, never-never time: Guinevere buying from merchants at a fair, Guinevere currying a horse, and so forth, until finally she responds that her father has just the thing, and he's not using it: the Round Table.

Messengers are sent out to the music of "Camelot," silhouetted against gorgeous sunsets, riding through forests, observed by picturesque peasants. Arthur and Guinevere pore over maps, stamping the places from which knights are beginning to pour in to assemble around the table in shadowy forms; carrier pigeons carry the message over seas, to Lancelot in faroff France. Lancelot is seen riding away to England, leading his horse, singing over a campfire, singing against the sky in a small boat as he crosses a remarkably placid

Two Films That Sparkle

From left to right, Lancelot (Franco Nero), Arthur (Richard Harris), and Guinevere (Vanessa Redgrave) in Camelot.

English Channel, riding toward Camelot on a white horse, until he meets Arthur and in the fervor of his unthinking devotion challenges and unseats Arthur himself in the name of Arthur. Arthur, amused, welcomes him to the Round Table, but Lancelot is as excessive in his abject apology as he was in his zeal to defend Arthur's honor.

The cinematic-musical interlude is over and the story resumes, with the unbending, serious Gaul demanding a mission, and being told that nothing much is going on now, the knights are all out with the Queen, who has gone a-Maying. In contrast to the stiff-necked righteousness of Lancelot, the Queen and her maidens appear decked with flowers and playing like children on swings and seesaws, being tossed in blankets in a most undignified manner, and generally behaving like the nobility in a picture by Fragonard. In the midst of this spring frolic, King Pellinore appears, the very image of a dotty English gentleman parodying a knight-errant. He once spent a fortnight "here" with Wart, in a real bed, and hopes to be invited again. In White as well as in Malory, Pellinore had a real role in the plot. He killed King Lot, and his son Lamorak had an affair with Morgause, Lot's wife, triggering some of the tragedy. But the movie has made him into just a comic but loveable old geezer with mutton chops, spectacles sliding down his nose, and a sympathetic clucking for the wayward youngsters in the court.

The action proceeds in a series of vignettes. Arthur appears with his new friend Lancelot, who condescends to Guinevere. Guinevere coquettishly asks Sir Lionel, Sir Sagramore, and Sir Dinadan each to challenge Lancelot in a tournament.

Arthur soliloquizes in song on how to handle a woman, the first hint of trouble in the marriage, and the scene shifts to a fair with puppets, masks, and acrobats providing visual charm. Then comes the critical scene, the turning point in the romance. Sir Lancelot unseats each of the knights in turn, but Sir Dinadan dies and Sir Lancelot, seeing the Queen's grief and confident of his own holiness, works a miracle to restore him to life. Though the miracle is in the sources, it comes at the end of the work, is performed in order to restore Sir Urry to health, and is used to reassure Lancelot that his repentance has been acceptable to God. Here, it is used to introduce a recognition scene.

When Guinevere looks into Lancelot's eyes, she sees his love and goodness, and kneels to him, and Arthur sees the look and knows the truth. Later, back in the castle, Lancelot, looking for Arthur, comes upon a disconsolate Guinevere and confesses his love just as Arthur comes upon them both. The second half of the film is filled with pain, the pain of three good people, each in love with the other two. This *menage à trois* is held in delicate balance until Mordred upsets it. The scene shifts again to the court, but this time the costumes are outlandish and the faces grotesque and evil-looking, reflecting the loss of innocence.

The pageantry of Lancelot's investiture is in long shot, with Arthur and Guinevere stony-faced, formal, and distant. Intimacy and warmth are gone, as well as innocence. Later, Arthur moves in soliloquy from pain to anger to understanding and finally to resolution to *be* a king, to reach for the stars. He responds to the highest law of all, God's law, where vengeance is neither the justification for the taking of a life nor the solution to the problem of pain. Church music swells in the background and another montage follows: knights assembled around the Round Table, cathedral windows in the background, the King making a progress, being worshiped by a grateful populace, Lancelot defending his honor by might,

Guinevere observing this and slipping away to a secret hideaway to meet Lance, to tell him to go away. They sing, "If Ever I Would Leave You," while the camera effectively summarizes the passage of time and the intimacy and duration of their affair. But they are never seen unclothed or in more intimate contact that an impassioned kiss.

Meanwhile, back in the throne room, Arthur sits, gloomy and alone. Pellinore enters with two unhappy tasks: to announce Mordred and to warn Arthur of the betrayal by Lancelot and Guinevere. Arthur rejects both messages, but Mordred enters anyway. The effect of Mordred's appearance is twofold: to remind Arthur of his own youthful transgression, increasing his tolerance for the misdeeds of the two people he loves most; and to allow his cherished concept of right for might to prove itself, by permitting his beloved Lance and Jenny to come to trial by law, confident that there will be no proof to condemn them. But there will be proof, circumstantial and rigged by Mordred, and there is no time for explanations, as Arthur, racing back to warn them, is almost run down by Lance escaping. Arthur's return to the castle to find Guinevere being led away in chains leads into another cinematic montage with the song "Guinevere" being sung softly, plaintively in the background: the trial, the pronouncement of the sentence, the preparation of the stake, Pellinore watching, Arthur on his throne listening to the tolling of the bells, waiting to give the signal for the execution, waiting for Lancelot to rescue her, Mordred taunting him with his dilemma, to kill the Queen or kill the law, the dramatic rescue, and the symbolic splitting of the table. The final scene returns to the opening scene, the dawn before the battle, which both the novel and the film stop short of portraying.

Both films, like the book on which they are based and the characters who inhabit them, are flawed, anachronistic, anarchic, sentimental, and idealized. They are only a few drops in the explosion of novels and films about Arthur, but oh, how they do sparkle.

WORKS CITED

White, T. H. *The Book of Merlyn*. Austin: Shaftesbury, 1977.

_____. *The Once and Future King*. 1958. New York: Berkley, 1966.

6.

Monty Python and the Medieval Other

David D. Day

The posters advertising *Monty Python and the Holy Grail* at its initial release in 1975 proclaimed, with appropriately comic bombast, that the film "set movie making back 900 years." The joke is of course an anachronistic absurdity—filmmaking is perhaps our most cherished form of modern artistic mimesis, the way in which we flatter ourselves that we can capture the essence of the object filmed absolutely: the final and conspicuously technological solution to the dilemma of artistic signification. And the thought of transposing this twentieth-century technological wonder into the Middle Ages is ridiculous enough to provoke a laugh. But the poster's claim is also representative of a larger satirical strategy followed throughout *Monty Python and the Holy Grail*, the deliberate exploitation of anachronism to attack all modern attempts to grasp the alterity of the Middle Ages and its artifacts. No sooner does the film evoke some definite idea about the Middle Ages than it juxtaposes against it the modern preconceptions or motivations that gave it rise, almost always with hilarious results. Ultimately at issue in *Monty Python and the Holy Grail* is our ability to know the Middle Ages at all, when every attempt we make ultimately betrays the traces of its modern manufacture.

The vehicle of *film* itself is just the first and most obvious target of this corrosive satirical method, the poster being one example of this particular attack. Another occurs in the film's first scene, which opens with the appearance on screen of large white uncial letters against a black background, reading "England 932 A.D.," accompanied by a rolling flourish of heroic music. The writing and sound set up an expectation, albeit one charged with a great deal of Monty Python-inspired apprehension, that the scenes to follow will in some fashion represent a medieval milieu, probably romantically with the usual paraphernalia of such representations—castles, knights on horseback, and so on. And the expectation is kept alive, at least for a moment. We first see swirling mist and then, emerging out of it, a sort of cryptic standard, a pole surmounted by what appears to be a wagon wheel, on which is stretched what may be a human body (perhaps a gesture toward the unromantic view of the Middle Ages as a time of draconian punishments, of extreme human cruelty). There follows yet another reinforcement of the romantic expectation through the medium of *sound*—we hear horse's hooves, and probably expect that the next thing to come out of the mist will be a knight on his destrier, in full chain armor and holding his pennoned lance. And this is of course what comes out of the mist, but with one of the film's more notorious modern modifications to the romantic myth of the knight. The knight (in this case, Arthur) has no horse, although he and his esquire studiously preserve the illusion of one by walking with a peculiar jog that mimics a horse's gait, and the esquire's clicking two coconut shells together. The film therefore undercuts its own earlier evocation of the knight of romance by visually portraying the Monty Python knight of limited absurdist film budgets: horses are expensive to keep and feed, one would expect. It is as if the Python troop, by this visual portrayal of the medium of sound, are admitting that they can afford to get the sounds right, but not the sights one would expect from a filmic view of the Middle Ages. Sorry, ladies and gentlemen, but the film is not the perfect medium of transmission you perhaps thought it was—perhaps you should try radio.

Monty Python and the Holy Grail in fact points out that this modern attempt to grasp the Middle Ages inescapably taints them with our modern concerns, whether those concerns are dictated by the emotional, intellectual, or ideological stake we have in seeing the Middle Ages as we do, or by the financial and aesthetic concerns governing the medium of expression. As always, the Python troop are here busily engaged in exploiting dilemmas that vex the much more serious concern of scholars and philosophers, but it is nevertheless interesting to note that this precise problem is of great concern to medievalists today.[1] How can we get outside ourselves enough to grasp the essence of the medieval Other? As Frederic Jameson puts it in "Marxism and Historicism":

> If . . . we decide that Chaucer, say, or a steatopygous Venus, or the narratives of nineteenth-century Russian gentry, are more or less directly or intuitively accessible to us with our own cultural *moyens du bord*—then we have presupposed in advance what was to have been demonstrated, and our apparent "comprehension" of these alien texts must be haunted by the nagging suspicion that we have all the while remained locked in our own present—the present of the *société de consummation* with its television sets and superhighways, its Cold War, and its postmodernisms and poststructuralisms—and that we have never really left home at all, that our feeling of *Verstehen* is little better than mere psychological projection, that we have somehow failed to touch the strangeness and the resistance of a reality genuinely different from our own. Yet if, as the result of such hyperbolic doubt, we decide to reverse this initial stance, and to affirm, instead and from the outset, the radical Difference of the alien object from ourselves, then at once the doors of comprehension begin to swing closed and we find ourselves separated by the whole density of our own culture from objects or cultures thus initially defined as Other from ourselves and thus as irremediably inaccessible (43-44).

Jameson argues here and elsewhere that a sufficiently sensitive Marxist interpretation of history as a dialectical process between differing modes of production may offer a way out of this dilemma of past ages' alterity/identity, the "hermeneutic circle," as it is sometimes called.[2] But *Monty Python and the Holy Grail* seems to anticipate such maneuvers in general and this one in particular. Consider the episode of Arthur and Dennis. This begins with Arthur riding over the crest of the hill seen in the film's first scene; the same cryptic standard continues to crown it, but this time it is seen against an overcast and dreary sky, while in the camera's foreground two peasants are kneeling in the mud, gouging at the ground with sticks and piling up "filth." The angle of the shot changes, and we see Arthur riding up behind Dennis as he trudges along, pulling a heavy cart; in the distance, we see a castle between the peasant and the King. Both these shots are ideologically "loaded"; their setups in each case

King Arthur (Graham Chapman) and his trusty steed Patsy (Terry Gilliam) in Monty Python and the Holy Grail.

present the peasants in the foreground working at some menial drudgery with a symbol of authority placed behind and slightly above them—in the first shot, the standard with its ill-defined human body, a vague reminder of authoritarian discipline; in the second, the brooding castle, sitting between the King and peasant. The overall effect is to realize in starkest visual terms yet another modern preconception of the Middle Ages, one underpinning the Marxist view of the feudal "mode of production," a tendency to regard the time as one of grim and barbarous tyranny, an age in which the lower class was ruthlessly exploited by its feudal overlords.

The King mistakenly accosts Dennis as "old woman," asking who the owner of the castle is. One expects, perhaps, a pulled forelock at the very least from this down-trodden medieval unfortunate, but Dennis is a touchy peasant and, as it turns out, an anarcho-syndicalist. He protests the King's "automatic treatment of him as an inferior," accuses him of "exploiting the workers" and of "hanging on to outdated imperialist dogma." Outdated by whose standards? Only from a modern perspective could one possibly accuse King Arthur of clinging to a royal prerogative in the least outdated; it would have just been coming into style in his day. The political coloring of the scene's visual presentation, portraying an expected typical condition of the medieval worker, is surrealistically juxtaposed with the socialist construct that at least in part produced such preconceptions—the Marxist model of history, which with its insistence on the linear progressivity of human achievement toward socialist perfection requires as a starting point a view of the feudal economy as exploitative. The effect of putting Marxist rhetoric into the mouths of medieval peasants is again to undermine this modern construct of medieval economic realities. What does it say for linear progress if the same Marxist rhetoric is being used by workers in the quintessentially exploitative Middle Ages as that used by the framers of Marxist historical theory?

To be fair to Jameson and other theoreticians who are trying to modify the positivistic tendencies of Marxist theory, it should be pointed out that this scene parodies an extremely overgeneralized and dogmatic variety of Marxism, the sloganeering sort that arrogantly assumes the correctness and finality of its interpretations of the past. This focus becomes clearer as the scene progresses and the level of conflict between Arthur and Dennis rises. Arthur becomes increasingly exasperated at Dennis's torrent of Marxist rhetoric, which grows more impudent and abusive with the arrival of reinforcements. A warty old woman enters with a cry of "Dennis, there's some lovely filth over here." Then, being informed that Arthur is her king, she wants to know how he got to be king—she "didn't vote for him." Arthur, his eyes turned heavenward, launches into a description of how he received his kingship by the supernatural sanction of "the Lady of the Lake, her arm clad in shining samite," who lifted Excalibur "aloft from the bosom of the lake" to bestow it upon him. As he speaks, a choir of angelic voices begins to sing in the background. Arthur's appeal to the supernatural for his right to rule is directly out of medieval political theory, which saw an anagogical reflection of the divine order in the structuring of the monarchical state. As Dante puts it, "When mankind is subject to one Prince it is most like to God and this implies conformity to the divine intention, which is the condition of perfection" (13). But any assertion of this alternative view of political legitimacy is ended with Dennis's derisive squawk, which debunks Arthur's appeal with what is literally a modern party line: "Strange women lying in ponds distributing swords is no basis for a system of government. You can't expect to wield supreme executive power just because some watery tart threw a sword at you!" A true statement of the case, perhaps, but so egregiously overstated that we have little sympathy with it. The viewer perhaps resents the thoughtlessness with which Dennis relegates Arthur's soliloquy to the rubbish-heap of political thought, not to mention his hypersensitive proletarianism before which Arthur is reduced to frustrated impotence—shaking the "bloody peasant" by the collar only to have this epithet turned against him. "Oh, that's a dead giveaway," says Dennis. "Did you see him repressing me?" One has a dreary sense that this kind of rhetoric can, and probably will, be prolonged indefinitely in tedious combat with any tendency, however innocent, to wish for a simpler time and a simpler way of doing things, any less complicated alternative ideology, which it will automatically dismiss as outmoded. As some Marxists would have it, Marxism may be salvable as a more sensitive, nuanced system for grasping the past. But some latter-day Dennises in the academic community are even today guilty of forcing the remains of the past into the overly restrictive mold of their ideology. As Lee Patterson notes of Marxist hermeneutics:

> The text serves not as the source of the historian's knowledge but merely as an occasion of its deployment. The interpreter possesses a knowledge of the Real (apparently derived from wholly extratextual sources) with which he will unmask the evasions and repressions of the text; he can say that which the text must always silence because he already knows that which the text refuses to (but, from another angle, must inevitably) say. Paradoxically but predictably, then, the historicism of the left comes round to meet that of the right: history ... tyrannizes the text and constrains its meanings within predetermined limits (47-48).

This analysis of the Arthur and Dennis episode should not be understood as an argument that the film has any sort of axe to grind when it comes to Marxism. *Monty Python and the Holy Grail* also satirizes less ideologically defined attempts to grasp the Middle Ages; indeed, it seems to level its guns in general at academic accounts of the Middle Ages. There is, for example, the very strange interlude following King Arthur's failure to take the French castle through the Trojan Rabbit ploy. A bespectacled and tweed-suited gentleman referred to in a subtitle only as "a famous historian," his generalized anonymity making him appear as a sort of academic Everyman, comes on screen to "explain" Arthur's subsequent strategy for taking the castle. This grey eminence gives his totally unnecessary explanation, made all the more strange and irritating by the scene's garish intrusiveness and artificiality, in the carefully modulated English of an Oxford don seen through the eyes of P. G. Wodehouse. His tone is animated, reinforced by frequent gestures; he seems totally absorbed in and enthusiastic about his expository charge. Then there is a barely audible drumming of horse's hooves from off-screen, followed by the appearance of a knight on a real horse, in full thirteenth-century panoply of war, who flashes between the camera and the historian and cuts the old gentleman down with a single sword stroke. The brutality of the scene is shocking but also rather funny; it is easy to resent the historian's officious intrusion into the story where no explanation was asked for or needed, and his demise is not mourned. The scene seems to reverse the sound/sight opposition invoked at the film's beginning; there, the romantic view of the Middle Ages is aurally invoked only to be visually undercut. Here, the modern words of the "famous historian" are just so much professorial wind to be cut violently short by the visually invoked medieval other, as if to point out that we medievalists talk a good game, but to ask how we would fare when confronted by the actuality of the Middle Ages, personified by its most imposing figurehead, the knight, the "terrible worm in an iron cocoon." The answer suggested here is of course that we would fare poorly; tweed-suited urbanity is not much of a defense against cold steel. And so the necessity of a safe, modern starting point for our academic expositions is required, lest we fare as the "famous historian."

But this scene has another importance beyond its character as an attack on academic medievalism. The thread of self-reflexivity noted in the advertising poster and the first scene is here picked up, and begins to run as a subversive subnarrative behind the continuing story of Arthur's quest. Following the murder, a middle-aged woman in a cardigan and skirt rushes onto the screen crying for help; we briefly see her standing over the body wringing her hands, then the scene changes to the "Tale of Sir Robin." The narrative again briefly alludes to this new subplot several scenes later, when the first part of Arthur's episode with the Knights Who Say "Ni" is followed by a brief shot showing the same woman standing over the historian's body with several policemen, gesticulating and plainly telling them

King Arthur (Graham Chapman) and one of the Knights Who Say "Ni" (Michael Palin) in Monty Python and the Holy Grail.

the events surrounding the killing. We next see the policemen standing by the shrubbery plot of the Knights Who Say "Ni," following the explosion of the Holy Hand Grenade of Antioch, the sound of which alerts them to the medieval film being made nearby. They appear again following Arthur's outwitting of the Bridge Keeper, shaking Lancelot down as he leans with his hands against the roof of their squad car, the static and scratchy voices of their two-way radios providing the shot's only sound. And their final and most important appearance is of course in the film's last scene when their car with sirens blaring pulls up in front of Arthur's advancing army; the last shot is of Arthur being led away in handcuffs, obliterated finally by a policeman's peremptory bark of "that's enough," followed by his palm covering the camera to terminate the film.

In these scenes, *Monty Python and the Holy Grail* seems to acknowledge that it is implicated in the very strategies it satirizes, for it is a modern film about the Middle Ages and cannot escape from its own modernity. The enterprise of filmmaking is after all motivated by an intrinsically modern desire to make the historically distant apprehensible to the eyes and ears through technologically ensured mimesis, to capture its essence through some metaphysically perfect medium of transmission. But one can do this no more than one can transpose the medium of film "back 900 years." The very effort to do so leads to an incident of violence on which the modern authorities frown; the film self-consciously acknowledges its status as a medieval fiction depending for its existence on the modern milieu that surrounds it—a milieu in which one cannot kill medieval historians with impunity. The modern world will not, cannot, be shut out of the film's enterprise of trying to capture the Middle Ages, and its intrusions eventually overload the efforts of *Monty Python and the Holy Grail* to sustain itself as a medieval fiction.

It would not be too extreme to see the real quest of the film as an effort to say something genuinely medieval about the Middle Ages, but unlike the actual quest for the Grail, there is no Galahad to act as *deus ex machina* and find the proper medium for saying it. Galahad here is certainly but quite understandibly possessed of impure thoughts, as the episode at Castle Anthrax demonstrates, and the characters are usually thwarted by the modernity of the very film they move and act in.[3] Not all the humor in the film fits into the pattern I have charted here, and to insist that it does would be to ignore a great deal of the inspired lunacy that graces the movie. But much of it does fit, not only the scenes I have discussed but others as well: the cartoonist's coronary that saves Arthur's party from the Black Beast, or the Rambo-esque, grotesque juxtaposition of modern military hardware and medieval religious artifacts in the Holy Hand Grenade of Antioch with its biblical instruction manual, the Book of Armaments. Moments like these demonstrate that there is a broad method to the madness of *Monty Python and the Holy Grail*; a ruthlessly comic tendency to point out modern constructs for grasping the medieval Other that is our shadow, constructs that prove only the shadows of our own age.

NOTES

[1] See, for example, Lee Patterson's book *Negotiating the Past: The Historical Understanding of Medieval Literature* (Madison: University of Wisconsin Press, 1987); or the essays collected by David Aers in *Medieval Literature: Criticism, Ideology and History* (Brighton: Harvester, 1986); in addition, both Patterson and Aers joined with Sheila Delany at the 1989 MLA Convention to give papers at a special session entitled "Politicizing

the Middle Ages in Theory and Practice," led by R. James Goldstein. Patterson, Aers, and Delany all argue that this problem of the "hermeneutic circle" is inescapable; the alternative is therefore a criticism that frankly admits its ideological motivations and preconceptions even as it uses them to interpret the past. "To acknowledge this [one's ideological stance and the effects it has on one's criticism] is to acknowledge severe problems. But these are simply unavoidable, and they are best confronted openly" (Aers 2).

[2]Most notably in *The Political Unconscious* (Ithaca: Cornell University Press, 1981).

[3]Perhaps ironically this idea of a quest for the ideal system of signification has recently been proposed as the guiding principle of *Piers Plowman*, another story of a frustrating quest that ends ambiguously. See Laurie Finke, "Truth's Treasure: Allegory and Meaning in *Piers Plowman*," *Medieval Texts and Contemporary Readers*, ed. Laurie A. Finke and Martin B. Shichtman (Ithaca: Cornell University Press, 1987), pp. 51-68.

WORKS CITED

Aers, David. *Medieval Literature: Criticism, Ideology, and History.* Brighton: Harvester, 1986.

Dante Alighieri. *Monarchy*, trans. Donald Nicholl. London: Weidenfeld and Nicholson, 1954.

Finke, Laurie A. "Truth's Treasure: Allegory and Meaning in *Piers Plowman*." *Medieval Texts and Contemporary Readers*, ed. Laurie A. Finke and Martin B. Shichtman. Ithaca: Cornell University Press, 1987. 51-68.

Jameson, Frederic. "Marxism and Historicism." *New Literary History* 11 (Autumn 1979): 41-73.

Patterson, Lee. *Negotiating the Past: the Historical Understanding of Medieval Literature.* Madison: University of Wisconsin Press, 1987.

7.

The Ironic Tradition in Arthurian Films Since 1960

Raymond H. Thompson

The high-minded ideals of Arthurian romance have over the centuries proven an inspiration not only for chivalrous behavior but also for irony and humor. After all, actions that impress one person as noble and self-sacrificing may strike another as foolish and impractical. The Holy Grail was a source of religious inspiration for Arthur's knights, to whom it represented the highest quest. Yet who in his right mind, one might ask, would spend years seeking an object of such disputed appearance and uncertain location? Weighing these factors, Hank Morgan, the nineteenth-century protagonist of Mark Twain's *A Connecticut Yankee in King Arthur's Court*, concludes, "There was worlds of reputation in it, but no money" (78).

The ironic tradition in Arthurian literature has remained strong throughout the centuries, from Chrétien de Troyes and the Gawain-poet in the Middle Ages to Mark Twain and Thomas Berger in more recent times, and thus it is not surprising to find it intruding into the medium of Arthurian films. Since 1960, four films have adopted an ironic approach to Arthurian legend. *The Sword in the Stone*, an animated feature directed by Wolfgang Reitherman for the Disney Studios in 1963, is loosely based upon T. H. White's *The Sword in the Stone* (1938); *Monty Python and the Holy Grail*, directed by Terry Gilliam and Terry Jones for Python Pictures in 1975, draws upon general Arthurian tradition rather that any one source; *The Unidentified Flying Oddball* (released in Great Britain as *The Space-*

man and King Arthur), directed by Russ Mayberry for Disney Studios in 1979, and *A Connecticut Yankee in King Arthur's Court*, directed by Mel Damski for Consolidated Productions and shown on NBC Television as a 1989 Christmas holiday special, are both based on Mark Twain's *A Connecticut Yankee in King Arthur's Court*, published a hundred years earlier in 1889.

Of the four films, *Monty Python and the Holy Grail* has achieved the most enduring popularity and critical recognition. The passage of time has not been kind to *The Sword in the Stone*, as critics have observed: "Though well-received when it came out, and grossing $4.5 million, *The Sword in the Stone* has sunk out of sight since it came out in the early 1960s. It is seldom mentioned in discussions of Disney's work and no character in it evolved into a Disney favorite" (Nash 7:3250). *The Unidentified Flying Oddball* has received even less critical attention, nor is *A Connecticut Yankee in King Arthur's Court* likely to do any better. By contrast, *Monty Python and the Holy Grail* is recognized as the finest film by the Monty Python troupe and has remained a perennial favorite with the devoted fans of their work (Proudy 4:1633-1637; Burns 86-97). As a study of all four films reveals, their success has depended upon the skill with which they use the ironic techniques so central to their vision of the Arthurian legend.

The failure of the film adaptation of *The Sword in the Stone* to develop into a Disney favorite is disappointing, because the book is well loved by readers and would seem to lend itself readily to the Disney fantasy touch. The film, however, borrows little from the book beyond the basic situation of the young Arthur, or Wart as he is known, learning valuable lessons about life while magically transformed into various creatures by his tutor, Merlin the Magician.

Both Wart's first transformation, into a perch, and the wizard's duel with Madame Mim are also found in the book, but the details are changed. In the former episode, Wart's conversation with the huge pike is replaced by an exciting and at times humorous chase. This allows the film to replace words with action yet still make essentially the same point about the dangers of power as does the book. It also provides many opportunities for irony, as the expectation by both pursuer and audience that Wart the perch will be caught is repeatedly, and often comically, frustrated.

Unfortunately, exciting and humorous chases occur both frequently and at considerable length throughout the film, by the wolf, the squirrel, the hawk, and Madame Mim (in various shapes). Consequently, the novelty palls despite the ingenuity of the individual situations depicted. Moreover, because so much time is spent on chases, particular devices recur predictably. Thus, on several occasions, a friendly creature pulls on the pursuing predator's tail, slowing it just enough to allow Wart to evade snapping jaws or clutching talons by inches: Merlin (in the shape of a tench) and the owl Archimedes both hinder the pike, the female squirrel the wolf, and Archimedes the hawk.

The message of these chase scenes is that smaller creatures can escape and even defeat a physically stronger foe through quick wits and courage. This philosophy is a firm favorite with Disney, dating back to his early cartoons, and it is developed with great success in classics like *Cinderella* and *The Jungle Book*. It is central to *The Sword in the Stone*, however, not only because so much of the film is devoted to chases, but also because of Wart's domestic situation. In White's novel, Wart is loved by everyone, even Kay in his own way, and he enjoys a glorious childhood in a community where everybody is happy. In the film, by contrast, he becomes a Cinderella figure, bullied by both the blustering Ector and the oafish Kay. Yet just as he eludes the larger animal predators, so he confounds Ector and Kay. Despite their low opinion of him, he rises to heights undreamed of, becoming king of England. They, by contrast, discover they have less to be proud of than they think, when they are soundly defeated by the ensorceled kitchen mops and dishes.

Merlin is another example of adult incompetence, setting off in the wrong direction for Ector's castle, and arousing the mirth of Archimedes when he tangles his model airplane in his beard. Yet like Wart he also demonstrates how those discounted by others as being of little consequence can achieve more than expected, when he defeats Madame Mim by turning into a tiny but potent germ.

This pattern in which the weak overcome the strong affords ample opportunity for irony, but it does grow tiresome through repetition. Moreover, it obscures other ideas that are present in the film. The transformations teach Wart a number of lessons, but they are forgotten amid the hectic action of chases and neglected in the aftermath. Wart learns the power of love when he is pursued through the trees by an amorous female squirrel, but his vigorous defense of Merlin against the criticism of Ector emphasizes the importance of open-mindedness rather than love for his tutor. And Merlin's transformations in the wizards' duel focus upon the comic effect of his bumbling impracticality, rather than the message that knowledge and wisdom bring power. The result is a film that offers little beyond the one basic message, and through repetition it grows tiresome, despite the charm of individual scenes.

The Disney Studios returned to the Arthurian legend in *The Unidentified Flying Oddball*. Although based upon Twain's *A Connecticut Yankee in King Arthur's Court*, it too borrows little more than the essential situation: in this case, a modern man with advanced technological skills who travels back in time to the days of King Arthur. As in the novel, he survives burning at the stake, is befriended by Clarence the page, makes an enemy of Merlin, and falls in love with Sandy, but that virtually exhausts the similarities. Instead, action centers upon a plot by Mordred and Merlin to usurp Arthur's kingdom. It is foiled because the hero, Tom Trimble, employs such modern devices as rockets and electromagnets to support the King.

The irony in the film arises from a number of sources. There are unexpected parallels with features that we associate with the modern age: for example, the speeches of one knight recall those of Winston Churchill, and Merlin's chambers are modeled on a doctor's office, complete with receptionist, who primly announces, "The magician will see you now." There are also examples of naive behavior by the people of Arthur's era: Sandy believes, on dubious circumstantial evidence, that her father has been magically transformed into a goose; and Arthur, reproving Gawain for unguardedly turning his back on the enemy, commits the same mistake himself while pulling out a spear that has pinned the knight's cloak to a door. Fortunately, the butt of the spear accidentally knocks down the onrushing soldier.

Most of the irony, however, is caused by the bewilderment of Arthur and his followers over Tom's modern gadgetry and language usage. Tom survives burning at the stake, thanks to his heat-resistant space suit, and he flies about in a one-man rocket-powered propulsion unit, attacking the enemy where they least expect it. His fondness for jargon based upon such features of contemporary life as fast food and baseball, together with an inability to discern what information is really important for his listeners to know, cause them great confusion.

The problem here, as in *The Sword in the Stone*, is overkill. The idea of magnetizing Mordred's sword and then attaching metal objects to it until it grows too heavy to wield is a clever example of how modern scientific knowledge can defeat physical superiority, in spite of most people's expectation of victory for the latter, but the

Alisande (Sheila White) and Spaceman Tom Trimble (Dennis Dugan) in The Unidentified Flying Oddball.

actual fight scene is prolonged unduly. Moreover, the idea surfaces again at the climax of the action, when Tom's look-alike robot companion uses their spacecraft's electromagnets to immobilize Mordred's armored troops. The scene in which they are drawn back to the craft, one after another, is extended at far too great a length. Once the results of an action cease to be unexpected, there is no longer any irony.

The same failure mars the joust between Mordred and the robot. The ability of the machine to keep functioning despite the loss of an arm certainly confounds the spectators, who believe it is Tom, but the dismemberment continues until the irony becomes merely gruesome. Arthur speaks for us all when he urges Mordred to put an end to the "butchery."

Nor is Tom's use of modern jargon any more successful. People cannot be expected to understand language based upon developments that lie in the future. The audience realizes this after a couple of conversations have taken place, and it is baffled that Tom, for all his mechanical skill, does not.

Thus, the irony generated by the interaction of ancient and modern attitudes fades as responses become predictable through repetition. The novelty palls rapidly because the individual incidents lack the ingenuity of those found in *The Sword in the Stone*. There just is not enough variety to sustain interest, despite the occasionally funny moment.

A Connecticut Yankee in King Arthur's Court is the most recent adaptation of Twain's novel to the screen. Released on television as a Christmas special for younger viewers, it stars Keshia Knight Pulliam, the youngest daughter in *The Bill Cosby Show*, as Karen Jones from Hartford, Connecticut. This version adopts not only the basic idea of a modern person traveling back to Arthur's day but also a number of specific details and incidents, such as Karen's use of the solar eclipse to escape burning at the stake, taking the name Sir Boss, traveling with the King disguised as peasants, and being rescued by knights on bicycles. Here too, however, the action focuses upon a plot by Mordred, Morgana de la Fey, and Merlin to seize Arthur's throne.

Irony again stems from the interaction of modern and Arthurian culture. When Karen teaches aerobic dancing, karate, and the equality of women to Guinevere and her ladies-in-waiting, we relish the incongruity of such elegant aristocrats "working out." The same incongruity is achieved by the sight of Arthur's knights in full armor riding on bicycles.

Yet too often the effect is marred by carrying the superstitious response of Arthur's court to excessive lengths. Their astonishment and fear at such modern inventions as the Polaroid camera and tape recorder, both of which, they believe, trap a part of themselves that can be harmed, seem unwarranted. While Twain's novel also stresses the credulity of people in the sixth century, Hank Morgan has to demonstrate his powers more devastatingly, not only with the eclipse (which occurs at the outset of the story, not near its conclusion as in the film), but also by blowing up buildings and people from time to time.

The contrast can be seen in the episode where the King and the Yankee, disguised as peasants, are attacked by knights for failing to show proper respect to their social superiors. In the novel, Hank blows up the two knights with a dynamite bomb, and "during the next fifteen minutes we stood under a steady drizzle of microscopic fragments of knights and hardware and horse-flesh" (272). In the film, Karen frightens off their single assailant by recording and playing back his speech. He flees, proclaiming that she is a "voice witch." Hank's violence would be out of character in Karen, who encourages the Queen and her ladies to decorate cushions with the motto "Save the Elephants" (in itself an ironic contrast with the views of Hank, who is willing to exploit everything), but it does much more to account for his reputation as a powerful magician who should be treated with healthy respect. Presumably in an attempt to compensate for the lack of convincing motivation, some of the actors compound the problem by overacting (though in fairness it must be admitted that any fear they demonstrate might strike the audience as excessive).

The naivete of the characters is not confined to their response to modern wonders. Arthur trusts Mordred and Morgana, despite warnings from knights like Lancelot, and he is easily outwitted by the plotters. Without more justification than the script offers, this behavior taxes the belief of the audience. A king unaware that his people are being taxed ninety percent of their income would hardly have survived even as long as he has. But then perhaps it was assumed that only a monarch so out of touch with reality would make a young girl one of his knights. One does not look for reality from a fantasy, especially since it all may be no more than a dream resulting from a blow to the head, but one certainly expects the motivations of the characters to be convincing, even if only in their own terms.

Monty Python and the Holy Grail is the creation of the comedy troupe comprising Graham Chapman, John Cleese, Terry Gilliam, Terry Jones, Eric Idle, and Michael Palin. Their popular comedy series *Monty Python's Flying Circus*, ran on British television from 1969 to 1974, and they went on to make a number of films. Their style, which has been described as "comic anarchy" (Proudy 4:1634), is offensive to some, but it has built up a devoted and enthusiastic following. In the film, the Grail quest serves as a narrative frame for a series of comic sketches, in which members of the troupe play several different roles.

As in the other films, the Arthurian borrowing for the narrative frame is confined to the basic situation: this time, the quest by the knights of the Round Table for the Holy Grail. Although probably borrowed from Malory, at least indirectly, the story is freely adapted, adding, for example, such non-traditional knights as the cowardly

Sir Robin. Some of the motifs it employs are found in more than one source. Thus, the voyage of Arthur and Bedivere on the mysterious vessel recalls that of Galahad and his companions, not only in Malory, but in other accounts based on his source, the French Vulgate *Queste del Saint Graal*.

The sources of the comic sketches within the narrative frame are even less easy to identify. The Camelot dance scene evokes Lerner and Loewe's musical *Camelot*, and Castle Anthrax recalls the Castle of Maidens in both Malory and Chrétien de Troyes. Most of the episodes, however, seem to be based upon general romance tradition rather than any one account; for example, Arthur's fight against the Black Knight, who refuses to yield despite the amputation of all his limbs, derides the exaggerations of knightly combat that occur everywhere. Others, like the witch hunt, come from outside Arthurian tradition entirely.

Most of the irony is aimed at the many conventions that occur in medieval romance, especially those connected with deeds of valor. The mindless enthusiasm for fighting is mocked not only in Arthur's encounter with the Black Knight, who dismisses the loss of an entire arm as "just a scratch . . . I've had worse," but also in Lancelot's "rescue" of the prince in the tower "I sometimes get a bit carried away," he confesses, after slaughtering many of the wedding guests, including such inoffensive figures as the garlanded maidens dancing in a circle. The knights are not always so fierce, however. They are forced to beat an ignominious retreat when bombarded with livestock by the French soldiers, and Sir Robin's flight from the three-headed knight is celebrated in song by his accompanying minstrels. Nor do they have much success against the rabbit that guards the cave.

Despite the special attention to knightly combat, few romance conventions are spared the Monty Python irony. Love and the rescue of maidens in distress are mocked in Lancelot's rescue of the prince, whom he mistakes for a princess, in the tower; mysterious and perilous castles, by Castle Anthrax, which is filled with damsels only too eager to be ravaged; the imposition of difficult tasks upon the hero, by the demand for a shrubbery by the Knights Who Say "Ni"; religious devotion, by God's irritable command that the knights seek the Holy Grail; magicians, by Tim the Enchanter, who can set off explosions yet fears a rabbit; the unthinking assumptions of feudal authority, by Arthur's argument with a subject from an "anarcho-syndicalist commune."

The Ironic Tradition in Arthurian Films 101

Nor is the irony confined to romance conventions. The need to answer difficult questions before passing over the Bridge of Death is a motif from folklore and legend; the call to "bring out your dead" is from history; and the commentary of the scholar is from the television documentary (or the lecture room).

This variety certainly helps to avoid the predictability that mars the other films. Nevertheless, so wide a range of targets might have caused confusion in the mind of the audience had not certain ironic techniques been deployed to link the material more closely. First of all, the extensive use of double reversals integrates the action within the individual episodes. When Bedivere reasons with the peasants who accuse a young woman of being a witch on very flimsy evidence, we expect him to expose the folly of their accusations. The charge by one of their number, that he had been turned into a newt but had "got better," seems improbable even to his companions. Instead, Bedivere concludes by proposing the equally ridiculous test of weighing her against a duck. Yet this does not prove her innocent, as we might confidently assume, for woman and duck turn out to weigh the same: "It's a fair cop," she wryly admits.

In search of the Holy Grail, Galahad pounds at the door of the sinister Castle Anthrax, but expectations of either dire perils or mystical revelations are dispelled by the warm welcome from its nubile inhabitants. Galahad resists their overtures and seeks to escape, until urged to spank them all, then engage in oral sex. At this invitation, his resistance unexpectedly melts, and he decides to "stay a bit longer" after all. Any prospect of an orgy is denied, however, by the arrival of Lancelot and another knight, who rescue him from his "deadly peril."

This series of reversals is further enriched by associations with Arthurian tradition. Recollections of the Castle of Maidens in Chrétien de Troyes's *Conte du Graal*, with roots in tales of the Celtic Otherworld, or of demons in disguise seeking to seduce the Grail knight to his eternal damnation, are contrasted with attitudes that belong in an English girls' school. The tradition of purity associated with Galahad's initial resistance contrasts with his eager anticipation of the orgy. And instead of the perfect Galahad defeating all foes, not only is he the one who must be rescued, but he is most reluctant to leave: "I want to face perils and trials," he protests, "I can handle them"; to which the eager damsels chorus, "Yes, handle me, handle me."

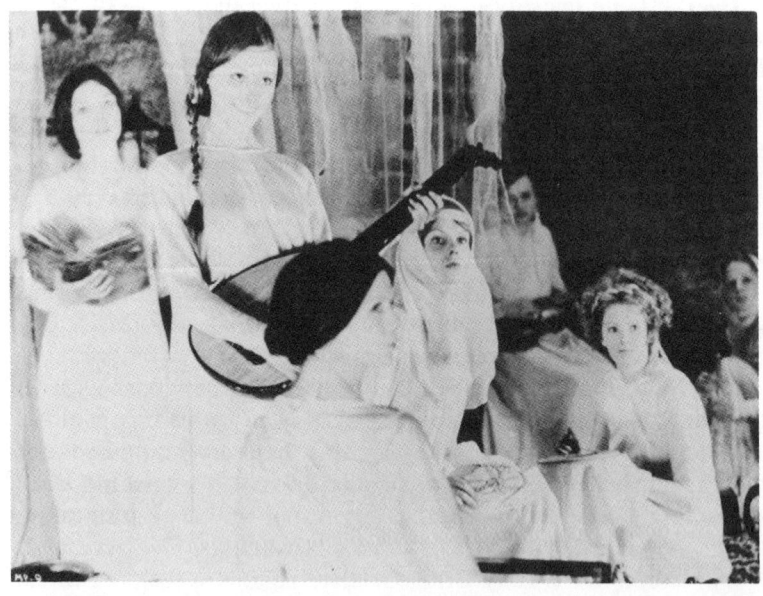

Zoot (with her lute) and "the equally delectable Girlies" who inhabit Castle Anthrax in Monty Python and the Holy Grail.

At the conclusion of the scene, he accuses his father of homosexual inclinations, and this adds irony and humor to Lancelot's embarrassed discovery that the princess whom he comes to rescue from the tower in a later episode is in fact an effeminate young prince. This technique is extended into the running joke in order to link episodes together.

When Arthur engages in the frustrating conversation about the swallow and the coconut with the guards on the castle wall in the opening scene, we enjoy the incongruity of the King of the Britons kept waiting while his social inferiors debate obscure details of natural history. The humor of this exchange is recalled by the allusion to swallows during the narrative bridge between Galahad's adventure at Castle Anthrax and the visit to the soothsayer by Arthur and Bedivere. And when Arthur uses the information he has gained about swallows to outwit the guardian of the Bridge of Death, we not only remember the earlier dialogues, but enjoy the King in the unfamiliar role of trickster.

The Ironic Tradition in Arthurian Films

In the episode where the villagers are summoned to "bring out your dead," one man arrives carrying a body that is still alive. While he tries to persuade the body collector to take this unusual "corpse," very much as a modern British houseowner might cajole a dustman into taking an item barred by regulations, the old man keeps interrupting: "I'm not dead yet... I'm getting better... I'm feeling quite well now." Eventually, the body collector knocks him on the head with a club and adds him to his pile. This pattern, in which a "dying" man stages a miraculous and unwelcome recovery, is reenacted several times in the episode where Lancelot rescues the prince: first by Lancelot's servant after he is hit by an arrow; then by the father of the bride after he has been cut down by Lancelot; and finally by the prince himself, who survives a fall from the tower.

The other three films all make the mistake of repeating a particular formula until it becomes predictable, and thus no longer ironic. *The Sword in the Stone* shows how the weak may overcome the strong; *The Unidentified Flying Oddball* and *A Connecticut Yankee in King Arthur's Court* explore the confusion caused by modern technology to people of an earlier age. *Monty Python and the Holy Grail* avoids this trap by tackling a variety of targets. Because one never can be sure what is coming next, the irony retains its force.

At the same time, *Monty Python and the Holy Grail* avoids much of the disjointedness of other films by the Monty Python troupe for two reasons. First of all, it makes effective use of such ironic techniques as the double reversal and running joke to link the material together. Second, it employs a narrative frame that permits the inclusion of a wide variety of episodes while still advancing the story. Indeed, the narrative style of the film is not unlike the interlacing that marks medieval prose romances of the Holy Grail.[1]

It may be that the other three films are assuming that the younger audience at which they are aimed can only understand lessons that are repeated over and over again. If so, it is time filmmakers realized that boredom is as deadly an obstacle to learning as it is to irony. *Monty Python and the Holy Grail* has its faults, as critics have noted: "Ninety minutes is simply a long time to sustain their nonstop goofiness.... The constant flood of absurdity can become wearing" (Proudy 4:1637). Yet its skillful and varied use of irony demonstrates just how effective this approach to the Arthurian legend in film can be, deflating our pretensions by exposing our penchant for romanticizing our heroes—and ourselves.

NOTES

[1]For a discussion of interlacing, see, for example, Eugene Vinaver, "The Questing Knight." *The Binding of Proteus: Perspectives on Myth and the Literary Process* (Lewisburg, Pa.: Bucknell University Press, 1980), pp. 126-140.

WORKS CITED

Burns, E. Jane. "Nostalgia Isn't What It Used to Be: The Middle Ages in Literature and Film." *Shadows of the Magic Lamp: Fantasy and Science Fiction in Film*, ed. George Slusser and Eric S. Rabkin. Carbondale: Southern Illinois University Press, 1985. 86-97.

Nash, Jay Robert, and Stanley Ralph Ross. *The Motion Picture Guide, 1927-1983*. 9 vols. Chicago: Cinebooks, 1987.

Proudy, Howard H. "Monty Python and the Holy Grail." *Magill's Survey of Cinema: English Language Films*, ed. Frank N. Magill. Series 2. 6 vols. Englewood Cliffs, N.J.: Salem, 1981. 4:1633-1637.

Twain, Mark [Samuel L. Clemens]. *A Connecticut Yankee in King Arthur's Court*, ed. Bernard L. Stein. Berkeley: University of California Press, 1979.

8.

Camelot Twice Removed: *Knightriders* and the Film Versions of *A Connecticut Yankee in King Arthur's Court*

Kevin J. Harty

The legend of Arthur has readily found a home in the American imagination. The best American example of Arthuriana from the late nineteenth century is Mark Twain's *A Connecticut Yankee in King Arthur's Court*, the only version of the legend "that fully realises the social and historical forces of its period" (Knight 187). Not surprisingly, the novel has several times been the source for Arthurian films. In both the novel and the films derived from it, the main character moves back in time to the sixth century to encounter the Arthurian legend. In contrast, in George Romero's *Knightriders*, arguably the most "American" contemporary Arthurian film, the legend moves ahead in time to the twentieth century.

Mark Twain's works have been a favorite source for filmmakers in search of good story lines since 1907, when Vitagraph made a one-reeler called *A Curious Dream* from the Twain short story of the same title. Twain, who lived to see the film and authorized Vitagraph to make it, wrote that he found the film "frightfully and deliciously humorous" (Roman 20). A half-dozen other films based on Twain's works found their way to the screen between 1907 and 1920, when Fox made the first film version of Twain's tale of Hank Morgan, a silent feature entitled *A Connecticut Yankee at King Arthur's Court*.

Twain might not at first have recognized many of the details of this film as being inspired by his novel.[1] The hero, Twain's Hank Morgan, "a Yankee of the Yankees" (Clemens 8), has in the film become Martin Cavendish (played by Harry Myers[2]), a wealthy young man who is in love with his mother's secretary, Betty, at the same time that his socially conscious mother wants him to marry Lady Gray Gordon. One night, as he sits reading in the drawing room, Cavendish is attracted to a suit of armor. As his mind turns back to the days when knighthood was in flower, a burglar quietly enters the house. Cavendish discovers him, the two scuffle, and Cavendish is knocked unconscious as the thief stands over him, threatening him with a lance. When Cavendish opens his eyes again, he has taken a leap of more than twelve hundred years backward in time and is lying under a tree, as a mounted knight, Sir Sagramore, is jabbing him with a lance.

Following the novel, Sir Sagramore marches Cavendish off to King Arthur's court at Camelot. Cavendish is clearly bewildered at the antique English spoken by his captors, while his use of the latest American slang is equally surprising to them. Condemned to death, Cavendish saves himself in the well-known scene involving Merlin and the solar eclipse.[3] Made a knight with the title of Sir Boss, Cavendish proceeds to modernize Camelot with the latest inventions, including telephones, electric lights, modern plumbing, and automobiles manufactured from discarded armor. The knights themselves soon punch time clocks and spend their lunch hours shooting craps.

Impressed by Cavendish's ingenuity, Arthur sends him to rescue the beautiful Lady Alisande ("Sandy"), who is being held captive by the King's half-sister, the wicked and, as portrayed by Rosemary Theby in the film, the vampish Morgan le Fay. The rescue ensues but only after Cavendish rejects the amorous overtures of Morgan and uses his trusty six-shooter to good advantage. Back at Camelot, Cavendish accepts a challenge to meet Sir Sagramore in the lists. Instead of wearing armor and using a lance, Cavendish appears dressed as a cowboy armed only with a lariat. He soon yanks Sir Sagramore from his horse and chases the rest of the armor-clad knights from the field. Getting the King to disguise himself, Cavendish conducts him on a tour of his domain so he can see for himself that "all this nobility stuff is bunk." When the King and Cavendish are captured by the "four horsemen of the eucalyptus" in the employ of Morgan le Fay, they are rescued by Lancelot and Sandy. Finally,

Cavendish comes to, discovers that his experiences have been nothing but a dream, and, to settle matters, elopes with Betty.

Despite the liberties it takes with its source, *A Connecticut Yankee at King Arthur's Court* garnered much critical praise. Burns Mantle dubbed the film the second-best screen comedy of the year, counting Chaplin's *The Kid* as the first (51),[4] while other critics commented that the film, directed by Emmett J. Flynn, proved the screen's potential for intelligent comedy rather than only for simple-minded slapstick (Patterson 143-144). In adapting Twain's novel, those responsible for the film missed no opportunity to add touches of contemporaneity to the screenplay. References abound to the Volstead Act, Tin Lizzies, and the Battle of Argonne. The army of rescuing knights arrives on motorcycles, headed by Lancelot driving a flivver, rather than on bicycles as they did in the novel. The film was made on a lavish scale. An announcement in the program for the film states that "every available motorcyclist around Los Angeles was drafted for the big rescue scene, that 370 pounds of nitroglycerine were used to destroy a castle built in the hills, and that two miles of roadway were constructed for the march of the motorcycle army" (Review, *New York Times* 14). In addition, the film required sets big enough to support scenes in which as many as a 1,000 people appeared ("Special Service" 1673).

Both novel and film are clearly dream stories, but the film is for its time a dream story with a twist. Practice dictated that the fact that the events in a film were a dream was to be concealed from moviegoers with a view to giving them a surprise ending. *A Connecticut Yankee at King Arthur's Court* never deludes the viewer into believing that any of the fantastic things ever took place, and yet, as one contemporary critic noted, the effect is as enjoyable as if they had actually happened (O'Dell 249-250).

The artistic and commercial success of this 1920 silent version of Twain's novel doubtless contributed to Fox's decision to remake the film eleven years later.[5] This second version, simply entitled *A Connecticut Yankee*, with Will Rogers as the Yankee,[6] Myrna Loy as Morgan, and Maureen O'Sullivan as Sandy, again takes considerable liberties with the plot of Twain's novel.

Here, the Yankee becomes Hank Martin, a repairman called to fix a radio for a slightly crazed customer who thinks he is listening in on discussions from King Arthur's court. Knocked out when a suit of armor falls on him, Martin awakens to find himself in Camelot. Familiar events follow. Martin's incantations to "make" the eclipse begin—"Prosperity! Farm relief! Freedom for Ireland and light wines and beer!"—and then end—"Coolidge, Hoover, and Al Smith"—are only two of the more obvious contemporary additions to the dialogue. Other new twists to the novel include Hank's use of a cigarette lighter rather than a match to outwit Merlin, telephone switchboards staffed by flirtatious operators, messengers on roller skates, and, in a variation on a dry cleaners, an establishment that cleans and oils armor.

A joust once again matches Sir Sagramore in armor against Martin dressed as a cowboy. The event is even broadcast on radio, sponsored by the "Camelot Iron Works—Builder of Lanceproof Armor." In this film version, Morgan le Fay is also once again enamored of the Yankee, whose innocence and shyness are emphasized when he blushes scarlet on the screen. The film was of course shot in black-and-white, but David Butler, the director, had each frame in this attempted seduction scene especially tinted progressively darker shades of pink (Sterling 113).

The final battle scene used a fleet of automobiles—174 Austins in all ("Will Rogers" 8. 7) machine guns, sawed-off shotguns, tanks, heliocopters, and airplanes that level the castle and knock out Martin who then awakens in the present where a modern-day Clarence and Sandy need help in eloping. The film ends with Martin gladly lending a hand to assist young love. The film cost almost $750,000 to make (Review, *Variety* 20), a considerable sum for a film in its day, and proved a critical and commercial success. The *New York Times* named it one of the year's ten best films, and it was rereleased in 1936, when Myrna Loy's earlier pre-*Thin Man* career as a *femme fatale* had all but been forgotten.

Perhaps better known than either the 1920 or the 1931 version of Twain's novel is Paramount's 1949 film *A Connecticut Yankee in King Arthur's Court*, directed by Tay Garnett and starring Bing Crosby in the title role, William Bendix as Sir Sagramore, Sir Cedric Hardwicke as a buffonish King Arthur, and Rhonda Fleming as Sandy. As the film opens, Hank Martin visits Pendragon Castle and meets the present lord, a descendant of Arthur, to whom he tells in flashback his time-travel adventure. In that story, Hank, a happy-go-lucky New England blacksmith, is knocked unconscious when he and his horse collide with a tree during a violent rainstorm. Martin awakens to find himself face to face with Sir Sagramore, here subsequently cast as Martin's apprentice in the role of Clarence from the novel.

The Yankee (Will Rogers) and Morgan (Myrna Loy) in A Connecticut Yankee *(1931).*

Martin has the expected run-ins with Merlin, but thanks to a pocketful of kitchen matches he is able to better his sixth-century rival and to impress Arthur and his court sufficiently so that they leave him alone to open a small blacksmith shop on the outskirts of the kingdom. Plot complication next occurs in the film when Martin becomes infatuated with Sandy. Despite the fact that she is betrothed to Sir Lancelot, Sandy returns Martin's affection. Once Lancelot finds out about this mutual attraction, he challenges the peace-loving Martin to a joust. Given permission by Arthur to choose his own weapon, Martin renders his opponent helpless by entangling Lancelot in a lasso. Sandy, upset by Martin's use of such an unknightly tactic, rushes to Lancelot's side to comfort him. Next, Merlin and his accomplice, Sir Logris, try to take over the kingdom by kidnaping Sandy and holding her prisoner. Martin goes to her rescue but receives a blow on the head in the process that transports him back to the present.

A few months later, Martin arrives at Pendragon Castle, where he meets the descendant of King Arthur to whom he tells his adventures in Camelot. Not quite knowing what to make of Martin's story, the old lord tells Martin to visit the garden before he leaves so that he can meet his niece. Strolling into the garden, Martin is both surprised and delighted to discover that the girl is the image of his beloved Sandy.

The 1949 film is a movie musical pure and simple, showing both the strengths and the weaknesses of the genre, although for legal and financial reasons its score owes no debt to that of the 1927 stage adaptation of Twain's novel, which had been revived in 1943.[7] Truer in detail to the plot of its source than either the 1920 or the 1931 film, the 1949 film is nonetheless the least successful of the three. Crosby fans may applaud his amply displayed musical talents—indeed, the film seems primarily a vehicle for showcasing his singing abilities—but Tay Garnett, the director,[8] makes little use of the cinematic possibilities of his source. The directorial method throughout the film calls for the plot to advance not by dramatic interaction but rather by snappy tune mixed with rather silly dialogue: In attempting to instruct a sixth-century orchestra in some musical fine points, Martin exclaims for instance, "Putteth in the brass and taketh out the lead." Where the film does shine above its two predecessors is in its "outstanding art direction, set decoration and photography . . . and a spectacular studio recreation of Camelot" (Bookbinder 184).

Twain's novel returned to the screen in 1979 in a fourth but largely ignored film version released by Disney in the United States as *The Unidentified Flying Oddball* and in Great Britain as *The Spaceman and King Arthur*. In this film, a freak accident causes robotics engineer Tom Trimble to be launched along with a lookalike humanoid robot, Hermes, in the inaugural flight of a new spacecraft. Since the spacecraft travels faster than the speed of light, the reluctant astronaut finds himself, thanks to a NASA malfunction, traveling backward in time to the sixth century, where he meets a peasant girl, Alisande, and a goose, whom she is convinced is her magically transformed father.

Captured by the evil Sir Mordred and taken before Arthur's court, Tom is unable to explain to the court where he has come from, despite a rambling synopsis of history of the world. Imprisoned and condemned to be burned at the stake, Tom is saved by his heat-resistant spacesuit (elsewhere in the film, he uses magnets to disarm an array of foes). After accusing Mordred of treachery—the knight

The Yankee (Bing Crosby) and Lady Alisande (Rhonda Fleming) in A Connecticut Yankee in King Arthur's Court *(1949).*

is trying to corner the real estate market in Camelot—Tom is obliged to fight him in a joust. Tom subsitutes Hermes for himself, and Alisande looks on in horror as the figure she imagines to be Tom is cut to pieces. Hermes continues to fight, in a scene reminiscent of that involving the knight at the bridge in *Monty Python and the Holy Grail*, even after losing his arms, legs, and head. Tom then puts down the rebellion, is rewarded with a seat at the Round Table, but is obliged to return to the present. The film's closing scene has him turning back the spacecraft's clock to return to Camelot for Sandy.

At first glance, nothing could seem farther from Twain's novel than this Disney film. Closer consideration, however, shows that the film and the novel have a number of points in common. In the novel, Sandy is convinced that a herd of swine are really enchanted princesses, whom she requires Hank to treat royally (Chapter 20). In the film, Sandy is convinced the goose is her father. Twain's novel uses language, especially German, a tongue Twain regularly took to task, as the basis for much of its humor. So does the film. Tom's rambling survey of Western civilization delivered in schoolboy slang clearly baffles Arthur and his court, whose number include a Sir Winston, who looks, talks, and and carries himself like Churchill. Finally, Twain's novel examines what happens when modern technology is imposed on medieval England. The film carries this point farther by widening the gap: here, space-age technology meets medieval England. If not always the most successful screen adaptation of Twain's novel, this fourth film may be the funniest.

A fifth adaptation of Twain's novel, which aired on NBC as a Christmas special in 1989—coincidentally the hundredth anniversary of the publication of the novel—may be the silliest. In this made-for-television film version, the Yankee becomes Karen Jones, a Connecticut schoolgirl played by Keshia Knight Pulliam from *The Cosby Show*; Michael Gross from *Family Ties* plays Arthur. Knocked unconscious in a fall from a horse, Karen wakes up in Camelot and undergoes the Yankee's usual adventures. Additional updating of events in the novel can be seen in Karen's use of a Polaroid camera, Walkman, and tape recorder as her "magic weapons." She also teaches aerobics and karate to Guinevere and the ladies of the court, who gain a social conscience about endangered species. Previously, they carved ivory figures made from elephant tusks; with Karen's encouragement, they now embroider pillows that read "Save the Elephants." Some of the novel's dialogue survives in this film version, but too much of what Karen says ranges from being borderline-obnoxious to overly cute.

What all five films have in common is humor of varying degrees of success—all five attempt to be funny films. Twain's *Connecticut Yankee* is, among other things, a comic tour-de-force. But it is also much more. In writing the novel, Twain pulled together several strands of plot material: the Arthurian legend, the international novel depicting the confrontation between American and European cultures, the idea of time travel, barbed satire against the Church and the monarchy, and finally the attack on what Twain came to call "the damned human race."[9]

Twain began the novel out of an impulse to spoof Malory's *Morte Darthur*, a book he liked. "Dream of being a knight errant in armour in the middle ages," he set down in his notebook. "Have the notions & habits of thought of the present day mixed with the necessities of that. No pockets in the armor. No way to manage certain requirements of nature. Can't scratch.... Make disagreeable clatter when I enter church.... See Morte Darthur" (Clemens ix-x). As this note from 1885 suggests, Twain's original plan was somehow to introduce a contemporary American to European feudal society in order to ridicule the worship of the past. But the story took shape over the next four years in a very different form. As Stanek notes,

> While the balance of the comparison between past and present remained heavily in favor of contemporary American liberalism and innovation, the basic plot of his story caused a shift in mood. The satire of *A Connecticut Yankee* was ultimately directed against what Mark Twain would later call "the damned human race," not simply against Scott's or Tennyson's idealization of the past. While the Yankee's time travel to sixth-century England produced humorous, even light-hearted adventures, it ended on a darker note, with a cataclysmic battle using weapons of "modern" warfare (1).

All five films fail to deal with the dark side of Twain's novel. Indeed, in making the fifth film version of the novel, those responsible for the telemovie purposely softened Twain's message to make it more palatable to a television audience by eliminating "Twain's heavy social satire about the class sytem" and the novel's "propensity for violence" (Knutzen 4-5). The Disney version, however, is truest to that part of the novel which is simply lighthearted comedy. Biting satire, misanthropy, and carnage made possible by "modern" methods of warfare, film directors seem to have decided, do not play well in Peoria, or anywhere else.[10]

George Romero's *Knightriders* had the bad luck to be given a limited original release during the same week as John Boorman's *Excalibur* and disappeared from general release within a few weeks.[11] A second release on the midnight circuit and video has given the film a limited if loyal secondary audience, but *Knightriders* has not attracted nearly the audience and attention it deserves. Although Romero's surface debt is to the American film western by way of its subgenre the biker film, his deeper debt is to the long tradition that sees Arthur as the Once and Future King.

George Romero has made his reputation as the director of such horror films as *Night of the Living Dead*, *Martin*, and *Dawn of the Dead*. His earlier work as a director would at first suggest that he would be the last person to be interested in making an Arthurian film. But, like most film directors of his generation, George Romero grew up watching films: "I loved all genre films—horror movies as well as war pictures and cowboy films. Whenever one was at a neighborhood theatre or on television, I'd watch it" (Seligson 12). Old genre movies also awakened his interested in the Arthurian legend: "I'd give my eyeteeth to make an *Ivanhoe*. In *Knightriders*, I'm borrowing from all those Cornel Wilde, Robert Taylor movies" (Seligson 16). In addition, *Knightriders*, like other Romero films, examines a community under siege from without. The menace here is not from an army of zombies but rather from the creeping commercialism and hucksterism that threatens Billy and the utopian community he hopes to create, a community whose survival signals a potential rebirth of the power of the magical in the twentieth century.[12]

Knightriders tells the story of a troupe of dropouts from mainstream society who travel throughout rural Pennsylvania in the mid-1970s. The troupe consists of assorted artisans who peddle their crafts and a group of armor-clad motorcycle stuntpeople who travel from county fair to county fair to perform jousts and to hold tournaments. The latter members of the troupe seem to have taken their cue from the Society for Creative Anachronsim, whose members meet regularly for "medieval festivals" at which various "courts" assemble. The troupe is headed by Billy—Sir William, the film's Arthur—and Linet, his "Queen." Around him, Billy has gathered a

Camelot Twice Removed 115

ragtag group who have adopted names both Arthurian and not so Arthurian. While Billy's followers include Sirs Ban (of Boston) Hector (of Newark), Ewain, Bors, Marhalt, and Morgan (here, a man), as well as Merlin, there are also Alan, Tuck, and Little John from the legend of Robin Hood, Pippin from the legend of Charlemagne, and a Sir Rocky (a woman, though a match to any man with whom she "does battle").

The film's opening is striking. Before the initial titles appear, the camera shows a raven in flight—the raven will prove one of the film's central symbols—after which the camera cuts to a naked Billy and Linet lying in the forest. Billy is next shown flagellating himself and then kneeling before his upraised sword. Linet and he then robe, and just when we assume Billy has mounted his trusty steed, he is shown riding off on his motorcycle as the opening titles begin to roll.

Billy joins up with the members of his troupe, who are being shaken down by Deputy Cook. The corpulent officer demands a bribe before allowing the tournament to begin. Billy, in the first demonstration of his allegiance to his code, adamantly refuses to buy off Cook, who threatens retaliation. Pippin announces the rules of the tournament in a speech that begins with a reference to T. H. White's *The Once and Future King*, wherein "honor," Pippin explains, "is true king." The purpose of the tournament is to determine who is rightful king, and Billy and Morgan do eventually face off. Morgan has the edge because Billy still nurses a wound from a previous joust and because he has the advantage in weapons; his mace has the capability of doing serious harm to an opponent.

Thanks to the intervention of his knights, Billy retains the crown, but it is soon obvious that his community is not without its problems. Billy is approached by a young boy, also named Billy, for an autograph, which he refuses to give, since to do so would be to surrender to the commercialsim he sees as a threat to his utopian vision. The film is not always consistent as to what this vision and threat are, but Merlin links Billy's dream of a raven that will some day defeat him with the notion of destiny by telling the story from Malory of Arthur's unsuccessful attempt to avoid his destiny by ordering the slaughter of all male children to eliminate the prophesied threat to his throne from Mordred.[13]

Billy rejects the adulation accorded a hero because, he says, he is "not trying to be a hero"—he is trying "to fight the dragon." The dragon soon returns in the form of Deputy Cook, who arrests one of the troupe, Bagman, after planting drugs on him. Billy demands that

King Billy (Ed Harris) and Lady Linet (Amy Ingersoll) in Knightriders.

he too be arrested, and when he again refuses to pay Cook the demanded bribe, both he and Bagman are hauled off to jail, where Bagman is severely beaten by Cook. Released from jail, Billy attempts to explain his code and the loyalty he feels to it. He believes in fighting for his ideals and if necessary in dying for them, secure in the knowledge that the truth, or the code, lives on. People, he argues, cannot be allowed to walk on the ideals of others.

Billy's ideals provide, in Pippin's words, a kind of "spiritual fix" for his followers, or at least for some of his followers. Having outwitted Cook and threatened to even the score with him at a later date, Billy faces new dragons in the persons of a slick promoter and a rapacious television reporter, who want to manage, market, and thereby exploit the troupe for financial gain. Billy will have nothing to do with such activities, but the ensuing tournament nonetheless proves the downfall of Billy's community. In the midst of general mayhem, a knight, a Native American, bearing a shield with a raven appears. While Billy does defeat the knight, he sustains a life-threatening wound, and the crowds at the tournament become a howling mob egging on the increasing violence. Morgan and his followers split with the troupe to follow the promise of riches and slick promotional tours. Alan, the film's Lancelot, also leaves, and Billy's few remaining loyal followers sit and wonder what will happen next.

Eventually, Alan and Morgan and his followers return to Billy's side for a last tournament, at the end of which Morgan rightfully wins the crown and Billy gives Linet over into Alan's care. Billy then sets out with only the Native American as his companion. He settles his debt with Deputy Cook and makes his peace with young Billy by giving him his sword in a scene reminiscent of the episode between Arthur and Young Tom Malory in White's *The Once and Future King* (634-637). Billy then rides off down the highway, imagining himself transformed into a knight in shining armor riding his charger across a field. The fantasy ends abruptly outside Gettysburg, when Billy is struck and killed by a truck into whose path he unwittingly rides. The final scenes of the film take place at Billy's grave where a saddened troupe gather under Morgan's leadership to mourn Billy. The film's last frames once again show the raven, suggesting that Billy has finally achieved his goal of being the Once and Future King.[14]

Knightriders is not without its flaws. The film is clearly in need of editing. Originally almost three hours long, the film was released with a running time of 145 minutes. Billy's vision is not, as I have already indicated, always clearly articulated. But that vision is a version of the American dream, a utopian society that accepts people regardless of race, sex, affectional preference, or disability. *Knightriders* is a latter-day cinematic Arthurian romance. As Martin Sutton notes in his review of the film:

> Romero's central concern has always been with the direction and dilemna of civilisation, and in *Knightriders* he proposes an "optimistic" vision by invoking the rigorous morality, the Edenic virtues of Camelot. The hype of the media, the corruption of the law, the material overindulgence of the average citizen is contrasted with the selfless dreams and organic structure of Arthurian legend (38).

In *Knightriders*, Camelot successfully meets the American dream, and unlike the situation in Twain's novel and the films based on it, the Arthurian legend and the dream are compatible, since

Romero's film not only presents but also finally dispels a vision as dark as Twain's.

NOTES

[1] Roman quotes an unidentified critic who, when the film was released, remarked that "this Connecticut Yankee is William Fox's, not Mark Twain's" (25).

[2] The part was originally offered to Douglas Fairbanks, who turned it down. See the review in *Variety* 28 Jan. 1921: 40.

[3] See Chapter 6 in Twain's novel.

[4] Mantle's sentiments were echoed by the critic from the *New York Times*, who wrote: "So, although there are those who would rather see Charlie Chaplin in 'The Kid' than 'A Connecticut Yankee,' every one can see both and enjoy both, in different degrees and for different reasons, but with good measure in the case of each" (14).

[5] The 1920 film version of Twain's novel was also the inspiration for the very successful 1927 Broadway musical with songs by Rodgers and Hart.

[6] Interestingly, in reviewing the 1920 film, the critic for *Exceptional Photoplays* remarked: "Most of the acting comes up to the level of the picture. The role of the Yankee, it is true, simply cries out for Will Rogers (a Yankee from Oklahoma)" (2).

[7] See Nathan for an explanation of the complications surrounding the screen rights to the 1927 musical (1907).

[8] Garnett directed a second Arthurian film, *The Black Knight*, in 1954.

[9] Between 1900 and 1909, Twain worked on the manuscript of *The Damned Human Race* (Geismar 534). Publication of the work (text in DeVoto 209-232) was delayed because of the objections of Twain's daughter, Clara Clemens.

[10] Neither the full-length animated version (1970) nor PBS's abridged sixty-minute version (1978) of *The Connecticut Yankee in King Arthur's Court* remain any truer to the darker side of Twain's novel. Despite its title, the 1987 Russian film directed by Viktor Gres for Dovzhenko Studios, *Novye Prikluchenia Janke pri Dvore Korola Artura (The New Adventures of a Connecticut Yankee at King Arthur's Court)*, is, according to a location report, "not a screening of Mark Twain's novel, but a fantasy based on all his works" (Basina 18).

[11] The film was released in only three major markets, New York, Los Angeles and Florida, where a high concentration of college students were spending their spring breaks (Gagne 117).

[12] As Gagne points out, Romero's earlier film, *Martin*, laments the death of magic in the twentieth century. Gagne also argues that *Knightriders* is "more than a bit autobiographical" (108).

[13] See *Le Morte D'Arthur* Book I Chapter 27 (1: 58-59).

[14] An owl also appears in Merlin's company periodically, though with less frequency than the raven, throughout *Knightriders*. The owl can be seen as yet another allusion to White's novel, where Merlin's constant companion is an owl named Archimedes.

WORKS CITED

Basina, Natalia. "On the Spot Report." *Soviet Film* 6 (1987): 18-19.

Bookbinder, Robert. *The Films of Bing Crosby*. Secaucus, N.J.: Citadel, 1977.

Clemens, Samuel Langhorne [Mark Twain]. *A Connecticut Yankee in King Arthur's Court*, ed. Alison R. Esnor. New York: Norton, 1982.

DeVoto, Bernard, ed. *Mark Twain, Letters from the Earth*. New York: Harper and Row, 1962.

Gagne, Paul R. *The Zombies That Ate Pittsburgh: The Films of George Romero*. New York: Dodd, Mead,1987.

Geismar, Maxwell. *Mark Twain, An American Prophet*. Boston: Houghton Mifflin, 1970.

Knight, Stephen. *Arthurian Literature and Society*. London: Macmillan, 1983.

Knutzen, Eirik, "Michael Gross in a Royal Role." *Philadelphia Inquirer TV Week* 17-23 Dec. 1989: 4-5.

Malory, Sir Thomas. *Le Morte D'Arthur*, ed. Janet Cowen. 2 vols. 1969. New York: Penguin, 1977.

Mantle, Burns. Review of *A Connecticut Yankee at King Arthur's Court*. *Photoplay* 20 (June 1921): 51.

Nathan, Paul S. "Books into Films." *Publisher's Weekly* 153 (1 May 1948): 1907.

O'Dell, Scott. *Representative Photoplays Analyzed*. Hollywood, Calif.: Palmer Institute for Authorship, 1924.

Patterson, Frances Taylor. *Cinema Craftsmanship*. New York: Harcourt, 1921.

Review of *A Connecticut Yankee*. *Variety* 15 Apr. 1931: 20.

Review of *A Connecticut Yankee at King Arthur's Court*. *Exceptional Photoplays* 4 (Mar. 1921): 2.

―――――. *New York Times* 15 Mar. 1921: 14.

―――――. *Variety* 28 Jan. 1921: 40.

Roman, Robert C. "Mark Twain on the Screen." *Films in Review* 12 (1961): 20-33.

Seligson, Tom. "George Romero: Revealing the Monsters Within Us." *Twilight Zone* 1 (Aug. 1981): 12-17.

"Special Service Section on *A Connecticut Yankee in* [sic] *King Arthur's Court*." *Motion Picture News* 26 Feb. 1921: 1673-1682.

Stanek, Lou W. *A Teacher's Manual for A Connecticut Yankee in King Arthur's Court*. Berkeley: University of California Press, 1984.

Sterling, Bryan B., and Frances N. Sterling. *Will Rogers in Hollywood*. New York: Crown, 1984.

Sutton, Mark. Review of *Knightriders*. *Films and Filming* 334 (July 1982): 38.

White, T.H. *The Once and Future King*. 1958. New York: Berkley, 1966.

"Will Rogers and King Arthur." *New York Times* 29 Mar. 1931: 8. 7.

9.

Mythopoeia in *Excalibur*

Norris J. Lacy

Mythopoeia, not only the creation but also the renewal of myth, has from the beginning been a part of Arthurian literature and art. Reinterpretations and modifications of the legend are inevitable, and by ensuring its vitality and currency, they are its lifeblood as well. Especially in England and North America, where enthusiasm for Arthuriana has often approached the level of a cult, hundreds of literary and visual artists have reworked the story of the Once and Future King, drawing most often from Sir Thomas Malory's monumental *Le Morte Darthur* (1485), less often from Alfred, Lord Tennyson's *Idylls of the King*, for which Malory was in turn a primary source. In the process, many of them have invented new characters and events, have suppressed (or occasionally censored) others, and have otherwise modified the shape and meaning of the original.

But Malory's work itself is the "original" in a very limited sense: to compare his text, he adapted a number of sources, especially the thirteenth-century French Vulgate Cycle, including the *Queste du Saint Graal*, while those texts in turn went far beyond the first great French Arthurian poet, Chrétien de Troyes (late twelfth century). Chrétien departed strikingly from Geoffrey of Monmouth's Latin chronicle of Arthur (*Historia Regum Britanniae*, ca. 1136), which itself was formed out of oral legends, fragmentary written references, and especially Geoffrey's own imagination. In other words, the Arthurian myth, for better or for worse, is constantly being remade.

A number of recent authors and filmmakers, having transformed the temporal or cultural context of the Arthurian story, have shown themselves to be far more radically innovative than John Boorman.[1] However, among retreatments of the legend that maintain a more or less traditional context (knights, ladies, and castles in either Dark Age or medieval settings), Boorman's film *Excalibur* must surely be counted as one of the most original. On the face of it, that originality may not be entirely apparent, for Boorman himself claimed to tell "the whole story" of *Le Morte Darthur* (Kennedy 33), and his closing credits inform us that he and Rospo Pallenberg adapted the text of Malory, the quintessential Arthurian story for anglophones. While most viewers may accept such claims uncritically, even the briefest comparison of the film and the medieval text reveals that Boorman modifies the story in substantial and significant ways, innovating in fact and detail alike, in an evident if not entirely successful attempt to enhance the cinematic impact of his presentation.[2]

Indeed, if the film was based at all on Malory, the English author provided at most a source of inspiration rather than an actual model. The viewer who knows Malory reasonably well will find that the film produces shocks, large and small, all along the way. The fact is that, despite the claim made in his credits, Boorman makes only general use of Malory, and Shichtman has persuasively argued that the English text is not even his primary source, that his film is instead "pure Jessie Weston."[3] Consequently, there is little point in assembling a catalog of Boorman's departures from Malory: the result would be too extensive to be of value, and it would demonstrate little beyond Boorman's independence from his putative source. A few examples will suffice, and those I offer here are mostly drawn from the early part of the story, since my larger discussion to follow will deal with later stages.

• In Malory, Uther lies with Igrayne (begetting Arthur) several hours after her husband the duke was killed: ". . . the duke himself was slain ere ever the king came to the castle of Tintagel" (5).[4] In the film, the duke dies at the very instant of Arthur's conception. The juxtaposition of life ending and life beginning, emphasized by intercutting scenes of death agony and sexual intensity, produces a striking scene out of a small change from Malory.

• Boorman has Excalibur belong originally to Uther, who received it from Merlin. Before his death, according to the film, Uther plunges the sword into the stone, from which Arthur later withdraws it. In Malory, the Sword in the Stone is not mentioned until long

Mythopoeia in Excalibur

after Uther's death, when "there was seen in the churchyard opposite the high altar a great stone...; in the middle thereof was an anvil of steel a foot in height, and therein stuck a fair naked sword by the point" (8). Arthur draws the sword and eventually is declared king.

• For Boorman, the Round Table is Arthur's inspiration and invention. In Malory (63), it existed prior to Arthur's birth; it was originally a gift from Uther to Lodegraunce, Guinevere's father, who offers it to Arthur as a wedding present.

• Boorman makes Mordred the son of Morgan/Morgana, not of her sister Morgause, as in Malory.

Of course, a good many of Boorman's departures from the "orthodox" legend have precedents in texts, medieval or modern, other than Malory's. Boorman is not the first to conflate the figures of Morgan and Morgause, nor is he alone in simply doing away with the third sister, Elayne. And if he has Arthur invent the Round Table or replaces Galahad by Perceval as the Grail knight,[5] he has company in those changes as well. Consequently, my comments concerning innovations or departures from tradition are not intended to suggest that he is in every case creating something entirely new, only that he follows Malory sporadically if at all.

While Boorman simplifies a great deal by conflating some characters and motifs and by eliminating others, he also redefines some crucial elements of the traditional Arthurian story, especially the wasteland and the Grail quest, and creates at the same time a very complex vision. One of his more successful sequences (inspired, as noted, more by Weston than by Malory) involves the presentation of the wasteland, the causes and symptoms of which are traced in relentless detail and with memorable imagery. That wasteland is literal, of course, as the country is devastated and infertile, but as in Arthurian tradition it is also moral and perhaps even religious. The moral dimension is underlined by Lancelot when he defines Camelot's decadence ("We have lost our way, Arthur"), and it will be expressed clearly in the Grail scene discussed below.

Although a moral failure is the ultimate cause of the wasteland, Boorman presents a complicated cluster of causes, symptoms, and additional effects of that failure. Whether as cause or effect—and the distinction is not in every case clear—the crisis of the Arthurian world in Boorman's vision involves Arthur's ineffectiveness (and the later decline of his health and vigor), the lassitude and indolence of the knights, Lancelot's and Guinevere's fall into adultery,

Merlin's departure, Morgan's treachery, and Mordred's eventual treason.

Lancelot's reaction to the crisis of the court is to withdraw in order to rediscover his way alone, in the wilderness. His departure proves, however, to be an ironically destructive course, for Guinevere follows him into the forest. There they meet and yield, apparently for the first time, to their temptation. Their illicit love, emblematic of the decay of the Arthurian court, sows the seed of its ultimate destruction in a specific way, for Arthur discovers them together, sleeping nude in each other's embrace.

The scene is fascinating for reasons other than its eroticism and its destructive effect. Guinevere's flight into the woods in pursuit of Lancelot is accompanied by music from the prelude to Wagner's *Tristan und Isolde*. For viewers who do not recognize it, it is simply lush romantic music appropriate to the scene. For those many who do, it is a startling development implying some kind of parallel or conjunction of the two pairs of ill-fated lovers, or rather of two corresponding and equally destructive love triangles: Lancelot/Guinevere/Arthur and Tristan/Isolde/Mark. Love and the announcement of impending tragedy are united in the music.

This music also prepares, very subtly, the next step in the wasteland spiral, for Boorman employs a motif without parallel in Malory's account of Lancelot and Guinevere, but drawn instead from the Tristan story.[6] Finding the sleeping lovers in the forest, Arthur leaves his sword between them (plunging it into the ground in a scene visually reminiscent of Uther's thrusting it into the stone). Upon awakening, they realize with horror that they have been discovered by the King. The scene is doubly catastrophic, however: not only is their sin revealed to her husband and his king, but, more important, Arthur loses Excalibur.

The consequence of the sword's loss is explained by Lancelot, who exclaims: "The King without a sword—the land without a king!" This loss is a symbolic manifestation of Arthur's failing powers—Excalibur is the "symbol and sceptre" of leadership (Haller 2)—but it is also a precise, literal cause of what is to come. As is traditional, in accounts from Chrétien de Troyes to Jessie Weston, there is an immediate link between the king's health and virility and the fertility, or infertility, of the land; here, there is an additional link, between the king's sword and his virility. Arthur is without the sword created by Merlin, left to him by Uther, and accepted as the symbol and instrument of his authority.

The Arthurian world's decline into impotence is both hastened and signaled powerfully by Merlin's withdrawal from the world. Arthur is deprived not only of the power and authority associated with Excalibur, but also of the guidance provided by Merlin. Moreover, Merlin's withdrawal is all the more tragic because it is followed by Morgan's apprenticeship, by her success in extracting from Merlin the incantation that will effectively transfer his power to her. Thereupon, she, Arthur's sister, uses an enchantment to seduce the King and conceive Mordred, who will later kill his father.

Mordred's birth is followed by a curious scene in which Arthur is struck by lightning. The immediate cause of this physical disability is thus a physical event, but one that crystallizes the moral developments traced here. While the lightning strike may appear to be an unnecessary physical elaboration of the King's decline and Camelot's decadence, it is consistent with Boorman's method, which provides parallel sequences on the physical and moral levels. On the former, Arthur loses his strongest support when Lancelot and Merlin are separated from the court; he loses the instrument of his authority when he leaves Excalibur in the forest; and he is literally struck down by the lightning. The second, moral, level is no less clearly delineated: the demoralization of his knights, betrayal by his wife, his own incest. The wasteland is established with chilling thoroughness.

But not, of course, with finality. There is one solution, a solution familiar to every reader of Arthurian fiction. The Grail is their last hope, and Arthur announces: "We must find what was lost: the Grail. Only the Grail can restore leaf and flower.... Only the Grail can redeem us." Although viewers even remotely familiar with the Arthurian story will doubtless not be surprised that the Grail is the remedy, they must surely be struck by the fact that it has not been mentioned before and that, now that it is evoked, there is no explanation. Neither the identity nor the nature of the Grail is discussed; nor does Arthur explain how the Grail was lost, how he knows that it will redeem them, or, since he does know that, why he did not suggest its recovery earlier.

Boorman's inadequate preparation for the scene—a charge sometimes leveled at Malory as well—and his lack of explanation weaken a crucial sequence, almost suggesting that the Grail theme was an afterthought,[7] rather than the climax and centerpiece of the Arthurian story. Yet that sequence, although less than entirely satisfying, includes what is surely the most remarkable set of innovations in the film, and it is here that *Excalibur* raises, as a result, the

From left to right, Arthur (Nigel Terry), Guinevere (Cherie Lunghi), and Lancelot (Nicholas Clay) in Excalibur.

most complex questions of meaning and filmic vision, and moreover of viewer response.

In the quest episodes, Boorman's method of conflating characters and events from tradition is pursued almost to its logical conclusion. Most significant are the changes in the Grail imagery and, especially, in the identity of the Grail king. Specifically, Arthur himself replaces two or even three characters from more traditional accounts. In addition to being the king who directs the Grail quest, Arthur here also takes the role traditionally given to the wounded and disabled Fisher King, the restoration of whose health, and that of the land, depends on the quest's successful conclusion. This is a significant innovation—Shichtman notes (43) that this is the only treatment of the legend in which "Arthur himself becomes the helpless lord of the Wasteland"—and a major departure from Malory, where the quest occurs not when the realm is wasted, but instead when it is prospering (Shichtman 48, n. 22). And, most spectacularly, in the complex scene that depicts the culmination of the quest,

Mythopoeia in Excalibur

Arthur also appears to replace Christ. That scene merits some detailed discussion.

When Perceval first has an opportunity to complete the quest, he has a vision of the Grail, an elevated chalice glowing in an ethereal light. A disembodied voice asks, "What is the secret of the Grail? Whom does it serve?" Perceval flees without responding and then confesses, "Arthur, the secret was in my grasp. I failed you."

There is nothing either in Malory or in the tradition of Grail lore in general that could prepare viewers for Boorman's highly original treatment of Perceval's second Grail vision. On that second occasion, the question is repeated but this time is answered by Perceval:

—What is the secret of the Grail? Whom does it serve?
—You, my lord.
—Who am I?
—You are my lord and king. [Pause] You're Arthur.
—Have you found the secret that I have lost?
—Yes: you and the land are one.

During this exchange, the Grail is transmuted from a chalice into a luminous vision of an Arthur in armor, and then back into the chalice, but this time it is not an image but the object itself: the vessel that can be grasped by Perceval and brought to Arthur.

Here, Boorman is faithful to his earlier method of maintaining parallel physical and moral, or real and symbolic, lines. As noted, however, that method here involves dividing Arthur into two. On the one hand, he is the disabled king who directed the Grail quest and who awaits its conclusion. On the other hand, he is the Grail king himself. He is both a real king of flesh and blood and the spiritual being that, in a curiously self-reflexive development, provides for the restoration of his own physical incarnation. One Arthur-figure has the power to redeem the other, healing himself, as it were, but through the mediation of Perceval.

The episode raises other questions, concerning both meaning and method. Perceval reaches out and is able to seize the Grail, which had just taken Arthur's form; he then takes it to Arthur and announces, "You and the land are one. Drink." His next statement is the only instance in which the Grail is specifically called a chalice, and the intent is clear: "Drink from the chalice and you will be reborn, and the land with you." Not simply healed or restored: *reborn.* Arthur replies, ". . .I didn't know how empty was my soul—until it was filled." Thereupon, his strength and the land are restored, and soon after, Arthur visits Guinevere, who returns Excalibur, still instrument and symbol of his power, to him.

Haller comments about Boorman's Grail that "Christian significance is never suggested" (3), and Harty concurs that "the Grail is stripped of any Christian associations" (108). While it is correct that Boorman establishes no *explicit* connection with traditional Christian interpretations of the Grail, he does on the other hand provide hints that we can hardly ignore. The references to chalice, to rebirth, to emptiness of soul not only confirm that this is a mystical vision but also imbue the episode with a fundamentally religious resonance, and it is inconceivable that viewers will not supply the associations at which Boorman only hints.

Indeed, this is one of the points in the film where a "naive" (i.e., fully uninformed) viewing is virtually impossible, for the association of Grail with Chalice of the Last Supper, firmly established during the Middle Ages, has become so thoroughly entrenched, even in the popular mind, that reference to the Grail inevitably evokes Christian themes. Only more knowledgeable viewers will be able to appreciate fully the eccentricities of Boorman's presentation, but both his "hints" and our usual assumptions surely make it impossible to exclude all Christian associations.

And yet the filmmaker, all the while forging dialog and images to encourage such associations, manages to subvert them. Everything in the scene seems to have pointed toward a traditionally religious interpretation of the events surrounding the Grail, and indeed Perceval's response to the disembodied voice—"you are my lord"—appears to confirm that interpretation. But then, startlingly, he adds, after a slight pause, "You're Arthur." This substitution is a stunning and daring innovation, one of the larger shocks of the film.

On the face of it, the effect of combining King, Fisher King, Grail king, and, by implication, Christ into a single person concentrates extraordinary symbolic import in the figure of Arthur. He is the center of his world, whereas traditional Grail texts had largely displaced him as focus, in order to replace Arthurian chivalry by a higher order, a celestial chivalry based on devotion to a moral and religious purpose. Undeniably, Boorman produces a more concentrated if unconventional vision, with Arthur as sender and receiver, as director of the Grail quest and as its principal recipient, and as the character whose physical and moral health remains closely linked to, and directly responsible for, the state of his land.

But a more concentrated vision is not necessarily a more effective one, and the value of this conflation still bears consideration. Is the film symbolically impoverished because Boorman diminishes the connection of the Grail to Christ, and therefore that of Arthur to sacred history? Or, conversely, is it enriched by the apotheosizing of Arthur? In other words, is Boorman brilliantly innovative or hopelessly muddled?

One defensible reaction is that Boorman has largely trivialized the legend by severing it from one of its most productive elements: its explicit relationship to sacred history. Medieval versions of the Grail story, as far back as the twelfth century, tended to open it up "vertically," adding layers of symbolic and mystical meaning by setting it within universal history and by pointing not only toward a physical restoration and a moral rebirth but also toward a spiritual ascension.[8] Arthur is a significant part of that process, but his role is simply an aspect of the historical process working toward a triumphant redemption.

In fact, it could be argued that the mythic appeal of the Grail legend derives precisely from the complex association of an ancient myth, the identity of land with its ruler, with the central religious beliefs of the West. Boorman intimates a tenuous connection with the latter beliefs, in his references (for example) to an empty soul, but without establishing them with the clarity they may call for; and Arthur's supplanting the deity at the conclusion of the quest appears to obscure the meaning of the Grail.

On the other hand, the result of that substitution is the apotheosizing of Arthur: Boorman raises him beyond the status of wise ruler and able soldier, even beyond the status he could attain with Merlin's magic. Instead of being a pawn, albeit a key one, in the quest ordained by God, he is central to the quest in every sense: he conceives and orders it, he (along with the land in general) is the beneficiary of it, and—most important—he is finally the power behind it. From this point of view, the figure of Arthur is expanded, both horizontally, in that he subsumes identities and roles elsewhere taken by others, and vertically, in that his role transcends the usual limits of his humanity. In other words, Boorman is in effect expanding the *Arthurian* legend at the expense of the *Grail* legend.

Ultimately, while we can easily enough identity Boorman's innovations, we can make no objective evaluation of their effectiveness. Along with other variables, such as personal taste and appreciation of cinematic technique, that influence the reaction to any film,

Merlin (Nicol Williamson) in Excalibur.

the level of knowledge a viewer is likely to bring to *Excalibur* is a crucial determinant of response. This principle logically holds for any retreatment of tradition: obviously, only those conversant with the tradition can fully appreciate and evaluate a work of art that exploits it. But Boorman's film constitutes a particular problem, owing both to the ubiquity of the legend and to his radical departures from earlier accounts of Arthur. The Arthurian story is so firmly established in Western, especially anglophone, culture and in the popular mind that everyone has at least a vague notion of how it is supposed to "go."[9] Beyond the most basic response, however, our evaluation of Boorman's vision and of the strengths or flaws of his film will naturally vary a good deal with the extent of the viewer's acquaintance with Malory, with Jessie Weston, or with Arthurian tradition in general.

To offer a simple example of the relationship of response to knowledge of the tradition: viewers unfamiliar with earlier texts will surely find nothing amiss when Arthur asks Perceval to throw the sword into the lake. Yet those who know Arthurian legend reasonably well must wonder why Perceval replaces the Bedivere of English tradition (who incidentally replaced Girflet in the French account).[10] This is a question with a perfectly good answer—eliminating Bedivere, Girflet, and even such characters as Galahad helps to concentrate the film's focus—but few are the viewers able to supply or appreciate that answer. Similarly, as I noted above, whether the use of Wagner's *Tristan und Isolde* simply sets a romantic mood or instead establishes a complex overlay of themes prefiguring both passion and death depends quite simply on the viewer's recognition of the music.

But the most complicated problems of response in this film are related to the Grail and to Arthur's multiple roles: as the impotent or "maimed" king, the instigator of the quest, and the image that implicitly replaces Christ. At least in the case of the Grail, even a rudimentary awareness of precedents, such as almost everyone has, transforms the viewer into an active participant, who brings some degree of knowledge and experience to the viewing. In regard to other sequences and themes, viewers' knowledge of Arthuriana, and thus their responses to the film, are likely to vary from the most informed readings of medieval literature and modern fiction to the vaguest associations drawn from popular culture.

By no means has it been my intent to criticize Boorman for his originality. He cannot be faulted for having modified the legend he inherited from others, for, as I suggested, Malory and most of the others did no less; in fact, only constant renewal can ensure the continued vitality of the Arthurian story. If Boorman is to be either praised or faulted, it must be for the effect of his innovations and for the overall quality of his creation. I do indeed find the film deeply flawed in a number of ways, but I also consider it to be among the most fascinating treatments of the legend. Boorman is highly original in his conception but far less successful in his execution. For those who have seen it, and especially for those who know the tradition reasonably well, it is material for a case study in cinematic response, and in any event it provides a singular illustration of the power cinema has to remake even our most profoundly held myths.

NOTES

I wish to express my gratitude to Kevin J. Harty, who facilitated the preparation of this essay by providing valuable advice and bibliographical assistance.

[1] Examples are transpositions into the sports or motorcycle culture. George Romero's film *Knightriders* (which appeared in 1981, the same year as Boorman's) depicts modern Arthurian "knights" on motorcycle. The best-known, and most subtle, retreatment of Arthurian legend in the context of sport is Bernard Malamud's *The Natural* (1952), which uses the Perceval story as underlying structure. Babs Deal, in *The Grail: A Novel* (1963), relates the Grail quest to the endeavors of an American football team.

[2] Although the film has a good many champions, particularly among French critics, it had an equal number of detractors, one of the most severe of whom was Vincent Canby, who described *Excalibur* as a "gigantic, overblown, overlong, pompous, essentially boorish reworking of the Arthurian legends" (Canby, "Of a Hit," 13). Although Canby's judgment is harsh, I agree that the film is far from flawless: it is overlong, often structurally unclear, at times thematically confused. While problems of clarity and meaning are the crucial matters, the film is also frequently jarring by its anachronisms and other distractions, which sometimes border on silliness. Examples are Mordred's gold armor and pseudo-classical mask, which appear (as Canby notes, 10 April 1981: 3. 11) "left over from Mr. Boorman's science-fiction film 'Zardoz.'" Boorman himself admitted the resemblance of Mordred's mask to those of *Zardoz*, commenting that "perhaps there was a lack of imagination on our part!" (Ciment 201).

[3] Shichtman 41; the reference is to Weston's *From Ritual to Romance* (1920; Garden City, N.Y.: Doubleday, 1957), a study in cultural anthropology that is best known as the primary inspiration for T.S. Eliot's *The Waste Land*. Weston links Grail themes to ancient nature rituals; the specific connection to Boorman's film is provided by her consideration of "the intimate relation at one time held to exist between the ruler and his land" (114). It must be noted that Boorman himself has acknowledged his debt to authors other than Malory; they include Weston, T. H. White, John Cowper Powys, T. S. Eliot, Chrétien de Troyes, and "the most fascinating and modern of them all," Wolfram von Eschenbach (Ciment 185, 192).

[4] For convenience and clarity, I quote Malory in Lumiansky's modernized edition; for the original text, see the edition by Vinaver.

[5] In Boorman's mind this was not a substitution but an additional conflation, the combining of Perceval and Galahad to permit the solution of a number of cinematic problems; see Tessier 31.

[6] For Béroul's Old French treatment of this motif, in his *Tristan* (late twelfth century), see Lacy, ed., 97. The Tristan legend is evoked elsewhere in the film, both by the use of Wagner's music and, as Jessica Yates (30)

notes, by the sequence in which Lancelot, escorting the Queen to Arthur's wedding, falls in love with her.

[7]Canby ("Of a Hit") notes that Boorman "introduces the search for the Holy Grail very late in the film as if the Grail were some misplaced lunchbox, not worth anything in itself but possessing sentimental value" (10). Canby is in my view mistaken about the lack of worth Boorman ascribes to the Grail, but his objection about the suddenness and lateness of its introduction is irrefutable. Yates acknowledges that the Grail episode is "fairly incomprehensible" but then defends Boorman's treatment by adding, "but then, so is the Grail legend" (30); it is hardly necessary to respond that incomprehensibility arising from divine inspiration is quite unlike incomprehensibility due to inadequate artistic preparation.

[8]The most dramatic example of this approach is the *Roman du Graal* (also known as the *Joseph d'Arimathie*) of Robert de Boron, a French poet writing at the end of the twelfth century or during the very first years of the thirteenth. It was Robert who first connected the Grail with the Chalice of the Last Supper; he also presented the Round Table as the third in a series that included the table of the Last Supper and a table established by Joseph of Arimathea, at the direction of the Holy Spirit, to celebrate the service of the Grail. Arthurian legend is thus linked to sacred history, and the Grail to the chalice of Christ.

[9]As Charles Champlin put it, the Arthurian legend "sticks like lint to generations of schoolboys and girls" (1).

[10]This role, incidentally, seems to be assignable to almost anyone. In the 1953 film *Knights of the Round Table*, it is Lancelot who returns Excalibur to the sea.

WORKS CITED

Béroul. *The Romance of Tristran*, ed. and trans. Norris J. Lacy. New York: Garland, 1989.

Canby, Vincent. "Of a Hit, a Series and the Word." *New York Times* 10 May 1981: D 13.

──────. Review of Boorman's *Excalibur*. *New York Times* 10 Apr. 1981: 3. 11.

Champlin, Charles. Review of Boorman's *Excalibur*. *Los Angeles Times* 17 June 1981: Calendar 1.

Ciment, Michel. *John Boorman*, trans. Gilbert Adair. London: Faber, 1986.

Haller, Robert A. "*Excalibur* and Innovation." *Field of Vision* 13 (Spring 1985): 2-3.

Harty, Kevin J. "Cinema Arthuriana." *Arthurian Interpretations* 2 (Fall 1987): 95-113.

Kennedy, Harlan. "The World of King Arthur According to John Boorman." *American Film* 6 (Mar. 1981): 30-37.

Malory, Sir Thomas. *Le Morte Darthur*, ed. R. M. Lumiansky. New York: Collier, 1982.

_____. *The Works of Thomas Malory*, ed. Eugene Vinaver. London: Oxford University Press, 1954.

Robert de Boron. *Le Roman de l'Estoire dou Graal*, ed. William A. Nitze. Paris: Champion, 1927.

Shichtman, Martin B. "Hollywood's New Weston: The Grail Myth in Francis Ford Coppola's *Apocalypse Now* and John Boorman's *Excalibur*." *Post Script* 4 (Autumn 1984): 35-48.

Tessier, Max. "Entretien avec John Boorman (sur *Excalibur*)." *Revue du cinéma* 363 (July-Aug. 1981): 31-34.

Weston, Jessie L. *From Ritual to Romance*. 1920. Garden City, N.Y.: Doubleday, 1957.

Yates, Jessica. "Boorman's Arthur." *Mythlore* 31 (Spring 1982): 29-30.

10.
Fire, Water, Rock: Elements of Setting in *Excalibur*

Muriel Whitaker

When the fifteenth-century knight-prisoner Sir Thomas Malory wrote the *Morte Darthur*, few doubted that Arthur was a real king who had unified Britain, led an army to the continent and become Roman emperor. William Caxton, who published the *Morte* in 1485, pointed in a prologue to the tomb at Glastonbury, his seal in Westminster Abbey and his Round Table at Winchester as evidence that "there was suche a noble kynge named Arthur" (Spisak 2). In the text, references to architecture, costume, and arms and armor, to the military campaigns of the Hundred Years War and the Wars of the Roses, to commercial details and to the use of cannon fix Arthurian society in the late Middle Ages. Lacking the concept of historical perspective, author and audience visualized the past in contemporary terms. Because the *Morte Darthur* is the definitive English version, modern audiences accept this fifteenth-century world as the conventional Arthurian milieu.

In the late twentieth century, however, the question of Arthur's historicity is also relevant to visualization. Archaeological excavations like those at South Cadbury in Somerset[1] have popularized the idea that Arthur was a sixth-century *dux bellorum* who led the Britons against invading Saxons. Novelists like Rosemary Sutcliff, Henry Treece, and Victor Canning have striven to recreate a wild and barbarous land in which a few Britons, galvanized by the hero

Arthur, struggle to maintain the fading Roman culture.[2] Romance and history, then, project conflicting visions.[3]

When Orion offered the British film director John Boorman the chance of making an Arthurian film in 1979, he had at his disposal still another model, one developed by the Victorians. Approved by Queen Victoria and Prince Albert and promoted by Alfred, Lord Tennyson in *Idylls of the King* was an English historical myth that treated King Arthur not as historical reality or romantic hero but as the progenitor of a relevant "national identity." Tennyson gave Boorman a way of combining the primitive world of Dark Age Britain with the myth of a hero who for a brief period established peace, truth, and justice. Though doomed to defeat, the hero survives in the imagination as an ideal of human achievement. Tennyson saw Arthur as "a man who spent himself in the cause of honour, duty and self-sacrifice, who felt and aspired with his nobler knights, though with a stronger and clearer conscience" (Hallam Tennyson 1. 193). For both Tennyson and Boorman, myth is didactic: "Listen carefully to the echoes of myth. It has much more to tell us than the petty lies and insignificant truths of recorded history," the director told an interviewer on the set of *Excalibur* (Strick 168).

Tennyson provided a mythic time scheme that links the progress of Arthur's life to a seasonal cycle, making it possible to use the world of nature as a source of mood and symbol. Winter signifies the barbarous world into which Arthur is born, to be carried immediately through a treacherous forest of twisted roots, bare branches, muddy banks, and thorny thickets. (Boorman's visualization of the Perilous Forest is one that Arthur Rackham established in illustrating *The Romance of King Arthur and His Knights of the Round Table* [1917]).[4] At Easter, eighteen years later in linear time, the hero succeeds in the sword test, flourishing Excalibur in a leafy forest hung with banners. Guinevere comes to Camelot amid the flowers of May. The chivalric summer finds Lancelot riding through a sunlit glade carpeted with bluebells. He and Guinevere consummate their love to the accompaniment of birdsong. Mordred's milieu is the dark world of autumn, where bare branches and brown bogs signify oppression and sterility. The last battle takes place at the year's end in a setting that Boorman seems to have based closely on Tennyson's lines:

> Then rose the King and moved his host by night,
> And ever push'd Sir Mordred, league by league,

> Back to the sunset bound of Lyonnesse—
> A land of old upheaven from the abyss
> By fire, to sink into the abyss again;
> Where fragments of forgotten peoples dwelt,
> And the long mountains ended in a coast. . . .
> And there, that day when the great light of heaven
> Burn'd at his lowest in the rolling year,
> On the waste sand by the waste sea they closed. . . .
> A deathwhite mist slept over sand and sea:
> Whereof the chill, to him who breathed it, drew
> Down with his blood, till all his heart was cold
> With formless fear; and ev'n on Arthur fell
> Confusion, since he saw not whom he fought.
> "The Passing of Arthur" ll. 80-99

Both productions conclude with the image of the barge sailing into light as "the new sun rose bringing the new year." Cyclical time allows for the possiblity that Arthur will return. Though Malory's *Morte Darthur* is credited as the source for *Excalibur*, the *Idylls of the King* was equally influential in shaping the imaginative construct.

In addition to the myth of sovereignty, Boorman is fascinated by the myth of the Holy Grail. He ignores Malory's hero Sir Galahad, a representation of thirteenth-century Cistercian mysticism, preferring to reach back through T. S. Eliot, Jessie L. Weston, Wagner, Wolfram von Eschenbach, and Chrétien de Troyes to the primitive vegetation myth that related the prosperity of a land and its people to the health of the ruler. In the earliest medieval adaptations, Perceval is the savior who, by finding his way to the Grail castle and asking the right question, restores the Maimed King and his wasted land. The secret that the film Perceval learns from the Grail and carries back to Arthur is "You and the land are one." When Arthur (Nigel Terry) drinks from the chalice (both a pagan vessel of healing and a Christian symbol of grace), he is physically and psychologically revitalized. Boorman equates the "achievement" of the Grail with humanity's repossession of ancient magic through a transcendent experience independent of the materialistic world (Yakir 49).

The film's aesthetic patterning depends on a series of polarities explored through aspects of setting. A state of barbarism is briefly ameliorated by a golden age of chivalry. The powers of ancient, pagan magic, which Merlin (Nicol Williamson) and Morgana (Helen Mirren) can tap, are diminished by the newly established Christianity to which Arthur, Lancelot, Perceval, and Guinevere adhere. The world of pristine nature is modified by the "emerging world of man." Fire, water, rock, dragon, sword, and chalice—these are persistent motifs within the matrix of forest, the perilous realm of romance.

Tennyson commenced "The Coming of Arthur" with a scene of desolation, rapine, and confusion as "a heathen horde/Reddening the sun with smoke and earth with blood" lays waste the land. The opening scene in *Excalibur* shows bare-branched trees and black knights in pig-snout helms (a fifteenth-century style) silhouetted against a lurid sky. Steam from the horses' nostrils condenses in the frosty air. Torches flicker in the hands of knights who charge into misty battle behind a wall of flame. Few subsequent scenes lack their fires. Balls of flame hurtle though the air as knights attack. Gas-fed jets enclose the bed where Uther (Gabriel Byrne) engenders Arthur on Igrayne (Katrina Boorman), shoot from the cauldron in the lair of Morgana, flare on the battlements where Arthur learns of his queen's adultery. Dragon flames synthesize the lovers' embraces, which rob Arthur of his power, and Merlin's submission, which allows Morgana to claim the dragon's power. Fire is an essential element in the aesthetic of violence and the aesthetic of magic, evoking the primitive, the destructive, and the passionate.

Fire can be used apocalyptically, too. Merlin's brightening staff symbolizes the light of civilization, a significance reinforced by the curtain of white candles that illuminate the Round Table in Arthur's new hall and the bright knights who sit down to feast wearing complete plate armor. The lights dim as the King's power fades.

Believing that the Arthurian world should be pristine and magical, Boorman chose to film the movie in Ireland, that misty, moisty country with a mythology that lies at the heart of Arthurian legend. Rain endows grass, leaves, and mosses with a luminosity that the technicians enhance by using filters and green gel. Green is the faerie color.

In Irish myth and medieval romances with Celtic motifs, water in some form—lakes, rivers, fountains, ocean, mist, rain, fog—marks the boundary between the mundane world and the magical otherworld. Boorman uses the association between water and the supernatural to point up scenes of heightened experience that transcend everyday life. The sea pounds on Tintagel's cliffs when Uther, magically changed to Cornwall's appearance, approaches Igrayne. Arthur, about to be knighted, stands knee-deep in a castle moat—the parallel to Christ's baptism is probably unintentional. The young

Uryens (Keith Buckley) and the mounted Mordred (Robert Addie) in Excalibur.

Guinevere (Cherie Lunghi) tends the young King beside a clear pool, bathing his wounds with water from a fountain. Arthur meets Lancelot for the first time beside a waterfall and sparkling stream. Filled wtih envy and anger, he insists on fighting, with the result that he breaks Excalibur. It slips away into the pool. In the underwater world, which represents in Jungian terms Arthur's subconcious, the sword is mended and restored by the Lady of the Lake to symbolize the King's suppression of anger, pride, and envy. In the wasteland, Perceval's Jungian victory over doubt and fear is conveyed when he emerges from the perilous underwater passage, clean and almost naked, to enter the Grail castle. Mist is the sign of Morgana's magic, rising from her cauldron to obscure Merlin. The wizard's taunt, "I see no mist," forces her to chant for the last time the spell of change that transmutes her into a hag while filling the battlefield with fog. The film's most magical scene shows Excalibur breaking through the water to hover, a shimmer of blue and green, in the pure white of off-stage lights. The simulated magic depended on shooting the sword from an underwater platform with a charge that sent it speedily into the air. A special camera recording 280 frames a second caught the images (Yakir 49).

While the lakes, waterfalls, and rushing streams are real, the castles are not. They are incomplete constructions of timber, plywood, polystyrene, and paint representing bits of battlement, cavernous passageways between stone slabs, some ceremonial staircases, and Romanesque pillars with zoomorphic designs on the capitals. Like Malory, Boorman recreates only the parts of castle architecture that are relevant to the action. Great blocks of "stone" oppose attacking knights, enclose devious intruders, or, shaped grotesquely into stalagmites and stalactites, incarcerate Merlin. Beyond the castles, County Wicklow's boulder-strewn landscape evokes the primitive world of the ancient Britons, as do the Stonehenge monoliths, which Boorman cannot resist when he composes a setting for Merlin's return to "the land of dreams." The blood-caked stones of the ultimate battleground demonically represent Malory's "colde erthe."

After Boorman's original title, *Merlin Lives*, had to be abandoned because of copyright problems, other familiar "icons"—Excalibur, the Grail, the Round Table—were "juggled into juxtapositions that might attract success at the world's box office" (Strick 168). The choice of *Excalibur* was an inspired one. The sword image dominates the film by combining history and myth, reality and fantasy, water and rock. A gift from the underwater world, it is held in rock to await its destined possessor. Because it represents sovereignty, it must be returned to the otherworld when the King's reign ends. Boorman expands the significance by relating the sword to Arthur's moral and spiritual condition. Broken in anger and envy of Lancelot, "the best knight in the world," it is restored when the King regains a virtuous equilibrium. It is lost, however, when, overcome again by anger and envy, he plunges it between Guinevere and her lover. Lancelot runs through the forest crying, "The king without a sword! The land without a king!" The cross-shaped Excalibur pierces through rock to "the coils of the dragon," the source of life.

Like so many of *Excalibur*'s archetypes, the dragon is ambivalent. It is the personal symbol of Uther and his son Arthur. In medieval chronicle, it derives from the victorious red dragon under Vortigern's tower, which presages Uther's defeat of the Saxons. Like Tennyson, the movie director turns the dragon to gold, embossing it on Arthur's shield and on the great scarlet banners that fly above the King's victorious army. A dragon sculpture guards Camelot's entrance, as in Tennyson's construct, where

> Both the wings are made of gold, and flame
> At sunrise till the people in far fields,
> Wasted so often by the heathen hordes,
> Behold it, crying, "We have still a King."
> "The Holy Grail" ll. 242-245

At the heart of the rock, and the heart of Boorman's myth, lies a more ancient dragon, the primal source of life. It represents the spirit of nature in all its forms—the snake descending from the branch, the owl, the centipede, the lizard, the fire, the rock. While the adolescent Arthur fears this spirit's manifestation, Merlin and then Morgana draw power from it. Merlin releases the dragon's breath so that Uther can lie with Igrayne and so that Lancelot can be healed. When Arthur, betrayed, drives Excalibur between Guinevere and Lancelot, the sword pierces through rock to "the coils of the dragon," causing a transfer of power from the forces of good (Merlin and Arthur) to the forces of evil (Morgana and Mordred). Only when Merlin, renewed by Arthur's love, challenges Morgana to "call the dragon; mend the sword; speak the spell of making" can the dragon's power end the fée's supernatural youth and beauty, restore Excalibur to Arthur's use, and release Merlin into Arthur's dream.

Excalibur is flawed by a lack of consistency, which Boorman defends by asserting that "the film has to do with mythical truth, not historical truth" (Yakir 49). Yet it is his treatment of myth that causes the problems. In mingling the Celtic mythology from which Arthurian romance derives and the Teutonic mythology that Boorman imposes by way of Tolkien and Wagner, the director sets up irreconcilable patterns of allusion. He sees Arthurian England as "a kind of Middle Earth in Tolkien terms" (Kennedy 33)—he directed the film version of *The Lord of the Rings*—ignoring the fact that Middle Earth is an Anglo-Saxon construct inappropriate both to the "historical" Arthurian sixth century, when the Saxons were the enemy, and to the French-dominated High Middle Ages, when Arthurian literature evolved. Merlin is presented as an Odin-Gandalf type of spiritual adviser, complete with ravens. Worst of all, musical quotations from Richard Wagner's *Ring* cycle, *Parsifal*, and *Tristan und*

Isolde, as well as from Carl Orff's *Carmina Burana*, underline the false analogy between Arthurian romance and Teutonic hero tales.

Another kind of inconsistency occurs when the director interrupts the cyclical time scheme that he has adopted from Tennyson's *Idylls*. Though there is too much water in evidence, the wasteland images of snow, brown grass, and grey trees from which dangle the bodies of hanged knights[3] are appropriate to the season of late autumn, with its resonances of approaching death. But after drinking from the Grail, the invigorated Arthur with his loyal followers rides through blossoming apple orchards on his way to Almesbury and the last battle. True, the scene conveys both the physical and psychological restoration that Perceval's achievement of the Grail quest has effected, while referring obliquely to Glastonbury's identification with Avalon, the *insula pomorum*; but it is an inappropriate prelude to the day of doom that swiftly follows. Perhaps it is intended as a promise that the "fair time may come again." Boorman has commented that "a filmmaker functions as a Merlin in the sense that he tries to organize the world" (Yakir 50). Whether the motifs of fire, water, and rock are sufficient to provide unity, only the viewer can judge.

NOTES

[1] See Leslie Alcock, '*By South Cadbury is that Camelot...*': *Excavations at Cadbury Castle 1966-1970* (London: Thames and Hudson, 1972).

[2] See Raymond H. Thompson, *The Return to Avalon: A Study of the Arthurian Legend in Modern Fiction* (Westport, Conn.: Greenwood, 1985), especially Chapter 3, "Realistic Fiction."

[3] For a study of Arthurian illustration, see Muriel Whitaker, "The Illustration of Arthurian Romance," in *King Arthur Through the Ages*, ed. Valerie M. Lagorio and Mildred Leake Day (New York: Garland, 1990), 2: 123-148.

[4] Alfred W. Pollard, *The Romance of King Arthur and His Knights of the Round Table Abridged from Malory's Morte Darthur* (London: Macmillan, 1917), p. 47. For the Perilous Forest, see pp. 47, opp. 59, 96. Compare also "How Queen Guenevere rode a-Maying into the woods and fields beside Westminster" (opp. p. 420) as a source of Guinevere's wedding procession and "How Mordred was slain by Arthur, and how by him Arthur was hurt to the death" (opp. p. 490) as a source of the last battle.

WORKS CITED

Kennedy, Harlan. "The World of King Arthur According to John Boorman." *American Film* 6 (Mar. 1981): 30-37.

Malory, Sir Thomas. *Le Morte Darthur*, ed. James W. Spisak. 2 vols. Berkeley: University of California Press, 1983.

Strick, Philip. "John Boorman's Merlin." *Sight and Sound* (Summer 1980): 168-171.

Tennyson, Alfred. *The Idylls of the King*, ed. J. M. Gray. New Haven: Yale University Press, 1983.

Tennyson, Hallam. *Alfred Lord Tennyson: A Memoir*. 2 vols. New York: Macmillan, 1897.

Yakir, Dan. "The Sorcerer." *Film Comment* 17 (May-June 1981): 49-53.

11.

Morgan and the Problem of Incest

Jacqueline de Weever

Morgan le Fay, Arthur's sister, who hates him and who challenges his court in several ways, may be said to inhabit the margins of Arthurian romance, even when she is the cause and mover of the action, as in *Sir Gawain and the Green Knight* (c. 1375-1400). Morgan has not, however, excited much critical attention.

From the beginning, Morgan is a character who may or may not be included in the story. She is absent from Geoffrey of Monmouth's *History of the Kings of Britain* (ca. 1136) but appears in his *Vita Merlini* (ca. 1150) as the wisest and fairest of the nine maidens who rule the Island of Apples. To this island Arthur is brought after the battle of Camlann to be healed. "Morgen" receives him with honor and agrees to tend his wounds (Jarman 97). Geoffrey imputes to her neither jealousy, animus, nor incestuous plans. She is also absent from Wace's *Roman de Brut* (1155) and Layamon's *Brut* (ca. 1180-1204), a retelling of Wace. By the fourteenth century, however, Morgan grows more powerful. In *Sir Gawain and the Green Knight*, she sends the Green Knight to challenge the court and to frighten Guinevere to death, and although she does not succeed in killing the Queen, she succeeds in her challenge because Gawain fails the tests of the castle of Hautdesert. In the fifteenth century, Malory portrays her as a constant irritant to Arthur and his knights; some she entraps, and others she enchants. Always, she seeks ways to destroy the court. Tennyson pays her no attention in his *Idylls of the King*, and T. H. White likewise ignores her in *The Once and*

Future King (1939). Wherever she does appear, she is a challenge to the court and, in later versions, one of the causes of its fall.

In film, with its need for contrasting characters to represent good and evil, Morgan makes her most dramatic and important appearances. Several films have emphasized in different ways Morgan's role as an opponent of Camelot, whether or not they make explicit the relationship between Arthur and Mordred. This depiction of Morgan as destroyer of the court of the Round Table appears, for example, in Richard Thorpe's *Knights of the Round Table* (1953) and in John Boorman's *Excalibur* (1981).

Bound up in the theme of Morgan's destruction of Arthur's court is the theme of incest. In both Wace and Layamon, the incest occurs between Mordred, the King's nephew, and Guinevere, the King's wife. In Wace's *Roman de Brut*, Mordred is

> a marvellously hardy knight, whom Arthur loved passing well. Mordred was a man of high birth, and of many noble virtues, but he was not true. He had set his heart on Guenevere, his kinswoman, but such a love brought little honour to the queen. Mordred had kept this love close, for easy enough it was to hide, since who would be so bold as to deem he loved his uncle's dame? The lady on her side had given her love to a lord of whom much good was spoken; but Mordred was of her husband's kin! This made the shame more shameworthy. Ah, God, the deep wrong done in this season by Mordred and the queen [Wace and Layamon 79].

Lancelot, a creation of romance, does not appear, and the dishonor of the court is created by the liaison between Mordred and Guinevere. Wace does not name Mordred's mother, except to say that she is the King's sister. Layamon, however, says that Walwain or Gawain, King Loth's eldest son, is Mordred's brother. This makes Morgawse his mother (Wace and Layamon 214-215, 260). Malory picks up this part of the genealogy and makes Morgawse Mordred's mother by her brother, Arthur.

By the time that films began to be made, however, the focus of Arthur's incest has shifted from Morgawse to Morgan. There are several ways that directors can deal with this troubling subject. They can remove it to the background, as Thorpe does in his *Knights of the Round Table* (1953), where Mordred is Morgan's "champion," implying that he fights her battles since, as a woman, she cannot fight

Morgan and the Problem of Incest

her own. They can name Mordred's mother but not explain that she is Arthur's sister, as in *Camelot* (1967). They can ignore it altogether, as in the satirical *Monty Python and the Holy Grail* (1975). They can make Morgan a man and thus eliminate the possibility of incest, as in Romero's *Knightriders* (1981). And they can meet the challenge head-on, as Boorman does in *Excalibur* (1981).

The dates of these films are important. Given the cultural and political climate of 1953, a director could not deal honestly with a source that included incest, especially with a subject of such popular interest as King Arthur and the Round Table. Richard Thorpe, however, states the issues at the very beginning of *Knights of the Round Table*. Morgan demands the kingdom because she is the rightful heir and Arthur is not. The issues are clearly drawn. Arthur has to prove that he is the heir by drawing the sword out of the stone twice. The great battle of Badon Hill, by which in the chronicles Arthur establishes peace in the kingdom, is fought at the beginning of the film also, but it is a battle demanded by Mordred. Arthur defeats him and accepts his allegiance, so Mordred lives to sow dissension in the kingdom and indeed becomes Morgan's champion as he carries out her schemes. She is determined to expose Lancelot's love for Guinevere, and thus she is at the very heart of the film.

The development of the plot hinges on her machinations. To escape Morgan, Lancelot leaves the court to fight the Picts. He marries Elaine to save the Queen's honor and moves with her to the Scottish border. But Elaine dies in childbirth; Mordred encourages the Picts to sue for peace because peace would force Lancelot back to Camelot, back to Guinevere, and back into Morgan's power. Merlin is against the plan, but Morgan kills him in his cell. Peace is declared, and Lancelot returns to court. Knowing that he is in danger, Lancelot avoids Guinevere, but she visits him at night and they are discovered. Humiliated at last, Arthur sends Guinevere to a convent and banishes Lancelot. Morgan and Mordred declare war, which brings about the destruction of the kingdom and Arthur's death. Lancelot returns to fight for the King and kills Mordred. Mordred's parentage is never revealed.

The film is singularly devoid of magic. Morgan is not Merlin's apprentice; she is not a sorceress. Merlin himself performs no magic. The only supernatural occurrence is the vision of the Grail, a theme treated near the end of the film.

The musical *Camelot*, based on T. H. White's *The Once and Future King* (1939), also ignores the incest theme. White follows Malory in making Morgawse, Arthur's elder sister, Mordred's mother, and he repeats Malory's statement that Arthur did not know that Morgawse was his sister when he accepted her invitation to share her bed. (We must remember also that Oedipus did not know that Jocasta was his mother when he married her, but ignorance of the true relationship does not make the deed less incestuous.) Lerner and Loewe, the lyricist and composer of *Camelot*, follow White in making Morgawse Mordred's mother but do not state that she is Arthur's sister. Arthur accepts Mordred as his son when the youth arrives from Scotland and tries to change his character, but Mordred refuses to adopt Arthur's ideals. The destruction of Camelot follows through Mordred's machination.

Knightriders, released the same year as *Excalibur*, 1981, is an inversion of the Morgan story found in Malory. Here, Morgan is a man, and the knights are part of a motorcycle-stunt circus. The magic is the result of the stunts. Like Malory's Morgan, a woman of many lovers, Romero's leaves his faithful girlfriend to go off with different women, though he always returns to her. Morgan's ambition is at the heart of the film (his refrain is "I want to be king"), and no Mordred is necessary to fight for him since he is well able to fight for himself. In all the motorcycle tournaments, he defeats Billy (the king) decisively, yet Billy will not give up the rule of the group. Morgan leaves to form his own traveling show with some of the group, but he returns when the group falls apart because of internal battles. Billy finally yields to Morgan, and when he is killed by a truck on the highway, Morgan's rule becomes total and legitimate. Morgan in this film is thus a combination of Morgan le Fay and Mordred, and the incest theme is bypassed altogether.

Excalibur's credits tell us that the film is based on Malory's account (Kennedy 30-37). Malory mentions Morgan briefly in book I.2, where he tells us that Morgan le Fay is one of three daughters of Queen Igraine. The eldest, Morgawse, marries King Lot and is Gawain's mother; the second, Elaine, marries King Nentres; and the third, Morgan, is sent to a nunnery, where she learns necromancy, and afterward marries King Uriens of Gore. She next appears in Book IV.6-16, an extended episode that shows her hatred of the King. She sends a hart to lure Arthur, King Uriens, and Sir Accolon of Gaul, who have been hunting in a great forest. When their horses die of exhaustion, the men follow on foot until Arthur kills the hart.

Tom Savini as Morgan the Black Knight in Knightriders.

Suddenly, on the edge of a lake, a ship appears and the three men board. Twelve fair damsels appear and entertain the King and his men until they fall into a deep sleep. They awake in separate cells of a dark prison, held by Morgan le Fay. Arthur is told by one of the ladies that he can deliver himself and the knights whose moans he hears by fighting a joust. He agrees and prepares for the contest. At the same time, a dwarf sent by Morgan delivers the same message to Sir Accolon. To ensure his victory, Morgan has sent him Excalibur, the King's sword, while sending Arthur only a copy of his sword. The joust goes ill for Arthur until he retrieves the real Excalibur. Accolon's life is forfeit, but the combatants reveal themselves to each other, and Arthur forgives Accolon, who later dies of his wounds. Morgan is later able to steal Excalibur's scabbard. Arthur pursues her, but she turns herself and her knights into huge stones to escape. She again makes an attempt on his life through the gift of a poisoned robe.

Three things are emphasized in Malory's Book IV: Morgan hates Arthur, her half-brother; she is a shape-changer who can turn herself into stone if she so wishes; she is determined to kill Arthur one way or another. The one thing Morgan does not do in Malory's version of the Arthurian story is seduce the King and bear him Mordred, a role filled by Morgan's sister Morgawse (Book I.19).

John Boorman's film is a variant of Malory's narrative. He supplies his own motive for Morgan's actions, actions that are directed mostly against Merlin for his creation of Arthur and thus for depriving her of her rightful inheritance.

Boorman's film becomes a revenge tragedy, as Sara Boyle has argued (42-43). Boyle suggests that in *Excalibur* Merlin's plan to give the Britons the ideal king does not take Morgana into account. Morgana is helpless against the forces unleashed by Merlin, "a woman shaped by treachery, twisted at the root, and determined to wield power" (Boyle 43). Morgana is about eight years old when her father, Golois, dies in battle with Uther Pendragon. She possesses second sight, and at the moment of her father's death, she cries out to her mother, "My father is dead." But almost immediately Uther in the form of Gorlois arrives, and Igraine says to Morgana: "No. See, your father is here." The child Morgana gives this "Gorlois" a knowing stare. She watches as Uther copulates with her mother, who cries out more in pain than in pleasure. When the real Gorlois is brought home dead, Morgana caresses his face, her own face expressionless as she seems to put the events together. When Arthur is born, Merlin appears to take him away, and Morgana asks him, "Are you the mother and the father of the baby now, Merlin?" Her question is merely rhetorical because she knows that Merlin is Arthur's creator. Igraine and Uther are only agents of his will.

Morgana next appears at Arthur's marriage to Guinevere. She leaves the ceremony to follow Merlin into the woods. In surprise, he asks her why she has left the wedding, and she replies, "I am a creature like you," and asks to be his pupil. The more Morgana learns from him, however, the more she wants to learn, and Merlin begins to fall in love with her.

After returning to Arthur's court, where she sows dissension by revealing Launcelot's love for Guinevere, Morgana leaves for her cavern. She wants desperately to learn the "charm of making," the secret of creation, which Merlin possesses. He finally agrees to teach her, but he tells her, "Here is desire and regret, knowledge and oblivion, in the total knowledge including love and hate." He warns

Morgan and the Problem of Incest

her that such knowledge would burn. "Then burn me," she replies. As he speaks the charm, she takes it from his lips and traps him in his own cave. "You fool," she exults. "You are trapped with the same sorcery you used to deceive my mother. You are nothing. You are not a man. I shall find a man and give birth to a god."

With these words, Morgana makes clear that her motives are threefold: to avenge her mother's rape by Uther Pendragon, to produce a god-king who will displace Arthur, and to achieve power. She puts a spell on Arthur and appears to him as Guinevere, while she seduces him. Just as she snatches the charms of making from Merlin, she snatches Arthur's seed from him to create Mordred, Arthur's nemesis. In all this, Morgana is the actor: she creates opportunities to work her will; she controls events more than Merlin does. But her power is used to destroy, not to create. This is illustrated by the Grail episode. Morgana sends the boy Mordred to lure the Grail knights to her castle, where she seduces them, then hangs them in trees for birds to pick out their eyes and the vultures to tear their flesh.

The King and his knights age throughout these episodes, but Morgana keeps her beauty. Nothing touches her, neither experience, nor emotion, nor events. She is an unearthly creature, and Merlin acknowledges her power when he returns from his cave. "You, madam, flow into a dream, a shadow—that comes and goes." He taunts her into speaking the charm of making, and as she speaks it, he takes it back. The breath of her mouth as she speaks becomes a fog that clouds the battlefield as Mordred faces Arthur's army. Morgana does not know that bereft of the charm she is now bereft of her beauty, and she goes to Mordred's camp to encourage him in his fight against Arthur. Mordred, seeing the hag who says she is his mother, strangles her on the battlefield.

By suppressing the love affair of Launcelot and Guinevere as the main cause of the Round Table's fall, Boorman enhances Morgana's role as a destroyer. Indeed, he frames the story with Morgana's presence: at the very beginning, she witnesses Uther's rape of her mother, which leads to Arthur's birth; she is present at the fatal battle, where Arthur and his kingdom perish; and in bringing down the kingdom, she destroys herself.

In the fourteenth-century poem *Sir Gawain and the Green Knight*, Morgan is the instigator of the action. Sheila Fisher (who cites the few scholarly articles devoted to Morgan's role in the poem) contends that despite her power Morgan is relegated to the margins

Morgana (Helen Mirren) and Merlin (Nicol Williamson) in Excalibur.

of the poem, appearing as an old hag sitting at the highest place at table with the lady of the castle. The Lady is Morgan's agent in Gawain's testing, not her husband's, as the poem at first suggests (79-80). Both Morgan and the Lady are therefore dangerous to Gawain. Fisher argues: "Proprietor of her castle, generator of the contracts and exchanges forming the poem's plot, Morgan has the power to displace both Bishop Bawdewyn and Bertilak, ecclesiastical and secular authority. In her powers of displacement lies the danger the narrative needs to displace. For this poem's particular construction of female sexuality and subjectivity inscribes a threatening otherness that is not only, and perhaps not primarily, sexual" (80). It is this enormous power that Bertilak acknowledges to Gawain at the end of the poem:

> I was entirely transformed and made terrible of hue
> Through the might of Morgan le Fay,
>   who remains in my house.

> Through the wiles of her witchcraft, a lore well learned,
> Many of the magical arts of Merlin has she acquired,
> For once she lavished her love delightfully
> On that susceptible sage, a sorcerer your knights know
> By name.
> So "Morgan the goddess"
> She accordingly became;
> The proudest she can oppress
> And to her purpose tame.
>
> (Fitt 4.XIX, Stone 122)

And yet, Fisher argues, this power, which displaces both chivalry and Christianity, is itself displaced, as the poem places Morgan in the margin. She continues: "Morgan's subsequent motivations, however, become increasingly dubious and increasingly trivial, because they are represented as increasingly dissociated from the values intrinsic to feudal, Christian ideology" (95). The poem's ambivalence toward its first cause, Morgan, is evident in the outcome. As Fisher writes:

> The poem concludes by linking the green girdle with betrayal, and specifically with the betrayal generated by women. The green girdle stands, then, as a warning against women and the currency of their tokens and even of their tokenism within the court. . . . For if Morgan could be effectively marginalized and if Guenevere could be reduced to permanent absence, the Round Table would not fall (99).

The theme that Fisher exposes in her discussion of the poem, the marginalization of the power of women to bring down the carefully constructed kingdom of Camelot, Boorman confirms in his treatment of Morgana in his film. Morgana does not reside in the margins but in the center. She deliberately sets out to destroy Camelot and succeeds. But she does not escape. The internecine strife that she engenders with her conception of Mordred is also the cause of her death. In this way, by emphasizing her power and her hatred, Boorman is saying that her death at Mordred's hands is deserved. She dies by what she has created. He thus places himself in the tradition of the antifeminist interpretations of the poem, that women's power is to be feared because it produces only evil.

A secondary theme not fully developed but only hinted at in Morgana's seduction of Arthur is the theme of doubling, generally linked with the theme of incest. Morgana transforms herself into a likeness of Guinevere, Arthur's wife, when she enters his bedroom to seduce him. Why Guinevere specifically and not just another beautiful woman? The double usually denotes another side of the character for whom it is the double and suggests that certain qualities belonging to Guinevere may also be found in Morgana. The film implies that Morgana would like to change places with Guinevere in Arthur's bed, although Morgana is given no overt longing for or sexual fascination with Arthur. The seduction is the only scene in which Morgana doubles as Guinevere. Short and decisive, it adds another dimension to Morgana's character.

In discussing doubling and incest in the *Mabinogi*, Andrew Welsh writes: "A purely psychological view of doubling in literature, such as Otto Rank's, explains it in terms of 'projection': unwanted instincts and desires, rejected aspects of the inner life (of a character or of the author, depending on the critic's focus), are dissociated from the self and then personified in the outer world" (347-348). He goes on to caution, however, that doubling in literature is not as simple as implied in Rank's explanation, a point explored in Welsh's discussion of the two Isoldes in the Tristan romance.

In *Excalibur*, Morgana's seduction of Arthur adds an unsuspected depth to the incest motif, something not found in any of the Arthurian legends, and is thus a decidedly post-Freudian addition, one that lends credence to Freud's statement that aberration is part of family romance. Arthur succumbs to Morgana's advances and is then horrified when she reveals her true self with a laugh as she leaves the room. Morgana is here a diabolical figure, powerful as the shape-changer Malory describes, wholly focused on destroying her brother, Arthur, who has robbed her of her kingdom, because incest, as Welsh writes, "creates serious confusion in social structures." He continues: "Incest is not ... a sign of familial unity or social vitality in *Oedipus Rex*, *Paradise Lost*, *Wuthering Heights*, or *Absalom, Absalom!* but of complex conditions of familial and social crisis: irruptions into the social order of the destructive will, defiant irrationality, or individual self-absorption; and the denial or disintegration of communal roles, duties, and bonds; or catastrophic intrusions into the world of nature and mankind by metaphysical evil or perverse fate" (357-358). Morgana's cold-blooded seduction of Arthur, involving no buildup of conflicting emotions or psychological torment, may be viewed as one of "irruptions" into the social order of Camelot, a defiant will to power through the son she would conceive and bear. The film makes it clear at the beginning that Morgana is older than Arthur but that a son would inherit Uther Pendragon's kingdom. Morgana, if there were no Arthur, would still be near to power through the husband chosen for her by her parents. With Arthur's birth, she loses any hope of even the appearance of wielding power. Arthur is an intruder sired by magic.

The story's feminist subtext emerges as readers and viewers ponder its meanings. Men cannot deny women their rightful inheritances and expect the world to live happily ever after. *Excalibur*, in depicting Arthur's creation so specifically as Merlin's attempt to provide a good king for the Britons, to the exclusion of Morgana, makes a point it may not have intended. Music from Wagner's *Götterdammerung* is used in the film to herald the end of one kind of world, the world of many gods, as Merlin calls it, but does not hint at what kind of new world will eventually emerge. The unintended point is that a world created upon a deliberate exclusion of a rightful claimant is just as doomed as the world it is intended to replace. Lerner and Loewe's *Camelot*, not brave enough to face the incest motif, places the blame for the destruction of the kingdom on Mordred as an embodiment of evil, as he taunts the King: "Kill the Queen or kill the Kingdom." *Excalibur* suggests a tantalizing paradox: that Camelot cannot stand, despite the power of the ideal king, because the seeds of its destruction have been sown at the very beginning, when Arthur is only an idea in Merlin's mind, brought to fruition precisely to save the social order, which is nevertheless doomed by his birth.

WORKS CITED

Boyle, Sara. "From Victim to Avenger: The Women in John Boorman's *Excalibur*." *Avalon to Camelot* 1 (Summer 1984): 42-43.

Fisher, Sheila. "Taken Men and Token Women in *Sir Gawain and the Green Knight*." In *Seeking the Woman in Late Medieval and Renaissance Writings*, ed. Sheila Fisher and Janet E. Halley. Knoxville: University of Tennessee Press, 1989. 71-105.

Geoffrey of Monmouth. *The History of the Kings of Britain*, trans. Lewis Thorp. Harmondsworth: Penguin, 1966.

Jarman, A. O. H., ed. and trans. *Geoffrey of Monmouth*. Cardiff: Wales, 1966.

Kennedy, Harlan. "The World of King Arthur According to John Boorman." *American Film* 6 (Mar. 1981): 30-37.

Malory, Sir Thomas. *Le Morte D'Arthur*, ed. Janet Cowen. 2 vols. Harmondsworth: Penguin, 1969.

Sir Gawain and the Green Knight, ed. and trans. Brian Stone. Harmondsworth: Penguin, 1959.

Wace and Layamon. *Arthurian Chronicles*, trans. Eugene Mason. 1912. New York: Dutton, 1962.

Welsh, Andrew. "Doubling and Incest in the *Mabinogi*." *Speculum* 65 (Apr. 1990): 344-362.

White, T. H. *The Once and Future King*. 1958. New York: Putnam, 1965.

12.

Blank, Syberberg, and the German Arthurian Tradition

Ulrich Müller
(translated by Julie Giffin)

Both Richard Blank's *Parzival* (1980) and Hans-Jürgen Syberberg's *Parsifal* (1981/1982) are films based on literary sources: the former on the early thirteenth-century *Parzival*, by Wolfram von Eschenbach, and the latter on Richard Wagner's opera, which premiered in 1882.

If the number of extant manuscripts is any evidence of contemporary popularity, then Wolfram's romance, surviving in almost ninety manuscripts, was the most successful courtly poem of the German Middle Ages. Wolfram based his romance on what was probably the last work of Chrétien de Troyes, a poet from northern France who wrote *Perceval*, or *Le Conte du Graal*, under the orders of Count Philip of Flanders. Chrétien's unfinished poem recounts the adventures of two heroes, Perceval and Gauvain.

When Wolfram was commissioned to retell and complete Chrétien's fragment around the year 1200, no one could have foreseen the range, merit, and significance of the result, which would overshadow every other work known at the time. Over the course of many years, Wolfram almost tripled the length of Chrétien's romance (from about 9,200 to 25,000 lines), completed the story in detail, added the early history of Perceval's father, and even gave a preview of the following generation of characters. *Parzival* was by far the longest known romance written in German up to that time.

Though generally faithful to Chrétien's plot, Wolfram changes so many large and small details that his *Parzival* becomes an independent work. It is neither a paraphrase nor a translation. Even his description and interpretation of the Grail are original: his Grail is a mysterious, powerful stone with divine origins, whereas Chrétien represents it as a golden vessel. References to the cup used at the Last Supper or to Christ's blood, references that became so important in the later tradition of the Grail, are completely missing in Wolfram's book, either because he was unaware of these connections (first made in the more or less contemporary *Estoire du Graal*, by Robert de Boron) or because he rejected them.

Like its source but unlike other courtly romances, Wolfram's poem has two main heroes, whom he calls Parzival and Gawan, and three central scenes of action: King Arthur's court and the realm of the Grail, as in Chrétien, and an original addition, the culturally equal if not superior world of the Orient. The whole narrative takes place in a magical time and a fantasy world that in many respects mirrors the geography and occasionally even the politics of Europe and the Orient.

Unlike Chrétien, who deals with strongly typified and often unnamed characters, Wolfram portrays a huge cosmos, a whole world, and his romance, which covers three generations of characters and events, gives the impression that there are countless characters with distinct personalities or at least personal "histories." The majority of them are related in the most complicated manner by blood, marriage, or political connections.

There is a unique trend in the German reception of the Arthurian legends: the story is retold without any mention of Arthur. Since the revival of interest in Arthurian materials in the early nineteenth century, German-speaking artists and authors have concentrated instead on the story of Parzival and his search for the Grail, and on the story of his son, Lohengrin. There are three reasons for this emphasis: the difficulty of exporting the British-national indentification with the legend of King Arthur; the German fixation on other "myths" of the Middle Ages; and the dominating influence of Richard Wagner on the reception of medieval myth in general.

The legend of Arthur and all its ramifications were not unknown to educated Germans at the end of the eighteenth and the beginning of the nineteenth centuries, albeit mostly through French and English versions. There was, however, little interest in these versions. Translations of Wolfram by San Marte (1835-1841) and Karl Simrock (1842) were responsible for first stimulating interest in the legend. Richard Wagner (1813-1883), who had been working with the Grail material since 1845, had an even stronger and more permanent influence on German Arthuriana. His "Bühnenweihfestspiel" ("Festival of Consecration in a Theater") *Parsifal,* when it premiered in 1882, confirmed the German practice of disregarding Arthur in place of Parzival.

Wagner omits King Arthur and Gawan, central figures in his source, Wolfram's *Parzival* (known to him through the San Marte translation and annotations). Instead, he focuses on the Searcher for the Grail, whom he calls "Parsifal." He reinterprets Wolfram's story, practically turning it upside down. He changes Wolfram's global and well-populated epic into a "Weltanschauung"-drama, one that concentrates on only a few characters. His "Bühnenweihfestspiel" advances the notion that sexual asceticism and the renunciation of the world are of the highest merit. The opera's hero is a searcher who overcomes himself by reducing his instinctual drives. Through aesceticism, he gains the power to acquire the Grail and takes on the role of redeemer.

Wagner's central idea, that a searcher can reach his goal through "purity"—"the pure fool, knowing through compassion..." ("durch Mitleid wissend der reine Tor . . .")—is not found in Wolfram's romance;[1] rather, it is one first found in late-medieval versions of the Grail story. The notion, which probably reached Wagner through his reading of San Marte's works, came to characterize all the later German reception of the Grail material.

Richard Blank's *Parzival* was first shown on West Germany's WDR (Westdeutscher Rundfunk) on November 11, 1980. Since then, it has been rebroadcast several times on the "Third Program" of ARD (Arbeitsgemeinschaft der öffentlichrechtlichen Rundfunkanstalten der Bundesrepublick Deutschland).[2]

While Eric Rohmer in his 1978 film *Perceval le Gallois* attempted an almost word-for-word adaptation of his medieval source, Blank[3] went in the opposite direction: he tried to actualize the medieval work. Like Rohmer, he was ambitious enough to make a film using and telling the *entire* story of his source.

Two performers, Wolfram Kunkel and Eva Schuchardt, play a majority of the roles in Blank's version. Using Wolfgang Mohr's translation (1977), they act out all essential parts of Wolfram's second generation of characters. Given that the length of the film is around ninety-two minutes, this is an astonishing achievement. It is also worth noting that Blank's film does not use rapid cuts or high-speed narration. The audience is never made to feel rushed because of the huge amount of material; instead, the director is able to project an "epic pace."

The film takes place partly in an imaginary, timeless Middle Ages, partly in the immediate present. The medieval segments are enacted in a large attic room, which like the prop room of a theater contains a few items indispensable to the story: dummies of horses, coats of arms, costumes.

The closed-off, windowless attic room is not only reminiscent of a theater prop room, but it also carries associations of a mythical picture of European philosophy and theology: the large "cavern of the memory" as presented and defined by Augustine in his *Confessions*. The plot emerges from this "mythical cave," whose tradition stretches from Plato to Jung, that is, from the collective memory of both the main actors and from their analysis and exposition of Wolfram's text.

Blank explicitly contrasts this "artificial Middle Ages" with the present. Shots from modern day cities and from the open country repeatedly show the reactions of a modern audience to the plot, and the film several times addresses ecological and environmental issues. Incorporated almost as "leitmotifs" are scenes in which the actor Wolfram Kunkel plays the hurdy-gurdy and sings *lieder* as commentary on the events.

The film thus meets the limitations of the television screen. It is not a period film with mass scenes in Hollywood style. Rather, the film stresses what the filmmaker saw as a "basic theme despite changed historical and social circumstances." As WDR's short commentary on the film notes: "Struggle and controversy still rule; women are still the main sufferers; human society has still not been realized."

The plot of Wolfram's work, though abridged, is basically unchanged. The film invents no themes that do not exist in the romance. Two important ideas from Wolfram's work are stressed: all humans are fundamentally "related," a constant theme in the romance, and women have special significance as sufferers and as a hope for a better future. Both points are brought together visually in the film's close, when all the important characters come together at the Grail Castle, in a huge celebration of reconciliation.

Hans-Jürgen Syberberg is one of the most prolific producers of the "new German Film."[4] His *Parsifal* is a complete adaptation of

Wagner's last opera, running almost four hours. For technical and aesthetic reasons, the film was originally supposed to be shown only in especially designed theaters. It has, however, since been shown on television and is also available on videocassette. The producer gave a detailed account of his project and its realization in a 1982 book and in subsequent lectures.

Before undertaking *Parsifal*, Syberberg had already dealt with Wagner and his ideology in three previous films: *Ludwig II: Requiem für einen jungfraülichen König* (1972), *Winifred Wagner und die Geschichte des Hauses Wahnfried von 1914-1975* (1975), and *Hitler: Ein Film aus Deutschland* (1977). Syberberg's five-hour documentary about Winifred Wagner, the director of the Bayreuth Festival during the Hitler era,[5] particularly angered some members of the Wagner family. It is unclear whether that anger was a factor in record companies' refusal to allow Syberberg to use existing recordings of *Parsifal* for his film. But Syberberg had the conductor Armin Jordan record a new production of the opera for Erato, one that compares favorably with other recordings of the work.[6] The film itself was made in the Bavaria Ateliers in Munich in 1981. It took only thirty-five days to shoot and had a budget of a little more than three million German marks (about $1.3 million).

Syberberg's *Parsifal* is completely original. He rejected any visual reference to theater and any note of realism. He did not want to make an "opera film" in the usual sense. "I did not make a *Parsifal* as a producer; rather, this *Parsifal* is one by Syberberg and is on film. I used Wagner for it, just as Wagner used the texts of the Middle Ages. Consequently, [the film was] a new creation" (Syberberg, "Filmisches" 76).

Syberberg's *Parsifal* takes place neither in a theater nor at any real site but is set in a place of fantasy, dream, and imagination. The stage floor used in several scenes and segments is a gigantic death mask of Wagner.[7] It is the film's "spiritual home" (Syberberg, *Parsifal* 14).

With two exceptions (Robert Lloyd as Gurnemanz and Aage Haukland as Klingsor), the roles of the opera are here assumed by nonsinging actors and actresses. The synchronization between the music and the film is astonishing; there is never the impression that the actors and actresses are only lip-synching. The achievements of Edith Clever as Kundry and Armin Jordan (the director of the soundtrack) as Amfortas are especially notable. Jordan proves himself to be an impressive and never pretentious actor under

The death mask of composer Richard Wagner that serves as the principal setting for Hans-Jürgen Syberberg's Parsifal.

Syberberg's direction; Clever, a famous actress on the Berlin *Schaubühne*, has worked with Syberberg for years, and they are the most fascinating and productive team in German film since Hanna Schygulla and Rainer Werner Fassbinder. Clever's Kundry ranks among the most impressive and most surprising of all interpretations of the role.

Wagner's *Parsifal* is a highly complicated and suggestive work. In Syberberg's "new creation," this aspect is emphasized through cinematic techniques that challenge the viewer to decode the content and music of the film while recognizing the relationships among its visual puzzles. These puzzles originate in part from one of Wagner's biographies: for example, the disproportionately large image of the composer's coat that appears several times, as well as "pictorial quotes" of Bayreuth, Ravello (where the opera was partly composed), and Venice (where Wagner died). Other signals refer to the effects of the opera; the ideology and politics of the nineteenth and twentieth centuries; Karl Marx, who knew Wagner's work but never met him; the Bavarian king Ludwig II; the Bayreuth Festivals; and National Socialism.[8]

There are also scenes that refer to Wolfram von Eschenbach and the Middle Ages. The viewer must recognize that the Grail throne and Kundry's seat are identical; that the world of the Grail and the world of Klingsor, asceticism and seduction, are like mirror images dependent on each other; that Amfortas and Klingsor suffer from their sexuality; that there are similarities between the "second Parsifal" and the medieval image of Christ; and that in death Amfortas and Kundry represent a medieval ruler and consort as they are shown on old gravestones. Syberberg expects his viewers not only to recognize these references but also to make sense of them.

Surprisingly, Syberberg avoids eroticism, even in the "most-feared scene of this opera" (Syberberg, *Parsifal* 127). This is the "flower girl" scene in the second act. Parsifal and the camera move through a gallery of statuelike girls, accompanied by lively music with seductive overtones and the beat of an "English waltz."[9] It almost seems that Syberberg here is portraying a fear of the erotic. One might question whether he is stressing the deep structure of Wagner's work too much and the seductive surface too little.

Syberberg's portrayal of Parsifal as androgynous caused much discussion. The role of Parsifal is performed by two impressive novice actors (Michael Kutter and Karin Krick). When Kundry kisses Parsifal, he feels sexual desire for the first time. Accompanying this feeling is the sudden realization of the relation between that desire and Amfortas's guilt, and a female Parsifal separates from the male figure. Both Parsifals, a feminine young man and a masculine young woman, are rejoined only at the film's end. This reunion leads to a scene that is at least partly shocking, when Parsifal sings a duet, as it were, with himself. Syberberg wants to break away from an idea that is generally representative of Wagner's work—"here evil woman, there redeeming man"—by portraying Parsifal as androgynous (Syberberg, *Parsifal* 56).

In a lecture, Syberberg summarized the main characteristics of his film:

> A few words about the things that I in part realized as important in the "Parsifal" movie. First of all, we have a young Parsifal, the like of which has not and could not have been on stage ever before. Furthermore, we have a division of Parsifal, which the stage had never delivered before.

There is a type of Kundry that had certainly never been on stage before and probably will not be again for a long time—unless on film: there is also a division of her voice and character. Then there is the "separierte Wunde."[10] This ... is incredibly significant. It is possible only when a closeup is possible, as it is with film; on stage, this form would simply be nonexistent. In addition, we had extraordinary voices at our disposal. This results in a clarity—Wagner's demands for distinctness are well known—that simply cannot be delivered on stage [which is characterized by] an eternal "long shot," indistinct speech, faces shrunk to the size of those of dolls. ... [This film attempted to] realize things that Wagner could only imagine. ... We really could show facial movement, expressions, etc. Therefore, for example, we tried in the "Good Friday Spell" to implement all of Wagner's directions and indications: the eye-dialogue of the three people and the gestures fit the music; it did not seem ridiculous. The Grail scene realized in Act I should also be mentioned: we projected an imaginary setting onto that character—something that would also be impossible in theater. ... And the projection onto this person makes reference to possibilities that psychoanalysis has introduced into this century, namely: to design a "projection" onto a person in addition to the projection of our ideas (Syberberg, "Filmisches" 67-68).

Syberberg's film has a fascinating power of expression that can be interpreted on many levels. A film of the highest quality, it furthermore is a valuable treatment of a Wagnerian opera, with whose innovative qualities no other screen adaptation (even from Bayreuth) can compare.[11] Occasionally shocking or controversial, it is in all events extraordinarily exciting.

NOTES

[1]Even Wagner's image of the Grail differs from Wolfram's. Whereas Wolfram's Grail is a stone with magical powers, Wagner's Grail follows Robert de Boron's tradition, in which the Grail is the vessel used both at the last Supper and to collect the blood of Christ at the Crucifixion.

Parsifal in both his male (Michael Kutter) and female (Karin Krick) forms arriving at the Chapel of the Grail in Act III of Hans-Jürgen Syberberg's Parsifal.

[2]Thanks to the efforts of Dr. Siegfried Schmidt (Salzburg), the Institute for German Studies at the University of Salzburg has a videotape of the film in its possession. The written documents I have at my disposal for the following discussion include an unpublished essay by Annelen Kranefuss, who inspired the film; a short text from WDR; and a few reactions from newspapers.

[3]Richard Blank was born in 1939 in Langenfeld in the Rhineland. After receiving his Ph.D. in Philosophy, he wrote radio plays and a few books. He also filmed documentaries before switching to the "literary" film. In addition to *Parzival*, he also made *Dracula* and *Peter Schlemihl, der Mann ohne Schatten*. Almost every year since 1978, he has been responsible for the screenplay and direction of a feature-length film (usually made for television). I would like to thank Dr. Blank for a long conversation about his film and his intentions.

[4]Syberberg, as quoted in *Opern und Opernfiguren* (1989): "Dr. Hans-Jürgen Syberberg, born on December 8, 1935, in Vorpommern, [in the former] East Germany. Spent childhood in the country until the end of the war; father landowner. Has lived since 1947 in Rostock (Ostsee), where he came into contact with theater, music, and cinema for the first time through films from the Russian Sowexport and DEFA. . . . He was also in contact with Benno Bresson from Brecht's Berliner Ensemble while in Rostock, and through him received invitation to go to Brecht in Berlin, where he produced his first 8 mm film (*Nach meinem letzten Umzug, Aufnahmen von der Bühne Brechts*, 1953). . . . Crossed from East to West Berlin in the same year (1953). . . . Produced over eighty television films . . . over the course of two years, starting in 1963. Made two-hour film about Fritz Kortner during rehearsals of *Kabale und Liebe*. Produced own films since 1965. Came into contact with Richard Wagner's music through the *Ludwig* film; plans for a trilogy: *Ludwig* (1972), *Karl May* (1974), *Hitler* (1977) (one hundred years of German and European history). . . ."

I would like to thank Dr. Syberberg for various conversations about his films and intentions. I would particularly like to acknowledge his participation in a seminar on German film that was held at the University of Salzburg in the 1988 summer semester and led by Professor Klaus M. Schmidt (Bowling Green State University) and the author.

[5]The Englishwoman Winifred Williams Klindworth (1897-1980) married Siegfried, a son of Richard Wagner, in 1915. After his death in 1930, she directed the festivals until the end of World War II. Her close ties with Hitler and National Socialism were incriminating, and she stepped down from her position.

[6]The singers for the main roles are Wolfgang Schöne (Amfortas), Hans Tschammer (Titurel), Robert Lloyd (Gurnemanz), Rainer Goldberg (Parsifal), Aage Haugland (Klingsor), and Yvonne Minton (Kundry).

[7]The death mask, designed by architect Werner Achmann, consisted of 40 tons of cement, was 15 meters long, 9 meters wide and 4.5 meters

high, and cost about 130,000 DM ($58,000.00) to make (Syberberg, *Parsifal* 17).

[8] The references to Hitler and National Socialism are recognizable but not obtrusive. The film is thus reminiscent of Syberberg's Winifred (1975) and Hitler (1977) films, where the producer made the connections between Wagner and National Socialism into a theme. Syberberg does not deal with the accusations of anti-Semitism made against Wagner's *Parsifal*.

[9] Wagner's original instruction was "wanting to sound American" ("amerikanisch sein wollend").

[10] Amfortas's "separierte Wunde," that is, that his wound is "separated" from his body, is reminiscent of the technique of the Christian votive picture as it is found in places of pilgrimage even today: a faithful and thankful Christ allows his healed body part to be depicted and hung as a picture in or on a church.

[11] In the realm of opera films, only Joachim Herz's version of the *Fliegender Holländer* (1964) can match the originality of Syberberg's cinematic techniques; cf. Sirikit Podroschko, "Senta."

WORKS CITED

Müller, Ulrich. "Parzival 1980—auf der Bühne, im Fernsehen und im Film." In *Mittelalter-Rezeption II: Gesammelte Vorträge des 2. Salzburger Symposions*, ed. Jürgen Kühnel et al. Göppingen: Kümmerle, 1982.

──────. "Gral 89: Mittelalter, Moderne Hermetik und die neue Politik der Perestroika: Zu den 'Parzival/Gral-Dramen' von Peter Handke und Christoph Hein." *Mittelalter-Rezeption IV: Gesammelte Vorträge des Symposions in Lausanne*. Göppingen: Kümmerle, forthcoming.

──────. "Moderne Gral-Questen: Vom Nachleben des 'epischen Mythos' der sinnsuchenden Reise: Fragmentarische Beobachtungen und Bemerkungen zu einigen modernen Dramen und Romanen sowie zu Science Fiction-Filmen von Stanley Kubrick und Andrej Tarkowskij." *Festschrift für Georg Mayer*, forthcoming.

──────, and Ursula Müller, eds. *Opern und Opernfiguren: Festschrift für Joachim Herz*. Anif (Austria): Müller-Speiser, 1989.

──────, and Peter Wapnewski, eds. *Richard-Wagner-Handbuch*. Stuttgart: Kröner, 1986.

Podroschko, Sirikit. "Senta, oder *Der Fliegende Holländer* von Joachim Herz: Ein Film nach Richard Wagner (1964)." In *Opern und Opernfiguren: Festschrift für Joachim Herz*, eds. Ulrich Müller and Ursula Müller. Anif (Austria): Müller-Speiser, 1989.

Syberberg, Hans-Jürgen. "Filmisches bei Richard Wagner." In *Richard Wagner: Millter zwischen Welten*, ed. Gerhardt Heldt. Anif (Austria): Müller-Speiser, 1990.

———. *Parsifal: Ein Filmessay*. Munich: Heyne, 1982.

———. *Syberbergs Filmbuch*. Munich: Nymphenburger, 1976.

Wolfram von Eschenbach. *Parzival*, trans. Wolfgang Mohr. 2nd ed. Göppingen: Kümmerle, 1979.

13.

Filming the Tristan Myth: From Text to Icon

Meradith T. McMunn

The story of the fatal passion of Tristan and Isolde is one of the best-known and most popular legacies of medieval literature. Twentieth-century films are only the latest transformations of this narrative, which has been translated from one language into another, from verse to prose, from oral performance to written text, and, most important for our consideration of modern films, from words to visual images. In this study, I shall examine some procedures and devices common to film narrative and to the "visual narration" that occurs in extensively illustrated medieval romance manuscripts (McMunn 277). Regardless of whether individual filmmakers were directly influenced by the illustrations of medieval romances, a comparison of the visual realizations of the story of Tristan and Isolde, including its underlying myth, in the two periods gives us a more precise understanding of the aesthetic psychology of both. The focus here is on a group of four film versions of Tristan and Isolde produced since 1940: *L'Éternel Retour* (1943), directed by Jean Delannoy; *Tristan et Yseult* (1972), directed by Yvan Lagrange; *Lovespell* (1979), directed by Tom Donovan; and *Fire and Sword* (1981), directed by Veith von Fürstenberg. These films demonstrate the considerable variety of options for filming this romance, from literal depiction of the narrative to an evocative use of icons, nearly devoid of narrative continuity.

The themes of consuming love and transfiguring death at the heart of the story have lost none of their emotional and aesthetic fascination. The challenge of interpreting the myth cinematically has proved formidable, and those directors who have taken the field have not completed the task to the satisfaction of most critics. Nevertheless, the cinema has been the major artistic medium for the exploration of Arthurian themes, including the Tristan legend, in the second half of the twentieth century (Mancoff 604).

Fire and Sword (Feuer und Schwert) or *Tristan and Isolde*, directed by Veith von Fürstenberg in 1981, is the most faithful to the legend narrative, and it has the most effective recreation of an early period. Filmed in color in Ireland, its scenes incorporate authentic medieval architecture and natural settings. The imagery of the title reflects its dual leitmotifs of passion and war. The film opens with the combat between Morholt and Tristan (the sword) and ends with the lover's funeral pyre—a touch of Germanic or even Wagnerian fire. Von Fürstenberg maintains the period atmosphere and literal interpretation of the medieval romance text, but the resulting lack of a personal style reduces the impact of the film. The story is presented linearly. The musical score by Robert Lovas provides continuity and emotional cues. Narrative summaries displayed on the screen supply additional continuity across skips in dramatic time.

Tristan and Isolde (Christopher Waltz and Antonia Preser) are well matched. The apparent youth of the actors, including the only young Brangane in any of the four films, gives verisimilitude to the self-absorption and self-indulgence of Tristan and Isolde, as well as their sometimes jejeune dialogue. Mark is portrayed as a sympathetic if weak man, unable to prevail against the headstrong duo.

Lovespell, too, is relatively faithful to the medieval plot. Also filmed in color in Ireland, it emphasizes the Celtic cultural setting of the legend by its score, which uses Irish folk music, its titles, based on the *Book of Kells,* and even Isolt's hawk, which is named for the medieval Irish hero Cuchulain. The script contains frequent references to Irish history and folklore.

Kate Mulgrew is cast as Isolt. She matches Richard Burton's Mark in appealing assertiveness and willful intensity. Perhaps in part because of the dynamism of the actors, these two characters dominate the film, shifting the balance away from Tristan (Nicholas Clay). The title should have been "Mark and Isolt." The film opens with their meeting in the fields near Isolt's home where she hunts alone with her tercel. Mark orders his companion knight to get the

Filming the Tristan Myth

tercel from the unknown girl who "must have stolen it." She rewards him instead by a blow with a grouse, which knocks him into the nearby stream. The incident may have been suggested by a historical event during the Third Crusade, when Richard the Lionhearted, riding through Calabria with only a single attendant, "rescued" a falcon from a peasant's hut and was chased by the villagers (Runciman 38). Throughout the film, the struggle for control between Mark and Isolt is sometimes friendly but increasingly bitter. Finally, she becomes an abused wife, first emotionally and then physically. The final shot of the film, after the death of the lovers, is of Mark, dressed in red and dominating the visual space.

Actions based on the medieval narrative are often provided with rationalized motivations in this film, as when Isolt gives Tristan the love potion to keep him from leaving her. They have earlier consummated their love without need of this device. The attempt at recreating the medieval period conflicts with the presentation of Isolt and with the intrusive modern psychological motivation supplied for all the major characters. The resulting tension produces a sense of anachronism that makes the medieval settings and costumes seem extraneous.

Tristan and Yseult was filmed in color in Ireland and France. It is the distinctive expression of its director, Yvan Lagrange, who aimed to create "the impressions of the theme of the myth—love, eternity, madness, fatality" (Selcer 45). Lagrange also wrote the screenplay and played the role of Tristan, opposite his wife Claire Wauthion, who played Yseult. This is the only film that does not attempt sequential narration. There is almost no dialogue, and Yseult speaks the only lines. Yseult dominates Tristan just as she controls the two greyhounds that accompany her on a leash in early sequences. Lagrange uses striking visual images of violence and explicit eroticism to convey the universal mythic dimensions underlying the romance. This is "the naked myth set beyond the anecdotal tradition," according to Jean-Marcel Parquette, who has given this complex film its most coherent reading. He interprets the principal themes of love and war as the "dreamed aspects" of the reproductive instinct and hunger, respectively. These themes are expressed iconically in static poses: Tristan and Yseult in front of stained-glass windows that represent Adam and Eve, or mimicking a pieta pose, or in repeated action sequences, such as the one in which Yseult is transformed into a warrior who "kills" Tristan, or an episode in which

Tristan (Yvan Lagrange) and Iseult (Claire Wauthion) in Lagrange's Tristan and Iseult. (Courtesy of the Film Stills Archive of the Museum of Modern Art.)

Yseult, wrapped in cellophane, is carried in Tristan's arms among carcasses hanging in a slaughterhouse.

L'Éternel Retour, with a screenplay by Jean Cocteau, was filmed in and around Nice during the German occupation of France. It is the only attempt at a modern-dress version of the medieval romance, and it retains the outline of the medieval story. On closer examination, however, even the modern settings are more like the archetypal settings of medieval romances ("the castle," "the island") and lack grounding in contemporary geography. There is a sensitive use of sound play to evoke the legendary characters. Tristan, played by Jean Marais, is called Patrice, and Iseult, played by Madelaine Solange, is called Nathalie. The last syllable of each name suggests the name of the character's medieval counterpart. Frossin, the surname of the dwarf Achille and his jealous family, is the same as the name of the medieval dwarf character. Marc, too, retains his legendary name, as does the bully Morolt (Lacy 115).

Tristan is clearly the dominant character. Camera angles emphasize his chiseled good looks and statuesque heroism. His moods alternate between gaiety and melancholy. His empathy with nature is reflected in his imitation of the nightingale's song and his rapport with his dog, Moulouk.

This is the only black-and-white Tristan film. The textured filming also serves to isolate the characters within a timeless "otherworld" of emotions and mythical elements. Light and shadow sculpt the figures, emphasizing their iconic qualities. Marais's hair was lightened to match that of Sologne, for example, and some extraordinary shots of the dwarf are the result of careful lighting and camera angles (Bazin 40; Marais 131-132). The final words of Cocteau's screenplay reiterate this merging of icon and myth. The film closes with the famous shot of the dead lovers on an improvised bier. "Death has sculpted them, enfolded them, lifted them onto a royal shield. They are alone, enveloped in glory... And so begins their real life" (Cocteau 99).

The evidence of medieval literature and art demonstrates that few narratives enjoyed such great popularity throughout the Middle Ages as that of Tristan and Isolde (Loomis and Loomis 42). Although its relationship to the Matter of Britain is tangential, this tragic story had become associated with the Arthurian legends as early as the twelfth century (Loomis 122; Batts 567). The popularity of both the Arthurian tales and the story of Tristan and Isolde was enhanced by their adaptation into the increasingly popular romance genre in the second half of the twelfth century. These early romance manuscripts, however, were unillustrated or contained only a few historiated initials or miniatures. (For example, see Paris, B.N. fr. 2186 or Munich, Bayerische Staatsbibliothek, cgm 51.) By the end of the thirteenth century, manuscripts that contained Tristan and other Arthurian romances often included extended programs of narrative illustrations, such as those in London, B.L. Add. 5474, Paris, B.N. fr. 750, and Malibu, Getty MS XV.5 (DeHamel 117-130; Stones 83-102). Narrative programs of the Tristan romance are also known to have been popular in tapestries and wall-paintings from the thirteenth through the fifteenth centuries, though relatively few examples are extant (Loomis and Loomis 42).

Medieval and modern visual recreations of the Tristan and Isolde narrative share many conventions. The following generalizations concerning the illustration of this romance are based primarily on illustrated manuscripts from the thirteenth through the fifteenth centuries and on modern films. The romance is the narrative form most closely associated with the legend of Tristan and Isolde, and so the conventions associated with this genre certainly condition both the technical and psychological elements chosen by the manuscript painters and later by filmmakers. The visual representation of Tristan material, like that of the Arthurian material, was structured by the literature, but the development of a visual narrative tradition came a century after the development of the verbal texts.

Technical excellence does not necessarily result in artistic success. A big budget did not ensure quality in the products of the medieval scriptorium any more than it does in those of the modern film-production company. In both instances, the artifact may be bigger, with more technical refinement and more lavish ornamentation, settings, and costumes, but the intangibles of imagination and aesthetic impact may still be lacking. The converse is also true of both medieval art and contemporary film. Technical limitations and flawed execution do not always negate the effect of creativity and originality.

To a large extent, the content and aesthetic of any work of visual or verbal art are determined by its intended audience or patron. The marked increase in the production of vernacular illustrated manuscripts beginning in the thirteenth century is usually attributed to the rise in the secular workshops working for lay patrons (Stones 359-360). Filmmakers, too, are affected by considerations of audience, though there is sometimes an apparent ambivalence toward the "general audience." Cocteau has explicitly stated that his intention was for a popular rather than a purely artistic or critical success with *L'Éternel Retour* (Cocteau 344). The fact that *Lovespell* was originally intended for television strongly suggests that it, too, was targeted for a popular audience. *Fire and Sword* contains little that would not be easily accessible to the general public. On the other hand, though Lagrange has not specifically addressed this issue of intended audience in his public statements on his film, he has admitted that his deliberate choice of complex imagery and paratactic structure create an interpretive challenge for the viewer (Selcer 49).

Since romance is usually situated in an "elsewhere," the settings must be evoked with as much richness of detail as possible. The authors often make up for the lack of specificity of geographic location by including a wealth of visual detail. The texts and pictures of most illustrated medieval Tristan romances are notable for their

Filming the Tristan Myth

portrayal of architectural spaces, natural settings, clothing, and armor. These miniatures often use intense, rich colors. The Tristan films likewise utilize vibrant colors and striking sets and costumes to create a self-contained world, even though these elements may not be historically "correct." Indeed, there are several "Middle Ages" to choose from when setting the romance: an early setting suggesting the period of the early Celtic tradition, a twelfth-century feudal society, a thirteenth- or fourteenth-century courtly context, or the late-medieval society of the fifteenth century, which was centered more on the town than the castle.

Extensively illustrated romances often mix stock and distinctive scenes. Scenes are "distinctive" when they are recognizable as illustrating a particular episode, such as Tristan rescuing Isolde from the lepers or Mark finding Tristan and Isolde in the forest asleep with a sword between them. Typical stock scenes are those showing two knights or two armies fighting, or two individuals talking—scenes that could illustrate any number of incidents in almost any romance (McMunn 278). Stock scenes may have provided a visual backdrop, like a stage or movie set, which prompted the visual imagination of the medieval reader. These two types of scenes may also be used by the artists in more complex patterns of repetition and interlace.

The cinematic treatments of Tristan also employ analogous stock scenes and distinctive scenes. The fight between Morholt and Tristan is a mounted combat of two knights with lances and swords in *Fire and Sword* or the fist-and-knife brawl between Patrice and Morolt in the bar on the island in *L'Éternel Retour*. These stock scenes could come from any number of films made in any number of studios. Scenes with Tristan and Isolde drinking the potion or Mark spying on the lovers at the fountains are distinctive to this particular romance and are immediately recognizable even in a modern-dress adaptation, such as *L'Éternel Retour*.

The medieval illustrations of Tristan romances most often depict the adventure narrative. In the Tristan films, however, the iconic elements are more prominent—more so even than they are in the medieval texts, and they more strikingly visualize the complex nature of the myth itself. In these four films, the theme of love and death becomes one of violence and domination. The nature of the conflict may be societal and the personal violence generalized to war (Lagrange and Von Fürstenberg), or the struggle may be between individuals and society and personalized to a conflict between individuals for dominance in marriage (Von Fürstenberg, Donovan,

Cocteau) or in the love relationship (Von Fürstenberg and Lagrange). The camera treatment identifies both the antagonists and the dominant character. The relative lack of personal vision or narrative focus in Von Fürstenberg's *Fire and Sword* results at least in part from his ambitious double focus of conflict, which is too broad for the scope of the film. Many medieval romances contain an emblematic or iconic use of key symbols, such as the love potion, the sword, and the black sails. This contrasts with the equally strong tendency to linear plot structure in romance adventure narratives. In films, the counterpart of these contrasting tendencies is generally the preference for one or the other process. This forms the basis for locating each film on a continuum from very literal to very iconic.

Psychological motivation and emotion are prominent in romance narratives. These features are difficult to convey in manuscript paintings but transfer well to cinematic adaptations, and modern directors, actors, and audiences find them appealing and "contemporary." The linking of psychology and symbolism intensifies the effect of both providing a rationalized interpretation for less easily accepted mysticism or allegory. The role of the "love potion" in the love affair, or the nature of the relationship between Mark and Isolde, are elements open to a variety of interpretations and permit significantly varied structures in the four films, depending on the interpretive choices assigned to them.

The prominence of nature has often been noted as characteristic of romance, where the proclivity for sensory details resulted in frequent descriptions of natural settings. Nature was also used symbolically to explore interior states and psychological relationships. Nature, often sentimentalized, is prominent in medieval manuscript paintings. Again, this medieval technique translates well into film. For example, animals are used thematically in each of the Tristan and Isolde films to develop characterizations of the principals, as well as to suggest the sometimes changing relationships among characters. The tercel in *Lovespell* has already been mentioned. In *L'Éternel Retour*, the dwarf Achille is both unnatural and antinatural. The handsome, gifted Patrice is favored by nature and is responsive to it. The contrasting characters of Patrice and Achille and their fundamental hostility to each other are defined by the contrasting opening shots of the dog that Achille has killed and the affectionate welcome of Patrice by his dog, Mouluk.

Finally, there are the two elements of motion and sound, which are intrinsic to modern films, but which are used very differently if

The final scene from L'Éternel Retour *showing the makeshift bier holding the bodies of Nathalie (Madeline Solange) and Patrice (Jean Marais). (Courtesy of the Film Stills Archive of the Museum of Modern Art.)*

at all by medieval painters. Medieval manuscript illustrators portrayed motion, often in a conventionalized manner. Medieval romances were sometimes performed to musical accompaniment. Nevertheless, the ability of the film medium to present visual motion and recorded sound distinguishes the films as a group from the illustrations in medieval romance manuscripts. These characteristics of film, however, are used differently in each of the four cinematic versions of Tristan and Isolde. Both *Fire and Sword* and *Lovespell* are "active" films. The movement is used to enliven the narration but rarely functions on a symbolic level. In *L'Éternel Retour*, the contrast between movement and its absence is used to create a rhythm in the narration and to isolate and intensify key images. In addition to the "real-time" representation in most of this film, there is a famous sequence that humorously plays on the fact that the film is a recorded artifact. To suggest Achille's haste in leaving Patrice's room, a sequence of "ellipsis in montage" shows a picture, a pack of cigarettes, and a necktie suddenly disappearing from their places (Clifton 151).

Lagrange's technique is even more self-consciously cinematic. He uses repeated movement ritualistically. Even at static moments, he draws the audience's attention to the movement of hair, hands, and eyes and thus contrasts realistic movement with the dreamlike stillness of these scenes, creating emotional and symbolic tension.

The musical scores are prominent in all of the Tristan films, but only Yvan Lagrange has used music as a substitute for dialogue. He subtitles his film "Opéra en scope-couleurs," and he uses the mesmerizing music performed by the rock group Magma as a leitmotif in scenes of love and war. The lyrics are deliberately unrecognizable. The driving intensity of the repeated scenes, especially the knights riding in the battle episodes, helps to confirm the haunting ritual-like impression. These repeated scenes function like theme and variations in music or like the *laisses similaires* of medieval *chansons de geste*, with shifts in perspective or setting that occur only after two or three repeats. The other films, especially *Fire and Sword*, use their musical scores in a more conventional, though still effective, manner to underline emotions and to indicate the passage of time.

This consideration of some of the strategies for visual realization of the story of Tristan and Isolde in medieval manuscript illustrations and in twentieth-century cinema continues the investigation into the relationship of text to image that is an active area of current medieval scholarship. Comparison of medieval and modern treatments of the visualization of the Tristan and Isolde story can tell us much about the creative aesthetic both of the Middle Ages and of our own time.

WORKS CITED

Batts, M.S. "Modern German Versions of Gottfried's *Tristan*." In Lacy et al., *Encyclopedia*, pp. 567-574.

Bazin, André. *French Cinema of the Occupation and Resistance*, trans. Stanley Hochman. New York: Ungar, 1975.

Clifton, N. Roy. *The Figure of Film*. London and Toronto: Associated University Presses, 1983.

Cocteau, Jean. *Three Screenplays*, trans. Carol Martin-Sperry. New York: Grossman, 1972.

DeHamel, Christopher. *A History of Illuminated Manuscripts*. Boston: Godine, 1986.

Lacy, Norris J. "Jean Cocteau." In Lacy et al., *Encyclopedia*, p. 115.

_____, et al., ed. *The Arthurian Encyclopedia*. New York: Garland, 1986.

Loomis, Roger Sherman, ed. *Arthurian Literature in the Middle Ages*. Oxford: Clarendon, 1959.

_____, and Laura Hibbard Loomis. *Arthurian Legends in Medieval Art*. New York: Modern Language Association of America, 1938.

McMunn, Meradith. "Translating the Medieval Romance Narrative: From Text to Image in the *Roman de Kanor*." *Romance Languages Annual* 1 (1990): 277-284.

Mancoff, Debra N. "Visual Arts." In Lacy et al., *Encyclopedia*, pp. 597-605.

Marais, Jean. *Mes quatre verités*. Paris: Éditions de Paris, 1957.

Paquette, Jean-Marcel. "The Final Metamorphosis of Tristan: Yvan Lagrange (1972)," *Tristania* (forthcoming).

Runciman, Steven. *The Kingdom of Acre and the Later Crusades*. Vol. 3 of *A History of the Crusades*. Corr. rpt. Cambridge: Cambridge University Press, 1955.

Scherer, Margaret R. *About the Round Table*. New York: Metropolitan Museum of Art, 1945.

Selcer, Robert. "Yvan Lagrange: Impressions of a Filmmaker." *Tristania* 4 (1979): 44-50.

Stones, M. Alison. "Arthurian Illuminated Manuscripts." In Lacy et al., *Encyclopedia*, pp. 359-375.

14.

Arms and Armor in Arthurian Film

Helmut Nickel

Among the aspects of Arthurian film that deserve special attention is its treatment of arms and armor. After all, Arthurian films are mainly about knights, and knights would not be knights without their armor. This essay will examine some typical approaches to the subject among these films and try to explain how arms and armor were handled, not only as far as selection of the period style is concerned but also in actual use of weapons in battle and tournament.

In reviewing costume and armor in cinema Arthurian, one must keep in mind that these films face problems different from those encountered by the average costume drama. Most historical films deal with an exactly datable timespan—say, Imperial Rome for *Ben Hur* or the fifteenth century for the campaigns of *Henry V* and *Richard III*—and therefore costumes, furniture, and weapons can be designed that should be reasonably accurate for the periods in question, provided that the designers did their research.

Arthurian films, by contrast, are not necessarily bound to such a fixed style period. Actually, the scriptwriter, the director, and the costume designer are free to choose from a timespan of almost a thousand years, if their ambition would call for historical accuracy. Given the legendary nature of the Matter of Britain, though, any flight of fancy concerning costume and setting could be equally well justified.

The version of the tales of King Arthur best known to the general public is Malory's *Morte Darthur*, written down in the fifteenth century, and for this reason costumes and setting in Late Gothic style might be considered to be appropriate. On the other hand, it is also well known today that the "historical Arthur" would have lived and fought at about the year A.D. 500, and a filmmaker aiming at historical verisimilitude would thus prefer a Dark Age background. Then again, most of the major Arthurian romances were composed during the twelfth and thirteenth centuries, and costume designers might see "around 1200" especially attractive as the right style period, because of its romantic association with the Crusades.

All these period styles could be shifted onto an imaginary plane by adding fanciful touches to otherwise quite realistically rendered costumes as *Verfremdungseffekt*, a trick amply used by nineteenth-century illustrators.

The medieval romances of chivalry are legitimate ancestors of both the Western novels and the Western movies, where the Lone Cowboy riding into town is the Questing Knight, the Sheriff and his posse are King Arthur and the companions of the Round Table, the villain in the showdown in Main Street is the Black Knight at the tournament, and the rancher's daughter is the Princess, whose fair hand is the prize at the happy end.

Every moviegoer knows and accepts the "white hats/black hats" rule of the Western horse operas. For the "knights in shining armor" films, the same rules apply in an appropriately modified form. The evil significance of the Black Knight is self-evident;[1] for balance, the Hero, who normally is also the star, not only has to ride a white horse whenever possible, he also has to wear an open-face helmet, in order to make absolutely sure that the audience gets a good look at the star's radiant brow, while the villain is hiding his sinister countenance behind a closed visor. Every so often, the hero is found fighting though raging battles without benefit of any helmet at all. This is usually made plausible by a fine touch of realism, when the hero's helmet gets knocked off his head as soon as the battle is under way.

All designers of costumes or armor, even those who rely largely on their own imagination, must necessarily have some models in mind upon which their creations are based. One of the problems with these models is that there are very few actual objects in the field of arms and armor that have survived from the periods in question. Practically ninety-nine percent of existing armor dates from after A.D. 1500. For this reason, a visit to even a major museum can be only of limited help, and therefore book illustrations would be the logical (and also easiest accessible) source for such models. Purists among designers could find their prototypes in the standard reference works of costume and armor, but those searching for the realm of myth and fantasy, if they would be willing to look for inspiration outside of their own imagination, presumably would prefer to glean their inspiration from the glorious illustrations provided by Howard Pyle, Arthur Rackham, Aubrey Beardsley, or N. C. Wyeth. The inspired use of such splendid material would contribute greatly to the success of a film.

Once in a while, a film is straightforwardly based upon fully prescribed pictorial material, which makes it both easy and difficult for the designers, who have to stay faithful to their source but have to use their own imaginations to flesh out the parts not preformed in the prototype. This is the case with *Prince Valiant* (1954), which was an adaptation of the comic-strip classic by Hal Foster. Foster, in his painstakingly precise drawings, had created his own vision of the Middle Ages, which even beyond the circle of his fans is widely taken for medieval reality. The setting of his *Prince Valiant* is as imaginary as his hero himself. Foster created him in the best tradition of medieval minstrels, who kept inventing new heroes and new adventures within the well-known and well-beloved Arthurian framework. This was done to enhance their performances and to catch the attention of their audiences in castle halls and county fairgrounds. The costumes and armor designed by Foster are of a medievalistic nature, vaguely "around 1200," with some highlights from earlier times, such as the Late Roman/Byzantine period, and of course—as would be expected in a story about a prince of Thule—with a generous dose of romantic Viking imagery.

The film designer of *Prince Valiant* faithfully adhered to the style created by Foster, down to such details as the armorial bearings of Sir Gawain (a highly, but quite unheraldically, stylized golden falcon on his green surcoat, doubtlessly chosen to fit the interpretation of Gawain's Welsh name, Gwalchmai, "Hawk of May"). It is interesting that, as far as I know, not one film designer ever made use of the "real" arms of the Knights of the Round Table that can be found recorded in romances, as illuminations in manuscripts, and even as regular rolls of arms from the thirteenth century onward. In all fairness, though, it has to be said that before Pastoureau's *Armorial*, published in 1983 (which mentions non-French material only in passing), reference to Arthurian arms was found mostly in scattered articles in heraldic journals.

The knights at the Great Tournament in *Prince Valiant* wear thirteenth-century-style mail armor with bucket-shaped *heaulms* and flowing armorial surcoats in bright colors. Shields are of the triangular "knightly" type, emblazoned with the champion's heraldic bearings, but Prince Valiant's own shield, with his badge of the red horse's head of Thule, is circular, to hint at his "Viking" heritage. A stickler for technical detail would insist that his shield is structurally closer to that of a Greek hoplite (a heavy-armored citizen soldier of classical antiquity) than to that of a Norseman. (Perhaps this can be explained as Mediterranean influence through his association with Aleta, the Queen of the Misty Islands in the Aegean Sea.) Shields in most films are not made of wood covered with leather, as actual medieval shields were, but are stamped out of sheet metal. Such construction has the advantages of faster and less expensive manufacture, of a neat and shiny look, and also of a pleasing acoustic effect, because these metal shields, when hit by sword or mace, give forth a resounding "Bang," instead of the less gratifying dull "Thud" of the wood.

The costumes of the invading and marauding Sea Rovers evoke the standard Viking image with shaggy furs and horned helmets; their chieftain, in his conspiratorial meeting with the Black Knight, Sir Brack,[2] has a winged helmet as mark of his rank. (Unfortunately, no archaeologist so far has unearthed a Viking helmet with horns, let alone with wings.)

As light campaign gear, fit equally for battle or quest, Hal Foster's knights are equipped with spiked steelcaps with mail curtains hanging down to protect nape and neck. Because the manufacture of mail is a time-consuming business—it means linking together by hand thousands of tiny rings—the costume designer of the film in what must have been a brilliant brainstorm was able to circumvent considerable labor expenses by simply obtaining a number of *khulakhud*, spiked helmets with camail of a traditional pattern (Robinson, *Oriental Armour* 31-52, 93-115), which were produced en masse in busy family armorers' shops in Persia and India up to the first half of this century. Made expressly for the tourist trade, they were sold in all the bazaars of the East, and they are still cluttering up antique shops and auction sales. These helmets resemble Foster's noble knightly gear quite admirably, as long as one does not look too closely for tell-tale Oriental feature, such as the paired plumeholders on either side of the moveable nasal.

An even more popular Arthurian film has been *Camelot* (1967). Admittedly, one reason for this popularity would be the fact that its model, the Lerner and Loewe musical *Camelot*, has become nostalgically linked with the presidency of John F. Kennedy (Knight 26-31). However, the lavishness of the film's production also guarantees its success. In the unpaginated illustrated souvenir booklet for *Camelot*, the costume designer, John Truscott, states that he "tried to make the film seem sophisticated but with elements which contradict sophistication." Truscott also claims that "materials were collected from all over the world." Though this comment evidently refers to the fabrics for the costumes to be made, it also applies to the armor in a surprising way.

Armor of knights and men-at-arms, a total of 361 suits, was designed to give it a "timeless" medieval look, but with generous use of *Verfremdungseffekt*, in order, in the words of the director, Joshua Logan, to "eliminate all the clichés that have surrounded castle-and-crusade pictures since the beginning of films."

The armor of the men-at-arms, to be seen only more or less on background figures in mass scenes, is vaguely fourteenth-century in style, with mailshirts, iron-studded leather jacks, and simple bascinets. The knights, as befitting their superior status, wear much more elaborate armor. Their articulated arm and leg defenses are also of the type in use since the fourteenth century (Blair 62-67), but the cuirasses and helmets of the main actors, Sir Lionel, Sir Sagramore, Sir Dinadan, and even of King Arthur himself, are derived from Central Asian and Chinese prototypes of the Wei, T'ang, and Ming periods (Robinson, *Oriental Armour* 32, 137-139, 151); a superlative *Verfremdungseffekt* indeed! In particular, Sir Lionel's lamellar helmet with its mask visor is clearly styled after an original of ca. A.D. 500, found in an Avar warrior's grave at Kertch in the Ukraine and now in the Historical Museum, Moscow (Robinson, *Oriental Armour* 55-56; Kirpičnikov 101-102). Presumably in order to make the bumptious Sir Lionel even a little more ridiculous looking, his visor is not hinged at the brow, to fold upward, as it should, but is made to open sideways, like the door of a pot-bellied iron stove.[3]

The bardings and trappings for the noble steeds of the three champions at the tournament, on the other hand, are in sixteenth-century European style. Their horses' chanfrons are magnificently crested: Sir Lionel's with a golden swan with spread wings, Sir Sagramore's with a splendid rack of stag's antlers, and Sir Dinadan's with a huge pair of curling ram's horns. These ram's horns are the clue for where the inspiration for these crests must have come from. Chanfrons with ram's horns as ear protectors are the leitmotif for horse armor made by a prolific Nürnberg armorer, Kunz Lochner (c. 1510-1567). Two of his horse armors are on display in museums at Madrid. One in particular is conspicuous as the very first in the array of a dozen equestrian figures of knights in full armor, man and horse, in the Great Hall of the Real Armeria, the ancient armory of the kings of Spain (Cortés pl. I and IV); the other has pride of place in the Armor Gallery of the Army Museum (*Museo del Ejercito* 35). When *Camelot* was filmed on location in Spain, using real castles in Spain for its scenery (the Castillo de Coca is Camelot; the Alcazar of Segovia is Lancelot's Joyous Guard), the designer seems to have found his inspirations for his horse armor in the Madrid museums. Having decided to adapt the impressive ram's horns for the chanfron crest of Sir Dinadan's charger, it would be only one further step to create the antler rack and the swan crest for the other champions as a "spinoff."

Lancelot's silver armor (he rides a white horse, of course) is topped by his helmet crest of a silver fleur-de-lys; this is to show not only that he is terribly pure but presumably also that he is French. The same "French" fleur-de-lys, set in a glory of rays, is displayed on his silver shield.[4] This shield has a bouche in its upper dexter corner, a cutout that served as a support for the lance in the charge.

A knight's shield was his main defense in the days of mail armor, which was too flexible to be shock resistant. To make the most out of the shield's protection, knights, especially in the formal combat of the tournament, charged each other left (shield) side against left side, their lances pointing diagonally across their horses' necks.

Unfortunately, fight coordinators in films are generally unaware of the technical function of the shield as a shock breaker. In sword fights, they let their combatants happily flail away, sword clashing against sword (the surest way to ruin a good blade), with their shields held out of the way as a mere ornamental nuisance, and in jousts the combatants all too often point their lances straightforward, meeting their opponents on their right sides unprotected by the ignored shields. Sad to say, in the wayside encounter of Lancelot with King Arthur, and also in his jousts with Sir Lionel and Sir Dinadan, the jousters charge each other right (but wrong) side against right side. Only Sir Sagramore manages to get on the proper side of the tilting barrier, a fine point appreciated by Queen Guinevere.

Arms and Armor in Arthurian Films

Another technical point regularly missed by illustrators of knightly tales and fight coordinators alike is that of the broken lance. Inevitably, the loser in the joust falls off his horse ingloriously, his broken lance dangling limply, while the victorious champion's shaft is boldly pointing up- and foreward at a triumphant angle. This is for us moderns understandable from the point of view of Freudian symbolism, but it is quite wrong from the technical point. A shattered lance was the best proof that the jouster had hit his opponent with the greatest force possible; a mere glancing blow or a miss would have left the shaft intact. As a fact, it was a score point carefully recorded by the heralds, whether a jouster broke his lance, even if neither combatant fell. Contemporary representations of jousts invariably show the victor's lance broken, and the loser's intact (Cripps-Day xxvii-xxx; Nickel, "Tournament" 216-217, 248).

In *Camelot*, King Arthur's great sword Excalibur is the sword he drew from the stone, as indicated by the Gothic script etched on its blade: "Whoso Pulleth Out This Sword of the Stone Is Rightwise King Born of All England." The Sword's cruciform hilt vaguely resembles that of a fifteenth-century sword with a grip "of one-hand-and-a-half." In an interesting pattern of mutual influence between the arts, the famous still photo of King Arthur enthroned, his fists clenched around the guard of Excalibur, has been adapted as the cover picture for the third novel, *Arthur*, in Stephen R. Lawhead's Pendragon Cycle (1989). The graphic artist exchanged Richard Harris's frowning brow for a more youthful countenance, and slightly—barely noticeably—altered the appearance of Excalibur by putting a purple gem in its guard, because the novel mentions an "eagle-carved amethyst" on its hilt. The amethyst in Excalibur's hilt has become an established detail, passed on and elaborated upon among Arthurian writers for fifty years, ever since Wart in T. H. White's *The Once and Future King* (1939) pulled at the Sword in the Stone, and "the light all about the churchyard glowed like amethysts."[5]

T. H. White's *The Once and Future King* has been the basis not only of *Camelot* but also of the Disney version of the story in *The Sword in the Stone* (1963). As an animated film, it is of course subject to rules totally different technically and aesthetically from those films already discussed. Therefore, nobody would expect anything resembling historical accuracy in such an esoteric subject as the arms and armor of the knights meeting at the Tournament toward the end of the picture. It is hard to swallow, though, that the cartoonist quite blithely let the Golden Knight couch his lance with his left hand and carry his round shield in his right![6]

Monty Python and the Holy Grail (1975) is even among satires "in a class by itself" (Lacy and Ashe 281). At first glance, the armor of its knights looks exactly like the medievalistic standard equipment of top-to-toe mail, helmets, and shields. In particular, the armor of King Arthur himself is not noticeably different from that which can be seen on dozens of effigies in dozens of churches and cathedrals all over what used to be Arthur's kingdom of Logres. The gisants of Robert de Vere, Earl of Oxford (d 1221), or of William Longespée (d 1228), in Salisbury Cathedral, might well have served as direct models. The jokes, in Monty Python fashion, are in silly details, such as Sir Bedivere's helmet with a visor open like a picture frame, funny armorial bearings like those of the Knight of the Red Herring or of Sir Robin Coeur-de-Poulet, the high-kicking ballet of the knights at Camelot, and of course the outrageous notion of having the knights galumph about on pretend horses. The armor of the Black Knight is probably styled after that of a sculpture of a knightly saint on the façade of Wells Cathedral (Blair 22; Norman 13). It would be interesting to know whether the black cross on the white shield of the knight in the fore of the battle array at Arthur's attack of the Grail Castle was chosen because this was the badge of the Teutonic Knights. This could well be one of those sometimes surprisingly subtle Monty Python gags, most likely arranged by Terry Jones, who also happens to be the author of an iconoclastic book about Chaucer's "parfit knyght" and his connection with the Order of the Teutonic Knights (Jones 49).[7]

The French film *Perceval le Gallois* (1978) takes its armor from the twelfth century. Not having seen this film, I know of it only from still photos. Reviewers have, however, praised it highly, because of its beautiful stylization using two-dimensional scenery props to create visual effects like the illuminations in a medieval manuscript (Lacy and Ashe 283). The film designer's puristic use of manuscript illustrations as his models is clearly evident in his treatment of armor. Those mail shirts not yet covered by surcoats, and the huge round-topped shields with simple heraldic charges painted in the Romanesque style of the late twelfth century are taken directly from miniatures in a devotional manuscript, the *Hortus Deliciarum* of the Abbess Herrad von Landsberg, ca. 1185. Although the precious original, once one of the treasures of the City Library of Strasbourg, was destroyed in a fire when this formidable fortress city was shelled

Arms and Armor in Arthurian Films

From left to right, Sir Bedevere (Terry Jones), King Arthur (Graham Chapman), Sir Lancelot the Brave (John Cleese), and Sir Robin the Not-Quite-So-Brave (Eric Idle) in Monty Python and the Holy Grail.

in 1870 during the Franco-Prussian War, we do have carefully made hand-colored lithograph copies of the miniatures from the early nineteenth century (Engelhardt n.p.; Martin 36-39).

Incidentally, when in *Camelot* King Arthur has his talk about Lancelot with King Pellinore,[8] he is toying with two armored puppets, which are so close in style to marionettes shown in one delightful miniature of the *Hortus Deliciarum*, where puppeteers are playing *ludus monstrorum*, that it is hard to believe that this similarity should be entirely coincidental (Nickel, "Little Knights" 170-183).

Though *Perceval le Gallois* has been much lauded for how closely it follows Chrétien de Troyes, it seems on the other hand to follow the "white hat" tradition, by letting its title hero ride a white horse, instead of a red sorrel or roan, as he should after he becomes the Red Knight. Very properly, the designer did not give Perceval's charger the flowing trappings so beloved by designers of "castle and crusade" films, because these trappings were not yet in fashion in

Chrétien's time (ca. 1170-1180). The first representations of knights on horses with trappings are from 1196.

While *Perceval* has its setting in the twelfth century of Chrétien de Troyes, the television series *The Legend of King Arthur* (1979) tries hard to evoke the background of the "historical Arthur" ca. A.D. 500. At times, it succeeds even a little too well in pointing out the rough edges of the Dark Ages; all too often, the Knights of the Round Table look rather more like the Stratford Inn's bane, Larry, his brother Darryl, and his other brother Darryl, from CBS's *Newhart*, than shining examples of champions at the foremost court of chivalry.

The armor designer for this series gave his knights body armor of the lamellar type, made up of small rectangular iron plates arranged in overlapping rows and laced together with leather straps. This was authentic Dark Age armor, introduced by the steppe tribes that came from the East during the Great Migration period (Robinson, *Oriental Armour* 4-10, 25-27, and *Armour of Imperial Rome* 163; Kirpičnikov 104-107; Gamber, "Kataphrakten" 7-44). In order to give the armor the "primitive" look appropriate for the Dark Ages, however, the designer seems to have turned these laced-together lamellar cuirasses inside out, so that the strap endings of the lacings dangle loosely (and messily) on the outside for the desired effect.

Primitive starkness was also uppermost in the designer's mind when the film's helmets and shields were created. The helmets with mask visors, cheek pieces, and neck guards are deliberately crude versions of the magnificent original from the fabled Sutton Hoo ship burial of the seventh century (Grohskopf 60ff.; Gamber, "Some Notes" 208-216; Bruce-Mitford 217-280; Nicolle 13). The helmet, now in the British Museum, is richly embellished by an overlay of embossed silver; its crest in shape of a dragon is stretched across the helmet bowl from its brow to the nape of the neck.[9] The helmet's most remarkable element is a visor wrought as a face mask with bristling moustache and garnet-inlaid lips. In the television series, the helmets are of the same type, with visor masks, but of starkly plain dark iron and without any decoration.

Shields in the series are circular, with a central boss sometimes surrounded by five or six smaller bosses that would be reinforcements and also ornamentation. Like the helmets, shields bear no distinguishing marks to tell one from the next. To tell friend from foe by painting shields with such markings was the reason for the rise of heraldry, necessary after the introduction of visored helmets

Arms and Armor in Arthurian Films 191

that made faces unrecognizable. For this reason, it is a truly amazing feat that Bors recognizes Lancelot's shield in the bundle that a groom, on Elaine's orders, tries to hide from him.

Arthur's legendary battle standard is a golden dragon; it probably was a windsock-like *draco* (a cavalry ensign of the Late Roman army), with a metal head and a fluttering fabric body (Tatlock 233; Esin 15; Nicolle pl. C; Robinson, *Armour of Imperial Rome* 17). In novels and films alike, Arthur's dragon banner is usually interpreted as a flag with a dragon's image embroidered or painted on it. One of the exceptions is the dragon standard, only fleetingly seen, that is shown in the television series. Here it is a sculptured dragon of metal, sitting on a cross-piece on top of a pole, in the style of the eagles and other signa of the Roman legions (Robinson, *Armour of Imperial Rome* 32, 34).

Quite likely, "for some tastes the most successful of the Arthurian films in English is *Excalibur*" (Lacy and Ashe 281). Its ambition is to tell the entire Arthurian story, including the Grail quest, in one fell swoop. It places an extraordinarily heavy emphasis on the representation of armor, to a degree that is unusual even among Arthurian films. *Excalibur* in fact indicates the rise, the glory, and the fall of Arthur's kingdom by changes in the appearance of the knights' armor. Not only are the knights in full armor practically all the time—Uther Pendragon keeps his armor on even while he rapes Ygraine, a wry reversal of the hoary old japes about chastity belts—but armor is ingeniously used as a vehicle to convey messages about the deeper meaning underlying the events. Stylistically, the film's armor is, with two exceptions, based on fifteenth-century models, but makes imaginative use of the *Verfremdungseffekt* of fanciful deviations from the traceable prototypes.

In the first episodes, the kingless interregnum and the no less brutal period of Uther Pendragon's rule are symbolized by warriors in black armor of monstrous shape, with oversize shoulder-pieces and elbow-cops, heavily studded with knobby rivets and wicked spikes. Helmets have bizarre visors of animal forms; Uther Pendragon's own is shaped as the snout of a wild boar. Here symbolism makes a clever play on the term "pig-faced" for this type of pointed visor (Blair 69); with the transformation of his helmet into a realistic boar's snout, Uther Pendragon's unbridled lust, both for power and for Ygraine, is unmistakably expressed in a literal and visual way. By contrast, Duke Gorlois's armor is recognizably based on an existing armor of ca. 1450-1460, now in the Historical Museum at Berne, Switzerland (Thomas and Gamber 51; Martin 122). As the wronged husband of Ygraine, Gorlois is the "good guy" and therefore does not qualify for the weirder bizarreries marking the more sinister characters.

After the foundation of the Round Table, the Knights appear in truly "shining armor," beautifully polished and styled in the best tradition of the illustrations of Arthur Rackham, as for instance in his "How Sir Launcelot fought with a fiendly dragon" (Pollard and Rackham pl. 10).[10] Rackham's illustrations did serve also as inspirations for entire episodes of the film, such as the hanged knights in the tree (Pollard and Rackham 96) and the climactic last fight at Camlann, derived from "How Mordred was slain by Arthur, and how by him Arthur was hurt to the death" (Pollard and Rackham pl. 16).

The symbolic value of the armor becomes fully evident when, during the Grail quest, the gradual breaking up of the Companionship of the Round Table is demonstrated by the rusting of the armor worn by the questing knights, until Perceval, after the achievement of the Grail, sheds his corroded armor altogether and returns almost naked, dressed only in loose breeches resembling the loincloth of Christ.

Equally, Lancelot's guilty conscience is brought out in the open through the medium of his armor. When resting in the forest, he is attacked and wounded with his own sword by a nightmare enemy, who turns out to be his own still shiny armor come to ghostly life. To demonstrate the fundamental difference between the brutal lust of Uther's rape of Ygraine and the guilty but pure love of Guinevere and Lancelot, armor is deftly utilized as symbolic props. Uther, disguised by Gorlois's armor, ravishes the naked Ygraine, after having ripped the clothes off her body; by contrast, Guinevere joyfully joins Lancelot in the enchanted forest glade, where the lovers embrace in almost chaste nakedness, with Lancelot's armor cast aside, never to be put on again. As a detail borrowed from Gottfried's *Tristan*, where King Mark is still noble and forgiving and not the despicable coward as in Malory (Surles 60-75), Arthur in the only scene in which he rides a white horse finds the guilty lovers asleep in the forest and, with broken heart, plants Excalibur between them, by this token giving up everything worthwhile in his life.

One of the most spectacular scenes of the film is the ride of the Knights of the Round Table to meet their destiny at Camlann in a blaze of glory. Their armor shining again, they follow King Arthur on his steed bedecked in golden scale armor, the huge banner of the Dragon floating above. There are few sights more stirring than a knight in sparkling plate armor galloping forth holding aloft a streaming banner of red and gold—and to top it off this sight is seen through a screen of apple trees in full bloom.

Interestingly, the scale armor of Arthur's steed is styled after an original cataphract (heavy-armored cavalry) armor found in the Late Roman fortress Dura Europos, Mesopotamia, and now on display in the Higgins Armory Museum, Worcester, Massachusetts. Fragments of such armor have been excavated at Newstead, the site of the Late Roman cavalry fort of Trimontium between Hadrian's and the Antonine Walls; they are now in the National Museum of Antiquities, Edinburgh. This scale armor for horses was introduced by steppe nomads taken into the Late Roman army as auxiliaries from A.D. 175 on.[11] The same steppe nomads, Sarmatians and Alani, introduced their tribal dragon banners as cavalry battle standards into the Roman army (Gamber, "Kataphrakten" 35ff.; Robinson, *Armour of Imperial Rome* 186, 190-195)

Arthur's knights ride to Camlann in shining armor, but the forces of evil, as represented by Mordred's followers, are in dark armor with bizarre elements. Their ensigns are ragged banners topped by skulls, identical to those from the period before Arthur's reign, signaling the lawless times to come.[12] The two glaring exceptions that do not fit the fifteenth century image of armor in *Excalibur* are Mordred's golden helmet and cuirass and the molded breastplate Morgan le Fay wears in her last scene of the film.

Mordred's golden helmet with its face mask and embossed curly hair is styled after Late Roman parade helmets in the Oriental fashion (Robinson, *Armour of Imperial Rome* 114-126, and *What Soldiers Wore* 26). One of the three helmets with visor masks found at Newstead might well have been its prototype. Mordred's muscle cuirass is also of Roman pattern (Robinson, *Armour of Imperial Rome* 147). With its embossed nipples, navel, and pectoral and abdominal muscles, it was designed to give the impression of heroic nudity. In antiquity, warriors of the most diverse cultures—Greek, Etruscan, Germanic, Celtic—went into battle naked, believing themselves to be invulnerable by virtue of invocation of the special protection of a deity. In societies where magic actually seems to work, this must have been a mighty deterrent to face such an enemy flaunting his powerful "medicine." More practical fighters, who wanted nothing left to chance with something as important as their own lives, preferred to wear such a muscle cuirass, which had the look of a naked body but gave solid real protection in addition to the

194   Helmut Nickel

Arthur and his knights in Excalibur.

magical one. Morgan le Fay's words, when she is arming Mordred—"No weapon forged by man can harm you, when you wear this armor"—clearly indicates the enchanted quality of this unusual armor. It is only Excalibur, the magic otherworld blade from the Lady of the Lake (no man!), returned to Arthur by Guinevere in their reconciliation scene before Camlann, that breaks the spell and kills Mordred.

Morgan's armor, mainly an abbreviated breastplate that looks as if it was designed by and for Cher, covers few of her vital parts and even fewer of her erogenous zones. When wearing it, she weaves her last and fatal spell, indicating thereby that it was meant to equal the ritual nakedness of witches. Judging by the expanse of skin exposed, she must have felt supremely confident in its magic defense value, probably against "weapons forged by man," though it proved to be useless against Merlin's greater power that led her into her own trap.

Arms and Armor in Arthurian Films

Mordred (Robert Addie) in Excalibur.

In conclusion, it can be said—not surprisingly—that the ways to approach the subject of arms and armor in Arthurian films are as many as there are costume designers, but that a blending of historical realism and fantasy seems to be the most successful, insofar as it corresponds to the image of the "knight in shining armor" every Arthurian carries in the heart.

APPENDIX

One of the first educational films ever made, *A Visit to the Armor Galleries,* was a project done in 1923 by Bashford Dean, Curator of the Department of Arms and Armor, Metropolitan Museum of Art, New York, and his assistant and eventual successor, Stephen V. Grancsay. This film attempted to dispel popular myths about armor that existed already before they became cast in concrete by Laurence

Olivier's *Henry V* and the television series about Henry VIII, where knights are hoisted into their saddles with derricks.

Armor is heavy, as can be expected from its being made of iron, but it is not so heavy that a knight would be unable to get up when thrown to the ground. A mailshirt with long sleeves weighs about twenty-five pounds, a full cap-à-pie plate armor of the fifteenth century, not more than sixty-five pounds. This weight, if properly "custom-made" and fitted to the body, represents no encumbrance for a well-trained man. In the armor film, the "knight" in fifteenth-century Burgundian armor gets up on his steed for a ride in Central Park (with the Belvedere Castle as an appropriate backdrop; the skyline was not yet cluttered up with high-rises), falls to the ground and gets up again, all unaided, though he had no previous training.

Terry Jones, in his *Chaucer's Knight* (273-274), states that in the filming of *Monty Python and the Holy Grail* most of the knights wore "imitation chain-mail made out of knitted wool, which was uncomfortable enough, but Graham Chapman, as King Arthur, wore a genuine metal chain-mail coif and found the weight of it unbearable for more than short periods." He also remarks that during the making of Eric Rohmer's film *Perceval le Gallois* "real chain-mail" was used. From my own experience, I can say that though a mailshirt is heavy it can be worn without major discomfort for hours, if this is done with a proper undergarment, a padded and quilted acton or pourpoint, which would prevent chafing on pressure points. It is also important to wear a tight sword-belt to take up the drag of the loose-hanging skirts, and to minimize the weight on the shoulders. Part of the problem with Graham Chapman's coif was that it was hanging loosely over the shoulders, with its full weight pulling down from the top of the head. Original coifs were cunningly tailored to fit around head, neck, and shoulders so as to distribute the weight; a padded skullcap was worn under the coif against the painful pressure of the steel rings (and catching of hair).

One designer of theatrical costumes in Berlin had "mail" made out of cheap brown-paper string in use after World War II, knitted with extra-thick needles by a group of nice old ladies whom his atelier had under contract. For the proper metallic effect, these shirts were dyed black and brushed with silver paint. Helmets and breastplates were hammered out of aluminum. Aluminum was also the material for the armor worn by Ingrid Bergman in her *Joan of Arc*. This armor in its entirety and the prototypes for the helmets and body defenses worn by the other "knights" were manufactured by the late

Leonard Heinrich, then armorer of the Metropolitan Museum (one of the great moments in the Department of Arms and Armor was when Ingrid Bergman came for measurements and fittings). "White" medieval armor was highly polished, and Master Heinrich did wonders with the aluminum elements. It turned out, however, that they were too dazzling under the lights, and—alas—had to be dulled.

Armor's main drawback is not so much that it is heavy as that it is hot. Wearing a quilted acton against the chafing of the metal elements, and a closed helmet in summer temperature, can be trying indeed, quite aside from the heat of the metal under the sun's rays. For the tournaments staged as part of annual summer community events at The Cloisters (the medieval branch of the Metropolitan Museum in upper Manhattan's Fort Tryon Park), we therefore had "mailshirts" made out of silver lamé, covered with colorful surcoats to eliminate the need for breastplates; shields of masonite; and helmets of fiberglass cast from originals in the Museum's collections. Because of this lack of body armor, "safety" lances—slim cones of rolled-up brown paper, slipped onto thin mailing tubes for handles—were used to be aimed against the shields only. The jousts were done by John Franzreb, the stuntman, who broke the Round Table in *Camelot* by jumping his horse onto it. He was, incidentally, also the White Knight in the old *Ajax* cleanser commercials. Ajax's white horse did participate in the Cloisters tournaments too, though not as a charger in the jousts, but—for reasons of advanced age—as the palfrey of the Lady of the Lake.

NOTES

Acknowledgments: For generously given assistance in locating material for this essay, I would like to express my thanks to my friend and colleague, Karl Katz, Consultant for Film and Television, and to Nadine Covert, Program for Art on Film, at New York's Metropolitan Museum of Art. Special thanks are due to Terry Geesken, Film Stills Archive, Museum of Modern Art, New York.

1. There are of course exceptions to this rule. In the film *The Black Knight* (1954), the Black Knight is the hero. The occasional Black Knight as a "good guy" goes back to the Black Knight in *Ivanhoe*, who turns out to be Richard Coeur-de-Lion in disguise, and lastly to the real-life Black Prince, Edward, Prince of Wales (1330-1376), who is considered, at least in English-speaking circles, to be Flower of Chivalry.

2. A still photo of Sir Brack at the Tournament was used for the back-cover illustration of the paperback edition of the fifteenth-century romance of chivalry *Tirant lo Blanc*, by Joannot Martorell and Marti Joan de Galba, translated by David H. Rosenthal (New York: Warner 1984).

3. Helmet visors opening sideways are a standard element in Howard Pyle's illustrations of *Otto of the Silver Hand* (1888). Here, though, they are not supposed to be used humorously, because they are found on the helmets of both the "good guys" and "bad guys."

4. Interestingly enough, the fleur-de-lys (which for us is the heraldic figure par excellence) does not occur in any of the fictitious arms attributed to the Knights of the Round Table before the eighteenth century.

5. The amethyst in Excalibur's hilt occurs also in Rosemary Sutcliff's *Sword at Sunset* (1963), Sanders Anne Laubenthal's *Excalibur* (1973), and Stephen R. Lawhead's *Arthur* (1989).

6. One of the questions invariably asked at any guided tour of the Armor Galleries or after a lecture is "What happened if a knight was left-handed?" There seems to be no answer to this problem; all armor that I know of was designed for the conventional combat with the opponents charging each other left (shield) side against left side. Even the sixteenth-century stalwart, Götz von Berlichingen "of the Iron Hand," had himself an artificial right hand made after he lost his right hand in battle, rather than fight with his left. On the other hand, in the collections of the Metropolitan Museum's Department of Arms and Armor there is one seventeenth-century Polish saber made for a left-hander.

7. One of the climactic events in "castle and crusader" dramas is a duel between knights fighting with two-handed swords, though these swords were strictly foot soldiers' weapons of the sixteenth century. Even in carefully researched films, such as *Joan of Arc*, with Ingrid Bergman, for which the Armor Shop of the Metropolitan Museum furnished prototypes for helmets and body armor (in aluminum), the fight coordinator could not resist the temptation to slip in such a duel. Therefore, the two-handed swords clashing away in the encounter with the Black Knight at the ford in *Monty Python* are practically unavoidable.

8. King Pellinore, with his bald head, flowing mustaches, and befuddled manner, is obviously modeled after the White Knight in Lewis Carroll's *Through the Looking-Glass*, as illustrated by John Tenniel. The spikes of the horse's armor and the horse-headed visors of the White Knight's and the Red Knight's helmets are like some armor to be found in *Excalibur*.

9. The armor found at Sutton Hoo corresponds in detail—parade lorica, circular shield, dragon-crested helmet—to the description that Geoffrey of Monmouth gives of Arthur's in his arming before the battle of Badon (*History* ix, 4) indicating that Geoffrey must have had some "ancient book" as his source for Dark Age arms. Armor in Geoffrey's own time ca. 1136, was quite different with mailshirts, triangular shields, and crestless helmets.

10. Rackham's illustrations seem to have been the source for the costumes in NBC's 1989 Christmas telefilm, *A Connecticut Yankee in King Arthur's Court*, with Keshia Knight Pulliam, the cute kid from *The Cosby Show*, as the Yankee who teaches karate and other black arts to Queen Guinevere and her ladies.

11. Of the 8,000 Sarmatians serving in the Roman army as the first heavy armored auxiliary cavalry, 5,500 were sent to North Britain to fight Picts, attached to the Legio VI Victrix, whose *praefectus* was a certain Lucius Artorius Castus. As late as A.D. 428, a kibbutz-like settlement of Sarmatian veterans is documented at Ribchester, Lancashire. These Sarmatians had the *draco* as their tribal battle ensign and worshiped a sword thrust upright in the ground as image of their war god.

12. The armor, A 78, in the Waffensammlung, Vienna, Austria, with its helmet sporting a mask visor shaped as an eagle's beak and batwing side elements, seems to have been the inspiration for some armors of the sinister characters at Uther's time, but also among Mordred's followers. On the other hand, Arthur's knights, in their "shining armor," have similar, non-functional batwing elements attached to their visors. Perhaps the costume designer got his inspirations from the catalogue of the Innsbruck exhibition of 1954, the only publication in which the "Gorlois" and the "batwing" helmets are illustrated together (Thomas and Gamber 51, ill. 1; 67-68, ill. 48 and 49)

WORKS CITED

Blair, Claude. *European Armour*. London: Batsford, 1959.

Bruce-Mitford, Rupert. "The Sutton Hoo Helmet-Reconstruction and the Design of the Royal Harness and Swordbelt." *Journal of the Arms and Armour Society* 10 (1982): 217-280.

Combs, Carl. *Camelot*. New York: National Publishers, 1967. [Souvenir booklet.]

Cortés, Javier. *Guia Illustrada de la Real Armeria de Madrid*. Madrid: Blass, 1950. [Museum guide.]

Cripps-Day, Francis Henry. *The History of the Tournament in England and in France*. London: Quarich, 1918.

Engelhardt, Christian Moritz. *Der Herrad von Landsberg, Äbtissin von Honberg und Odilienberg im Elsass, Hortus Deliciarum*. Stuttgart and Tübingen: 1818. [Portfolio.]

Esin, Emel. "Tös und Moncuk." *Central Asiatic Journal* 16 (1972): 14-37.

Gamber, Ortwin. "Kataphrakten, Clibanarier, Normannenreiter." *Jahrbuch der Kunsthistorischen Sammlungen zu Wien* 64 (1968): 7-44.

———. "Some Notes on the Sutton Hoo Military Equipment." *Journal of the Arms and Armour Society* 10 (1982): 208-216.

Grohskopf, Bernice. *The Treasure of Sutton Hoo.* New York: Atheneum, 1970.

Harty, Kevin J. "Cinema Arthuriana: A Filmography." *Quondam et Futurus* 7 (Spring 1987): 5-8.

———. "Cinema Arthuriana: Translations of the Arthurian Legend to the Screen." *Arthurian Interpretations* 2 (Fall 1987): 95-113.

———. "Cinema Arthuriana: A Bibliography of Selected Secondary Materials." *Arthurian Interpretations* 3 (Spring 1989): 119-137.

Jones, Terry. *Chaucer's Knight: The Portrait of a Medieval Mercenary.* New York: Methuen, 1980.

Kirpičnikov, A. N. "Russische Waffen des 9.-15. Jahrhunderts" *Waffen- und Kostümkunde* 2 (1986): 85-129.

Knight, W. Nicholas. "Lancer: Myth-Making and the Kennedy 'Camelot.'" *Avalon to Camelot* 2 (1986): 26-31.

Lacy, Norris J., and Geoffrey Ashe. *The Arthurian Handbook.* New York, Garland, 1988.

Martin, Paul. *Waffen und Rüstungen—von Karl dem Grossen bis zu Ludwig XIV.* Frankfurt am Main: Umschau, 1967.

Museo del Ejercito. Madrid, n.d. [Museum guide.]

Nickel, Helmut. "The Little Knights of the Living Room Table." *Metropolitan Museum Bulletin* 25 (1966): 170-183.

———. "The Tournament: An Historical Sketch." In *The Study of Chivalry,* ed. Howell Chickering and Thomas H. Seiler. Kalamazoo: Western Michigan University, 1988.

Nicolle, David. *Arthur and the Anglo-Saxon Wars.* London: Osprey, 1984.

Norman, Vesey A. B. *Arms and Armor.* New York: Putnam, 1964.

Pastoureau, Michel. *Armorial des Chevaliers de la Table Ronde.* Paris: Léopard d-Or, 1983.

Pollard, Alfred W., and Arthur Rackham. *The Romance of King Arthur and His Knights of the Round Table.* 1917. New York: Weathervane, n.d.

Robinson, H. Russell. *Oriental Armour.* London: Jenkins, 1967.

———. *The Armour of Imperial Rome.* New York: Scribner, 1975.

———. *What Soldiers Wore on Hadrian's Wall.* Newcastle upon Tyne: Graham, 1976.

Surles, Robert L. "Mark of Cornwall: Noble, Ignoble, Ignored." *Arthurian Interpretations* 3 (Spring 1989): 60-75.

Tatlock, J. S. P. "The Dragon of Wessex and Wales." *Speculum* 8 (April 1933): 223-235.

Thomas, Bruno, and Ortwin Gamber. *Die Innsbrucker Plattnerkunst.* Innsbruck: Museum Ferdinandeum, 1954. [Exhibition catalogue.]

15.

A Bibliography on Arthurian Film

Kevin J. Harty

This bibliography of reviews and other secondary materials relating to film versions of the legend of King Arthur supersedes my four earlier publications cited below under General Studies. The arrangement of the bibliography after the list of these general studies follows the chronology of the filmography that I originally published in *Quondam et Futurus*. (Again, I am grateful to Mildred Leake Day, editor of *Quondam et Futurus*, for her continued support of my work on Arthurian cinema and to Henry Hall Peyton III, editor of *Arthurian Interpretations*, for permission to reprint here revised versions of materials first published in that journal.) Film titles are given first—alternative titles are separated by a slash—followed by the name of the director (unknown in the case of one silent film), the name of the production company, and the date. Information on the availability of films for rental appears in parentheses; a simple notation of "V" indicates that the film is available on videotape in Beta and VHS formats. Bibliographical entries under each film citation first group reviews of the film and then provide information on fuller discussions of the film, on screenplays, and on other secondary materials.

- **General Studies**

    Beatie, Bruce A. "Arthurian Films and Arthurian Texts: Problems of Reception and Comprehension." *Arthurian Interpretations* 2 (Spring 1988): 65-78.

de la Brétèque, François, ed. *Le Moyen Âge au cinema. Les Cahiers de la cinémathèque* 42-43 (Summer 1985). [Special issue.]

Durand, Jacques. "La Chevalerie à l'écran." *L'Avant-scène cinéma* 221 (1 Feb. 1979): 29-40.

Grellner, Alice, and Raymond H. Thompson. "Films." In *The Arthurian Encyclopedia*, ed. Norris J. Lacy et al. New York: Garland, 1986.

Harty, Kevin J. "Cinema Arthuriana: A Bibliography of Selected Secondary Materials." *Arthurian Interpretations* 3 (Spring 1989): 119-137.

_____. "Cinema Arthuriana: A Filmography." *Quondam et Futurus* 7 (Spring 1987): 5-8; 7 (Summer 1987): 18.

_____. "Cinema Arthuriana: Translations of the Arthurian Legend to the Screen." *Arthurian Interpretations* 2 (Fall 1987): 95-113.

_____. "Film Treatments of the Legend of King Arthur." In *King Arthur Through the Ages*, ed. Valerie M. Lagorio and Mildred Leake Day. 2 vols. New York: Garland, 1990. 2: 278-290.

Holley, Linda Tarte. "Medievalism in Film: The Matter of Arthur, A Filmography." In *Mittelalter-Rezeption III*, ed. Jürgen Kühnel et al. Göppingen: Kümmerle, 1988.

Lacy, Norris J. "Arthurian Film and the Tyranny of Tradition." *Arthurian Interpretations* 4 (Fall 1989): 75-85.

_____, and Geoffrey Ashe. *The Arthurian Handbook*. New York: Garland, 1988.

Richards, Jeffrey. *Swordsmen of the Screen from Douglas Fairbanks to Michael York*. London: Routledge, 1977.

Wehrhahn, Jürgen. "König Artus und die Ritter der Tafelrunde." *Retro* 12 (Nov.-Dec. 1981): 5-13.

●*Parsifal*
dir. Edwin J. Porter, Edison, 1904.

Bush, W. Stephen. "Possibilities of Synchronization." *Motion Picture World* 2 Sept. 1911: 607-608.

Niver, Kemp R. *The First Twenty Years, A Segment of Film History*. Los Angeles: Locare Research Group, 1968.

_____. *Motion Pictures from the Library of Congress Paper Print Collection, 1894-1912*. Berkeley: University of California Press, 1967.

"Parsifal." *Edison Films* July 1906: 50-53.

Spears, Jack. "Edwin S. Porter." *Films in Review* 21 (June-July 1970): 327-354.

Walls, Howard Lamarr. *Motion Pictures 1894-1912 Identified from the United States Copyright Office.* Washington, D.C.: Library of Congress Copyright Office, 1953.

●*Launcelot and Elaine*
dir. Charles Kent, Vitagraph, 1909.
Reviews:
Moving Picture World 27 Nov. 1909: 759. (Rpt. *Selected Film Criticism, 1986-1911*, ed. Anthony Slide. Metuchen, N.J.: Scarecrow, 1982).

New York Dramatic Mirror 20 Nov. 1909: 16.

"Lancelot [sic] and Elaine." *Bioscope* 15 Jan. 1914: suppl. xxxi.

"Launcelot and Elaine." *Moving Picture World* 27 Nov. 1909: 773.

"Launcelot and Elaine." *Vitagraph Bulletin* 949 (13 Nov. 1909): n.p.

"Notes of the Trade." *Moving Picture World* 23 Oct. 1909: 565.

●*Tristan et Yseult*
dir. Albert Capellani, S.C.A.G.L.—Pathé, 1909.
Review:
Bioscope 28 Sept. 1911: suppl. v.

Mitry, Jean. *Filmographie universelle: Tome deuxième. Primitifs et précurseurs 1895-1915. Première partie: France et Europe.* Paris: Institut des Hautes Études Cinématographiques, 1964.

●*King Arthur, or The Knights of the Round Table*
dir. ?, New Agency, 1910.
"New Agency." *Bioscope* 15 Sept. 1910: 39.

●*Parsifal*
dir. Mario Caserini, Ambrosio, 1912.
Reviews:
Bioscope 30 Oct. 1913: 427; 27 Nov. 1913: 811-813.

Moving Picture World 28 Dec. 1912: 1307-1308.

Jarratt, Vernon. *The Italian Cinema.* London: Falcon, 1951.

Leprohon, Pierre. *The Italian Cinema*, trans. Roger Greaves and Oliver Stallybrass. New York: Praeger, 1972.

•*The Quest of the Holy Grail*
dir. D. W. Griffith, unrealized project, 1916.

"Film Flashes." *Variety* 28 May 1915: 16.

"Griffith to Make Holy Grail Picture." *Moving Picture World* 1 May 1915: 769.

Stern, Seymour. *An Index to the Creative Work of David Wark Griffith. Part II: The Art Triumphant. (b) The Triangle Productions 1915-1916*. Special Supplement to *Sight and Sound*. London: British Film Institute, 1946.

Wagenknecht, Edward, and Anthony Slide. *The Films of D. W. Griffith*. New York: Crown, 1975.

•*Knights of the Square Table; or The Grail*
dir. Alan Crosland, Edison, 1917.

Reviews:

Moving Picture World 4 Aug. 1917: 849; 11 Aug. 1917: 955-956.

New York Dramatic Mirror 4 Aug. 1917: 18.

Scouting 5 (15 July 1917): 11.

Wid's 26 July 1917: 474.

"Boy Scouts' Endorsement." *New York Dramatic Mirror* 25 Aug. 1917: 26.

Hanson, Patricia King, ed. *The American Film Institute Catalog of Motion Pictures Produced in the United States, Feature Films, 1911-1920*. Berkeley: University of California Press, 1988.

Horowitz, Rita, and Harriett Harrison. *The George Kleine Collection of Early Motion Pictures in the Library of Congress, A Catalog*. Washington, D.C.: Library of Congress, 1980.

"Praise for Scout Film." *New York Dramatic Mirror* 4 Aug. 1917: 24.

•*A Connecticut Yankee at King Arthur's Court*
dir. Emmett J. Flynn, Fox, 1920.

Reviews:

Exceptional Photoplays 4 (Mar. 1921): 2.

Exhibitor's Trade Review 12 Feb. 1921: 1065.

Life 77 (5 May 1921): 652.

Motion Picture News 12 Feb. 1921: 1383.

Moving Picture World 12 Feb. 1921: 792, 805.

New York Times 15 Mar. 1921: 14.

Photoplay 20 (June 1921): 51. (Rpt. *Selected Film Criticism 1921-1930*, ed. Anthony Slide. Metuchen, N.J.: Scarecrow, 1982).

Variety 28 Jan. 1921: 40.

Wid's Daily 6 Feb. 1921: 3.

Connelly, Robert. *The Motion Picture Guide, Silent Film 1910-1936.* Chicago: Cinebooks, 1986.

Hanson, Patricia King, ed. *The American Film Institute Catalog of Motion Pictures Produced in the United States, Feature Films, 1911-1920.* Berkeley: University of California Press, 1988.

Munden, Kenneth W., ed. *The American Film Institute Catalog of Motion Pictures Produced in the United States: Feature Films, 1921-1930.* New York: Bowker, 1971.

Nowlan, Robert A., and Gwendolyn Wright Nowlan. *Cinema Sequels and Remakes, 1903-1987.* Jefferson, N.C.: McFarland, 1989.

O'Dell, Scott. *Representative Photoplays Analyzed.* Hollywood, Calif.: Institute of Authorship, 1924.

Patterson, Frances Taylor. *Cinema Craftsmanship.* New York: Harcourt, 1921.

"Special Service Section on 'A Connecticut Yankee in [sic] King Arthur's Court.'" *Motion Picture News* 26 Feb. 1921: 1673-1682.

•*Tristan et Yseut*
dir. Maurice Mariaud, Nalpas, 1920.

Review:

Kinematograph Weekly 24 Nov. 1921: 73-74.

Abel, Richard. *French Cinema, The First Wave, 1915-1926.* Princeton: Princeton University Press, 1984.

Bardèche, Maurice, and Robert Brasillach. *Histoire du cinéma.* Rev. ed. 2 vols. Givors: Martel, 1953-1954. 1: 201-202.

Fescourt, Henri. *La Foi et les montagnes.* Paris: Montel, 1959.

Landry, Lionel. "La Reconstruction historique." *Cinemagazine* 3 (14 Sept. 1923): 368.

•*A Connecticut Yankee*
dir. David Butler, Fox, 1931.

> Reviews:
>
>> *Bioscope* 1 Apr. 1931: 18-19.
>>
>> *Film Daily* 12 Apr. 1931: 32.
>>
>> *Film Spectator* 11 (25 Apr. 1931): 11.
>>
>> *Illustrated London News* 20 June 1931: 1052, 1074.
>>
>> *Motion Picture Herald* 102 (21 Mar. 1931): 39.
>>
>> *National Board of Review Magazine* 6 (Apr. 1931): 15. (Rpt. From *Quasimodo to Scarlett O'Hara: National Board of Review Anthology, 1920-1940*, ed. Stanley Hochman. New York: Ungar, 1982).
>>
>> *New York Times* 11 Apr. 1931: 17; 4 May 1936: 16.
>>
>> *New Yorker* 7 (18 Apr. 1931): 75, 77.
>>
>> *Outlook and Independent* 157 (15 Apr. 1931): 539.
>>
>> *Photoplay* 39 (Apr. 1931): 48.
>>
>> *Picturegoer Weekly* NS 13 (22 Aug. 1931): 29.
>>
>> *Retro* 12 (Nov.-Dec. 1981): 20-23.
>>
>> *Rob Wagner's Script* 5 (30 May 1931): 10-11.
>>
>> *Time* 17 (20 Apr. 1931): 28.
>>
>> *Variety* 15 Apr. 1931: 20, 33.
>
> Hall, Mordaunt. "An Arlis Sans Monocle." *New York Times* 19 Apr. 1931: 8. 5.
>
> Korsilibas-Davis, James, and Myrna Loy. *Being and Becoming*. London: Bloomsbury, 1987.
>
> Nash, Jay Robert, and Stanley Ralph Ross. *The Motion Picture Guide, 1927-1983*. 9 vols. Chicago: Cinebooks, 1985. 2: 476.
>
> Nowlan, Robert A., and Gwendolyn Wright Nowlan. *Cinema Sequels and Remakes, 1903-1987*. Jefferson, N.C.: McFarland, 1989.
>
> Quirk, Lawrence J. *The Films of Myrna Loy*. Secaucus, N.J.: Citadel, 1980.
>
> Sterling, Bryan B., ed. *The Will Rogers Scrapbook*. New York: Grosset & Dunlap, 1976.
>
> _____., and Frances N. Sterling. *Will Rogers in Hollywood*. New York: Crown, 1984.
>
> "Will Rogers and King Arthur." *New York Times* 29 Mar. 1931: 8. 7.

•King Arthur Was a Gentleman
dir. Marcel Varnel, Gainsborough Films, 1942.

Reviews:

Kinematograph Weekly 10 Dec. 1942: 14.

Monthly Film Bulletin 9 (31 Dec. 1942): 153.

Motion Picture Herald 150 (16 Jan. 1943): Product Digest Section 1114.

To-day's Cinema 4 Dec. 1942: 5.

Askey, Arthur. *Before Your Very Eyes.* London: Woburn, 1975.

Everson, William K. "Arthur Askey." *Films in Review* 37 (Mar. 1986): 169-175.

Gifford, Denis. *The British Film Catalogue, 1895-1970.* Newton Abbot: David & Charles, 1973.

Martin, Roy, and Ray Seaton. "Gainsborough in the Forties." *Films and Filming* 333 (June 1982): 13-20.

Murphy, Robert. *Realism and Tinsel, Cinema and Society in Britain 1939-1948.* New York: Routledge, 1989.

Nash, Jay Robert, and Stanley Ralph Ross. *The Motion Picture Guide, 1927-1983.* 9 vols. Chicago: Cinebooks, 1985. 4: 1531.

Quinlan, David. *The British Sound Films, The Studio Years 1928-1959.* Totowa, N.J.: Barnes, 1984.

•L'Éternel Retour / The Eternal Return / Love Eternal
dir. Jean Delannoy, Discina International, 1943 (V).

Reviews:

Christian Century 67 (26 Apr. 1950): 543.

The Cinema 66 (13 Feb. 1946): 20.

Commonweal 47 (13 Feb. 1948): 448.

Film français 75 (23 Oct. 1943): 9.

Kinematograph Weekly 21 Feb. 1946: 25.

Monthly Film Bulletin 13 (28 Feb. 1946): 22-23.

New Statesman and Nation 31 (23 Feb. 1946): 136-137.

New York Times 5 Jan. 1948: 15.

New Yorker 23 (17 Jan. 1948): 62-63.

Newsweek 31 (19 Jan. 1948): 89.

Rotarian 76 (June 1950): 37.

Theatre Arts 32 (Feb. 1948): 44.

Time 51 (19 Jan. 1948): 102.

Variety 17 Dec. 1948: 8, 22.

Armengual, Barthélemy. *Le Mythe de Tristan et Yseult au cinéma*. Algiers: Travail et culture, 1952.

Auden, W. H. *The Dyer's Hand*. London: Faber, 1963.

Bardèche, Maurice, and Robert Brasillach. *Histoire du cinéma*. Rev. ed. 2 vols. Givors: Martel, 1953-1954. 2: 266-267, 428.

Bazin, André. *French Cinema of the Occupation and Resistance*, trans. Stanley Hochman. New York: Ungar, 1975.

Bianchi, Pietro, and Franco Berutti. *Storia del cinema*. 2nd ed. Rome: Garzanti: 1959.

"Brillantes Premières à Vichy et à Paris de 'L'Éternel Retour.'" *Film français* 75 (23 Oct. 1943): 7.

Cocteau, Jean. "L'Équipe de 'L'Éternel Retour.'" In *Oeuvres complètes*. 11 vols. Geneva: Marguerat, 1946-1951. 11: 442-444.

_____. "'L'Éternel Retour.'" In *Oeuvres complètes*. 11 vols. Geneva: Marguerat, 1946-1951. 10: 342-344.

_____. *Three Screenplays*, trans. Carol Martin-Sperry. New York: Grossman, 1972.

Hackett, Hazel. "The French Cinema During the Occupation." *Sight and Sound* 15 (Spring 1946): 1-3.

Magill's Survey of Cinema: Foreign Language Films, ed. Frank N. Magill. 8 vols. Englewood Cliffs, N.J.: Salem, 1985. 2: 1001-1004.

Manvell, Roger. "Films of the Quarter." *Sight and Sound* 15 (Spring 1946): 24-27.

Marais, Jean. *Mes quatre verités*. Paris: Éditions de Paris, 1957.

Nash, Jay Robert, and Stanley Ralph Ross. *The Motion Picture Guide, 1927-1983*. 9 vols. Chicago: Cinebooks, 1985. 3: 779.

Paris, James Reid. *The Great French Films*. Secaucus, N.J.: Citadel, 1983.

Sadoul, Georges. *Dictionary of Films*, trans. Peter Morris. Berkeley: University of California Press, 1972.

Steegmuller, Francis. *Cocteau, A Biography*. Boston: Little, Brown, 1970.

Topart, Robert. "L'Éternel Retour." In *Analyses des films*. Paris: Institut des Hautes Études Cinématographiques, [1948].

Vialle, Gabriel. "Trois Visages de Jean Cocteau." *Image et son* 214 (1968): 183-196.

Whithall, R. E. "Such Stuff as Dreams Are Made Of." *Film Quarterly* [London] Summer 1947: 26-29.

•*The Adventures of Sir Galahad*
dir. Spencer Bennett, Columbia (15-part serial), 1949 (V).

Reviews:

Monthy Film Bulletin 18 (Mar. 1951): 231.

Motion Picture Herald 178 (14 Jan. 1950): Product Digest Section 155.

To-day's Cinema 2 Feb. 1951: 10.

Barbour, Alan. *Cliffhanger*. New York: A&W, 1979.

_____. *The Serials of Columbia*. Kew Gardens, N.Y.: Screen Facts, 1967.

Catalog of Holdings of the American Film Institute Collection and the United Artists Collection at the Library of Congress. Washington, D.C.: American Film Institute, 1978.

Harmon, Jim, and Donald F. Glut. *The Great Movie Serials*. Garden City, N.Y.: Doubleday, 1972.

Kinnard, Roy. *Fifty Years of Serial Thrills*. Metuchen, N.J.: Scarecrow, 1983.

Richards, Jeffrey. *Swordsmen of the Screen from Douglas Fairbanks to Michael York*. London: Routledge, 1977.

Weiss, Ken, and Ed Goodgold. *To Be Continued*. New York: Crown, 1972.

•*A Connecticut Yankee in King Arthur's Court*
dir. Tay Garnett, Paramount, 1949 (V).

Reviews:

America 81 (16 Apr. 1949): 96-97.

Collier's 123 (19 Mar. 1949): 36, 73.

Commonweal 50 (22 Apr. 1949): 48.

Cosmopolitan 126 (Apr. 1949): 12-13, 92.

Extension 44 (July 1949): 40.

Film Daily 24 Feb. 1949: 6.

Good Housekeeping 128 (Apr. 1949): 303.

Hollywood Reporter 21 Feb. 1949: 3.

Monthly Film Bulletin 16 (3 Mar. 1949): 48.

Motion Picture Herald 174 (26 Feb. 1949): Product Digest Section 4513.

New Republic 31 (18 Apr. 1949): 31.

New York Times 8 Apr. 1949: 31.

New Yorker 25 (16 Apr. 1949): 965.

Newsweek 33 (18 Apr. 1949): 89.

Photoplay 34 (Apr. 1949): 22.

Rotarian 75 (Aug. 1949): 42.

Scholastic 54 (13 Apr. 1949): 25.

Senior Scholastic 54 (13 Apr. 1949): 25.

Sign 28 (Mar. 1949): 45.

Time 53 (25 Apr. 1949): 99-100.

To-day's Cinema 4 Feb. 1949: 11.

Variety 23 Feb. 1949: 10.

Woman's Home Companion 76 (Apr. 1949): 10-11.

Beylie, Claude, et al. "Les 44 Films de Tay Garnett." *Ecran* 57 (Apr. 1977): 27-38; 58 (May 1977): 40-45.

Bookbinder, Robert. *The Films of Bing Crosby*. Secaucus, N.J.: Citadel, 1977.

Garnett, Tay, and Fredda Dudley Balling. *Light Up Your Torches and Pull Up Your Tights*. New Rochelle, N.Y.: Arlington House, 1973.

Hirschhorn, Clive. *The Hollywood Musical*. New York: Crown, 1981.

Maeder, Edward. *Hollywood and History, Costume Design in Film*. Los Angeles: Los Angeles County Museum of Art, 1987.

Nash, Jay Robert, and Stanley Ralph Ross. *The Motion Picture Guide, 1927-1983*. 9 vols. Chicago: Cinebooks, 1985. 2: 476.

Nathan, Paul S. "Books into Films." *Publisher's Weekly* 153 (1 May 1948): 1907.

Nowlan, Robert A., and Gwendolyn Wright Nowlan. *Cinema Sequels and Remakes, 1903-1987*. Jefferson, N.C.: McFarland, 1989.

Thomas, Bob. "Tay Garnett: A Man for All Films." *Action* 7 (Sept.-Oct. 1972): 12-16.

Viviani, Christian. "Tay Garnett, 1898-1977." *L'Avant scène cinéma* 245 (1 Apr. 1980): 97-128.

Wachhorst, Wyn. "Time-Travel Romance on Film: Archetypes and Structures." *Extrapolation* 25 (Winter 1984): 340-359.

●*Parsifal*
dir. Daniel Mangrane, CineEspañol-Regents, 1953.
Review:
Film français 448 (13 Nov. 1953): 20.

●*Knights of the Round Table*
dir. Richard Thorpe, MGM, 1953 (V).
Reviews:
America 90 (16 Jan. 1954): 407.
Catholic World 178 (Mar. 1954): 460.
Celuloide 331 (Jan. 1982): 15-18.
Commonweal 59 (29 Jan. 1954): 427-428.
Extension 48 (Mar. 1954): 4.
Farm Journal 78 (Mar. 1954): 94.
Film Daily 23 Dec. 1953: 6.
Films and Filming 5 (June 1963): 37.
Films in Review 5 (Feb. 1954): 90-91.
Kinematograph Weekly 446 (20 May 1951): 19-20.
Library Journal 79 (15 Jan. 1954): 139.
Life 36 (25 Jan. 1954): 108-110.
Look 17 (29 Dec. 1953): 34.
Monthly Film Bulletin 21 (July 1954): 100-101.
Motion Picture Herald 193 (26 Dec. 1953): Product Digest Section 2117.
National Parent-Teacher 48 (Mar. 1954): 38.
New Statesman and Nation 47 (22 May 1954): 661.
New York Times 8 Jan. 1954: 17.
New Yorker 29 (16 Jan. 1954): 85-86.
Newsweek 43 (18 Jan. 1954): 88.
Saturday Review 37 (16 Jan. 1954): 32.
Scholastic 64 (3 Feb. 1954): 27.

Sign 33 (Feb. 1954): 64.

Spectator 192 (21 May 1954): 613-614.

Tatler 212 (26 May 1954): 462.

Time 63 (26 Apr. 1954): 112.

Times (London) 14 May 1954: 8.

Today 9 (Mar. 1954): 14.

To-day's Cinema 13 May 1954: 7-8.

Variety 23 Dec. 1953: 6.

de la Brétèque, François. "La Table ronde au far-west: 'Les Chevaliers de la table ronde' de Richard Thorpe (1953)." *Les Cahiers de la cinémathèque* 42-43 (Summer 1985): 97-102.

Dietz, Howard. "The Anomalous Sir Thomas Malory." *New York Times* 10 Jan. 1954: 2. 5.

Fraser, George MacDonald. *The Hollywood History of the World*. New York: Morrow, 1988.

Hudgins, Morgan. "Logistics of a Bivouac on the Liffey River." *New York Times* 22 Nov. 1953: 2. 5.

Knights of the Round Table: A Souvenir Booklet. New York: Al Greenstone, 1954.

Lambert, Gavin. "Actor on CinemaScope." *Sight and Sound* 23 (Oct.-Dec. 1953): 70.

Nash, Jay Robert, and Stanley Ralph Ross. *The Motion Picture Guide, 1927-1983*. 9 vols. Chicago: Cinebooks, 1985. 4: 1558.

Quirk, Lawrence J. *The Films of Robert Taylor*. Secaucus, N.J.: Citadel, 1975.

Richards, Jeffrey. *Swordsmen of the Screen from Douglas Fairbanks to Michael York*. London: Routledge, 1977.

●***The Black Knight***
dir. Tay Garnett, Columbia, 1954 (Williams Films, 2240 Noblestown Road, Pittsburgh, PA 15025).

Reviews:

America 92 (27 Nov. 1954): 259.

Catholic World 179 (Sept. 1954): 466.

Commonweal 61 (19 Nov. 1954): 188.

Film Daily 21 Oct. 1954: 6.

Hollywood Reporter 9 Nov. 1954: 3.

Kinematograph Weekly 449 (26 Aug. 1954): 21-22.

Monthly Film Bulletin 21 (Oct. 1954): 147.

Motion Picture Herald 197 (23 Oct. 1954): Product Digest Section 185.

National Parent-Teacher 49 (Jan. 1955): 38.

New York Times 29 Oct. 1954: 27.

Newsweek 44 (15 Nov. 1954): 44.

Sign 35 (Oct. 1954): 33.

Time 64 (8 Nov. 1954): 64.

To-day's Cinema 25 Aug. 1954: 10.

Variety 8 Sept. 1954: 6.

Beylie, Claude, et al. "Les 44 Films de Tay Garnett." *Ecran* 57 (Apr. 1977): 27-38; 58 (May 1977): 40-45.

Garnett, Tay, and Fredda Dudley Balling. *Light Up Your Torches and Pull Up Your Tights*. New Rochelle, N.Y.: Arlington House, 1973.

Halliwell, Leslie. "Putting a Name to the Place." *TV Times* (London) 126 (14-21 Feb. 1987): 34.

Henry, Marilyn, and Ron De Sourdis. *The Films of Alan Ladd*. Secaucus, N.J.: Citadel, 1981.

Nash, Jay Robert, and Stanley Ralph Ross. *The Motion Picture Guide, 1927-1983*. 9 vols. Chicago: Cinebooks, 1985. 1: 218.

Richards, Jeffrey. *Swordsmen of the Screen from Douglas Fairbanks to Michael York*. London: Routledge, 1977.

Viviani, Christian. "Tay Garnett, 1898-1977." *L'Avant scène cinéma* 245 (1 Apr. 1980): 97-128.

•**Prince Valiant**
dir. Henry Hathaway, Twentieth Century-Fox, 1954 (Arcus Films, 1225 Broadway, New York, NY 10001).

Reviews:

America 91 (24 Apr. 1954): 117-119.

Catholic World 179 (May 1954): 142-143.

Commonweal 60 (16 Apr. 1954): 41.

Film Daily 2 Apr. 1954: 6.

Films in Review 5 (May 1954): 241-42.

Hollywood Reporter 2 Mar. 1954: 3.

Kinematograph Weekly 6 May 1954: 16.

Library Journal 79 (15 Apr. 1954): 766.

Life 36 (25 Jan. 1954): 108-110.

Look 17 (29 Dec. 1953): 34-35.

Monthly Film Bulletin 21 (July 1954): 85-86.

Motion Picture Herald 195 (3 Apr. 1954): 30; 195 (10 Apr. 1954): Product Digest Section 2254-2255.

National Parent-Teacher 48 (June 1954): 38.

New Statesman and Nation 47 (1 May 1954): 598.

New York Times 7 Apr. 1954: 40.

New Yorker 30 (10 Apr. 1954): 93-94.

Newsweek 43 (19 Apr. 1954): 106-107.

Sign 33 (May 1954): 62.

Tatler 212 (12 May 1954): 356.

Time 63 (12 Apr. 1954): 106.

Times (London) 3 May 1954: 9.

To-day's Cinema 29 Apr. 1954: 6.

Variety 7 Apr. 1954: 6.

Brownell, William H., Jr. "Comics Come Alive." *New York Times* 1 Nov. 1953: 2. 7.

Canham, Kingsley. "Henry Hathaway: A Filmography." *Focus on Film* 7 (1971): 28-35.

Eyman, Scott. "'. . . I Made Movies. . . .'" *Take One* 5 (Feb. 1976): 6-12.

Fuchs, Wolfgang J. "Prinz Eisenherz." *Jugend, Film, Fernsehen* 19. 3 (1975): 183-184.

Kaminsky, Stuart M. "Legend of the Lost." *Velvet Light Trap* 14 (Winter 1975): 25-29.

Nash, Jay Robert, and Stanley Ralph Ross. *The Motion Picture Guide, 1927-1983.* 9 vols. Chicago: Cinebooks, 1985. 6: 2458.

Nogueira, Rui. "Henry Hathaway." *Focus on Film* 7 (1971): 11-27.

Reid, John H. "The Best Second Fiddle." *Films and Filming* 9 (Nov. 1962):14-16.

Richards, Jeffrey. *Swordsmen of the Screen from Douglas Fairbanks to Michael York.* London: Routledge, 1977.

A Bibliography on Arthurian Film 217

•*The Siege of the Saxons / King Arthur and the Siege of the Saxons*
dir. Nathan Juran, BLC-Columbia, 1963 (Arcus Films, 1225 Broadway, New York, NY 10001).

Reviews:

Daily Cinema 24 July 1963: 10.

Film Daily 8 Aug. 1963: 4.

Films and Filming 9 (Sept. 1963): 24.

Kinematograph Weekly 25 July 1963: 31-32.

Hollywood Reporter 22 Aug. 1963: 3.

Monthly Film Bulletin 30 (Sept. 1963): 133.

Motion Picture Herald 230 (4 Sept. 1963): Product Digest Section 884.

Variety 21 Aug. 1963: 17.

Chibnall, Bernard, and Michael Moulds, eds. *The British National Film Catalogue*. London: British National Film Catalogue, 1963.

Nash, Jay Robert, and Stanley Ralph Ross. *The Motion Picture Guide, 1927-1983*. 9 vols. Chicago: Cinebooks, 1985. 7: 2912.

•*The Sword in the Stone*
dir. Wolfgang Reitherman, Disney, 1963 (V).

Reviews:

America 110 (11 Jan. 1964): 55.

Commonweal 79 (13 Dec. 1963): 350.

Daily Cinema 4 Dec. 1963: 8.

Extension 58 (Dec. 1963): 8.

Film Daily 3 Oct. 1963: 14.

Film Facts 6 (9 Dec. 1963): 286-287.

Films and Filming 10 (Jan. 1964); 25-26; 352 (Jan. 1984): 42-43.

Furrow 15 (Aug. 1964): 539.

Hollywood Reporter 2 Oct. 1963: 3.

Kinematograph Weekly 5 Dec. 1963: 9.

Monthly Film Bulletin 31 (Feb. 1964): 22.

Motion Picture Herald 230 (16 Oct. 1963): Product Digest Section 913-914.

New Republic 149 (21 Dec. 1963): 29-30.

New York Times 26 Dec. 1963: 33.

Photoplay 21 (Jan. 1964): 21.

Tablet 217 (14 Dec. 1963): 1362.

Variety 2 Oct. 1963: 6.

Carey, Mary. *The Sword In the Stone*. Racine, Wisc.: Whitman, 1963. [Novelization.]

Duchène, Alain, and Odile Houen. "Merlin l'enchanteur ou le désenchantment." *Banc-titre* 40 (Apr. 1984): 33-35.

Frank, Thomas, and Ollie Johnston. *Disney Animation: The Illusion of Life*. New York: Abbeville, 1981.

Grant, John. *Encyclopedia of Walt Disney Animated Characters*. New York: Harper, 1987.

Krafsur, Richard P., ed. *The American Film Institute Catalog of Feature Films, 1961-1970*. New York: Bowker, 1976.

Leebron, Elizabeth, and Lynn Gartley. *Walt Disney, A Guide to References and Resources*. Boston: Hall, 1979.

Maltin, Leonard. *The Disney Films*. Rev. ed. New York: Crown, 1984.

Nash, Jay Robert, and Stanley Ralph Ross. *The Motion Picture Guide, 1927-1983*. 9 vols. Chicago: Cinebooks, 1985. 7: 3250.

Plas, Marc. "'Merlin l'enchanteur' de Walt Disney: du roman médiéval au conte de fées." *Les Cahiers de la cinémathèque* 42-43 (Summer 1985): 103-104.

•*The Sword of Lancelot / Lancelot and Guinevere*
dir. Cornel Wilde, Emblem, 1963 (V).

Reviews:

Commonweal 78 (6 Sept. 1963): 539.

Daily Cinema 3 May 1963: 5.

Film Daily 29 Apr. 1963: 8.

Film Facts 6 (10 Oct. 1963): 211-212.

Films and Filming 9 (July 1963): 24

Hollywood Reporter 29 Apr. 1963: 3.

Monthly Film Bulletin 30 (June 1963): 87.

Motion Picture Herald 229 (15 May 1963): Product Digest Section 809.

New York Times 10 Oct. 1963: 49.

Newsweek 62 (28 Oct. 1963): 97.

Sign 42 (June 1963): 42.

Variety 1 May 1963: 6.

Chibnall, Bernard, and Michael Moulds, eds. *The British National Film Catalogue.* London: British Film Institute, 1963.

Coen, John. "Producer/Director Cornel Wilde." *Film Comment* 6 (Spring 1970): 53-61.

Gow, Gordon. "Survival!" *Films and Filming* 17 (Oct. 1970): 4-10.

Kaminsky, Stuart M. "Getting Back to Basics with Cornel Wilde." *Take One* 5 (Oct. 1976): 22-24.

Krafsur, Richard. P., ed. *The American Film Institute Catalog of Feature Films, 1961-1970.* New York: Bowker, 1976.

Lancelot and Guinevere. London: Rank Film Distributors, [1963]. [Press book.]

Nash, Jay Robert, and Stanley Ralph Ross. *The Motion Picture Guide, 1927-1983.* 9 vols. Chicago: Cinebooks, 1985. 7: 3251.

Richards, Jeffrey. *Swordsmen of the Screen from Douglas Fairbanks to Michael York.* London: Routledge, 1977.

●*To Parsifal*
dir. Bruce Baillie, Canyon Cinema Co-op, 1963.

Bragin, John. "The Work of Bruce Baillie." In *The New American Cinema,* ed. Gregory Battock. New York: Dutton, 1967.

"Bruce Baillie: An Interview." *Film Comment* 7 (Spring 1971): 24-32.

Curtis, David. *Experimental Cinema.* New York: Delta, 1971.

Nygren, Scott. "Myth and Bruce Baillie's *To Parsifal."* *Field of Vision* 13 (Spring 1985): 3-4.

Polt, Harriet. "The Films of Bruce Baillie." *Film Comment* 2 (Fall 1964): 50-53.

Sitney, P. Adams. "Bruce Baillie and the Lyrical Film." In *New Forms in Film,* ed. Annette Michelson. Montreux (Switz.): Corbaz, 1974.

"Special Section: The Films of Bruce Baillie." *Harbinger* 1 (July 1967): 15-36.

Whitehall, Richard. "An Interview with Bruce Baillie." *Film Culture* 47 (Summer 1969): 16-20.

● *Camelot*
dir. Joshua Logan, Warner Brothers, 1967 (V).

Reviews:

America 117 (11 Nov. 1967): 582-583.

Christian Century 85 (10 Jan. 1968): 52-53.

Columbia 47 (Nov. 1967): 29.

Commonweal 87 (17 Nov. 1967): 207.

Daily Cinema 17 Nov. 1967: 6.

Extension 62 (Jan. 1968): 38.

Film Daily 26 Oct. 1967: 3, 6.

Film Facts 10 (15 Nov. 1967): 280-281.

Film Quarterly 21 (Spring 1968): 56.

Films and Filming 14 (Nov. 1967): 15-17; 14 (Jan. 1968): 22.

Films in Review 18 (Dec. 1967): 649-650.

Harper's 236 (Jan. 1968): 81-82.

Hollywood Reporter 25 Oct. 1967: 3, 14.

Kinematograph Weekly 18 Nov. 1967: 10, 18.

Monthly Film Bulletin 35 (Jan. 1968): 3.

Motion Picture Herald 237 (1 Nov. 1967): Product Digest Section 737.

New York Times 26 Oct. 1967: 54.

Newsweek 70 (6 Nov. 1967): 90.

St. Anthony Messenger 75 (Mar. 1968): 8.

Senior Scholastic 91 (14 Dec. 1967): 21.

Sign 47 (Oct. 1967): 45.

Simon, John. *Movies into Film, Film Criticism 1967-1970*. New York: Dell, 1971.

Tablet 221 (18 Nov. 1967): 1208.

Time 90 (3 Nov. 1967): 100.

Variety 25 Oct. 1967: 6.

Vogue 150 (Dec. 1967): 175.

Borgzinner, Jon. "The Shining Pageant of Camelot" and "The Limerick Lad in King Arthur's Court." *Life* 63 (22 Sept. 1967): 70-76, 79-80, 84, 86.

Combs, Carl. *Camelot: The Movie Souvenir Book*. New York: National, 1968.

Hirschhorn, Clive. *The Hollywood Musical*. New York: Crown, 1981.

A Bibliography on Arthurian Film

_____. *The Warner Brothers Story.* New York: Crown, 1979.

Kaplan, Phillip J. *The Best, Worst and Most Unusual: Hollywood Musicals.* New York: Beckman, 1983.

Knee, Allan, ed. *Selections from Idylls of the King and Camelot.* New York: Dell, 1967.

Krafsur, Richard P., ed. *The American Film Institute Catalog of Feature Films 1961-1970.* New York: Bowker, 1976.

Lightman, Herb A. "Capturing on Film the Mythical Magic of *Camelot*." *American Cinematographer* 49 (Jan. 1968): 30-33.

Logan, Joshua. *Movie Stars, Real People, and Me.* New York: Delacorte, 1978.

Maeder, Edward. *Hollywood and History, Costume Design in Film.* Los Angeles: Los Angeles County Museum of Art, 1987.

Nash, Jay Robert, and Stanley Ralph Ross. *The Motion Picture Guide, 1927-1983.* 9 vols. Chicago: Cinebooks, 1985. 2: 339.

Schroth, Evelyn. "Camelot: Contemporary Interpretation of Arthur in 'Sens' and 'Matiere.'" *Journal of Popular Culture* 17 (Fall 1983): 31-43.

•*Tristan et Iseult*
dir. Yvan Lagrange, Film du Soir, 1972.

Reviews:

Cinéma 187 (May 1974): 138.

Ecran 25 (May 1974): 68.

Image et son 284 (May 1974): 103-104; 288-289 (Oct. 1974): 364-365.

Kino 9 (Jan. 1974): 60-61.

Téléciné 188 (May 1974): 27.

Variety 18 July 1973: 14.

Payen, Jean Charles. "Le *Tristan et Iseut* de Lagrange comme un anti-Tristan." *Tristania* 4 (May 1979): 51-56.

Selcer, Robert W. "Yvan Lagrange: Impressions of a Filmmaker." *Tristania* 4 (May 1979): 44-50.

Vialle, Gabriel. "Musique, la quatrième dimension." *Image et son* 291 (Dec. 1974): 10-12.

•*Gawain and the Green Knight*
dir. Stephen Weeks, United Artists, 1973 (FilmBank Distributors Ltd., Grayton House, 498-504 Fulham Road, London SW6 5NH, England).

Review:

Monthly Film Bulletin 40 (Apr. 1973): 168-169.

Berry, Dave. "Stephen Weeks." *Film* 37 (May 1976): 6-7.

Nash, Jay Robert, and Stanley Ralph Ross. *The Motion Picture Guide, 1927-1983*. 9 vols. Chicago: Cinebooks, 1985. 3: 952.

Richards, Jeffrey. *Swordsmen of the Screen from Douglas Fairbanks to Michael York*. London: Routledge, 1977.

Wood, Linda, ed. *The British Film Catalogue, 1971-1981*. London: British Film Institute, 1983.

•*Lancelot du Lac*
dir. Robert Bresson, Mara Films, 1974 (New Yorker Films, 161 W. 61st Street, New York, NY 10023).

Reviews:

Amis du film et de la television 224 (May 1975): 16-17.

Audience 7 (June 1975): 5-6.

Cinéma 190-191 (Sept.-Oct. 1974): 273-275.

Cinema pratique 134-135 (Nov.-Dec. 1974): 244-246.

Cinéma Québec 4 (May 1975): 34-35.

Cinema Nuovo 33 (Sept.-Oct. 1974): 366-368.

Ecran 29 (Oct. 1974): 57-59.

Ekran 12 (1974): 88-93.

Etudes 341 (Nov. 1974): 593.

[British] *Federation* [of Film Societies] *News* 33 (Dec. 1975): 5.

Film 22 (Jan. 1975): 3; 32 (Dec. 1975): 4.

Filmcritica 25 (May 1974): 162-163.

Film en Televisie 239 (Apr. 1977): 38.

Film français 1546 (6 Sept. 1974): 14.

Filmkritik 19 (Aug. 1975): 378-380.

Filmrutan 17. 4 (1974): 136-137.

Hollywood Reporter 7 Oct. 1974: 17.

Image et son 285 (June-July 1974): 29; 291 (Dec. 1974): 98-102; 292 (Jan. 1975): 2-3.

Independent Film Journal 75 (14 May 1975): 10.

Listener 94 (18 Sept. 1975): 381.

Monthly Film Bulletin 42 (Sept. 1975): 199-200.

New Statesman 90 (5 Sept. 1975): 287.

New York 8 (19 May 1975): 80.

New York Times 1 Oct. 1974: 33; 5 June 1975: 50.

New Yorker 51 (9 June 1975): 117-118.

Newsweek 84 (14 Oct. 1974): 131-133.

Partisan Review 41. 4 (1974): 581.

Positif 162 (Oct. 1974): 55-57; 163 (Nov. 1974): 71-74.

Revue du cinéma 291 (Dec. 1974): 98-102.

Sight and Sound 43 (Summer 1974): 128-130.

Skoop 11 (Mar. 1975): 34-35.

Tablet 229 (13 Sept. 1975): 869.

Take One 4 (Dec. 1974 [for Sept.-Oct. 1973]): 34.

Téléciné 214 (Jan. 1977): 13-14.

Thousand Eyes 2 (Mar. 1977): 7.

Variety 12 June 1974: 24.

Village Voice 31 Oct. 1974: 110.

Baby, Yvonne. "Metal Makes Sounds: An Interview with Robert Bresson," trans. Nora Jacobson. *Field of Vision* 13 (Spring 1985): 4-5.

Buchka, Peter, et al. *Robert Bresson*. Munich: Hanser, 1978.

Burns, E. Jane. "Nostalgia Isn't What It Used to Be: The Middle Ages in Literature and Film." In *Shadows of the Magic Lamp, Fantasy and Science Fiction in Film*, ed. George Slusser and Eric S. Rabkin. Carbondale: Southern Illinois University Press, 1985.

Comuzio, Ermanno. "Robert Bresson, 'Lancillotto e Ginevra.'" *Cineforum* 134 (July 1974): 537-553.

Crotta, Bruno. "Lancelot du Lac: la guerre, le simulcare de la vertu." *Camera/Stylo* 5 (Jan. 1985): 83-86.

Cugier, Alphonse. "'Lancelot du Lac' de Robert Bresson: Le Moyen Âge revisité ou la dimension tragique du XXe siècle." *Les Cahiers de la cinémathèque* 42-43 (Summer 1985): 119-124.

de la Brétèque, François. "Une 'Figure Obligé' du film de chevalrie: le Tournoi." *Les Cahiers de la cinémathèque* 42-43 (Summer 1985): 91-96.

Delmas, J. "Lancelot du Lac : Robert Bresson et ses armures." *Jeune cinéma* 82 (Nov. 1974): 19-24.

Dempsey, Michael. "Despair Abounding: The Recent Films of Robert Bresson." *Film Quarterly* 34 (Fall 1980): 2-15.

Estève, Michel. *Cinéma et condition humaine*. Paris: Albatros, 1978.

──────────. *Robert Bresson*. Rev. ed. Paris: Seghers, 1974.

Ferero, Adelio. *Bresson*. Florence: La Nuova Italia, 1976.

Gauville, Hervé. "Lancelot du Sang." *Camera/Stylo* 5 (Jan. 1985): 100-103.

Hanlon, Lindley. *Fragments, Robert Bresson's Film Style*. Rutherford, N.J.: Fairleigh Dickinson University Press, 1986.

Jutkewitsch, Sergej "Die 'Cinématographie' des Robert Bresson (3): Ein politischer Regisseur." *Film und Fernsehen* 11. 3 (1983): 45-49.

"*Lancelot du Lac*, un film de Robert Bresson." *L'Avant-scène cinéma* 155 (Feb. 1975): 46-50.

Le Dantec, Mireille Latil. "Lancelot." *Cinématographe* 10 (Nov.-Dec. 1974): 38-42.

Margetts, John. "Robert Bressons 'Lancelot du lac': Monotonie und Depression." *Mittelalter-Rezeption II*, ed. Jürgen Kühnel et al. Göppingen: Kümmerle, 1982.

Micciché, Lino. "Bresson: la scrittura di una situazione interiore." *Cinema Sessatina* 97-98 (May-Aug. 1974): 27-34.

Nash, Jay Robert, and Stanley Ralph Ross. *The Motion Picture Guide, 1927-1983*. 9 vols. Chicago: Cinebooks, 1985. 5: 1597.

Oudart, Jean-Pierre. "Un Pouvoir qui ne pense, ne calcule, ni ne juge?" *Cahiers du cinéma* 258-259 (July-Aug. 1975): 36-41.

Paquette, Jean-Marcel. "La Dernière Métamorphose de Lancelot." *Les Cahiers de la cinémathèque* 42-43 (Summer 1985): 113-118.

Prédal, René, et al. "Dossier: Robert Bresson." *Cinéma* 294 (June 1983): 3-32.

Pruitt, John. "Robert Bresson's Lancelot du Lac." *Field of Vision* 13 (Spring 1985): 5-9.

Robert Bresson. Madrid: Filmoteca Nacional, 1977.

Roud, Richard, ed. *Cinema, A Critical Dictionary*. New York: Viking, 1980.

Sémolué, Jean. "Lancelot du Lac." *Téléciné* 191-192 (Sept.-Oct. 1974): 23-26.

Schrader, Paul. "Robert Bresson, Possibly." *Film Comment* 13 (Sept-Oct. 1977): 26-30.

Sloane, Jane. *Robert Bresson, A Guide to References and Resources.* Boston: Hall, 1983.

Targe, André. "Ici l'espace naît du temps." *Camera/Stylo* 5 (Jan. 1985): 87-99.

Tinazzi, Giorgio. *Il Cinema di Robert Bresson.* Venice: Marsilo, 1976.

_____. "'Lancelot du Lac': a proposito di Bresson." *Cinema e cinema* 2 (Apr.-July 1975): 83-92.

Torri, Bruno. "Bresson: lo stile e la grazia." *Cinema Sessatina* 97-98 (May-Aug. 1974): 35-39.

Waters, John. "John Waters' Guilty Pleasures." *Film Comment* 19 (July-Aug. 1983): 20-23.

Williams, Alan. "On the Absence of the Grail." *Movietone News* 47 (Jan. 1976): 10-13.

●*King Arthur, The Young Warlord*
dir. Sidney Hayers, Patrick Jackson, and Patrick Sasdy, Heritage Enterprises, 1975 (V).

The Video Sourcebook. 5th ed. Syosset, N.Y.: National Video Clearinghouse, 1983.

●*Monty Python and the Holy Grail*
dir. Terry Gilliam and Terry Jones, Python Pictures, 1975 (V).

Reviews:

America 132 (31 May 1975): 428-429.

Amis de film et de la television 238 (Mar. 1976): 7.

APEC—Revue Belge du cinéma 13 (Apr. 1976): 38-39.

Byron, Stuart, and Elisabeth Weiss, eds. *The National Society of Film Critics on Film Comedy.* New York: Grossman, 1977.

Cineaste 7 (Fall 1975): 15-18.

Cinéma 205 (Jan. 1976): 143.

Cineforum 159 (Nov. 1976): 717-718.

Commonweal 102 (6 June 1975): 182.

Film Review 25 (June 1975): 8-9.

Films and Filming 21 (May 1975): 40.

Films Illustrated 4 (May 1975): 326.

Hollywood Reporter 13 Mar. 1975: 18.

Image et son 301 (Dec. 1975): 117.

Independent Film Journal 75 (30 Apr. 1975): 13-14.

Jeune cinéma 93 (Mar. 1976): 29-30.

Listener 93 (10 Apr. 1975): 480.

Los Angeles Times 23 July 1974: 4. 1.

Monthly Film Bulletin 42 (Apr. 1975): 84-85.

New Republic 172 (24 May 1975): 20.

New Statesman 89 (4 Apr. 1975): 458.

New York 8 (5 May 1975): 76.

New York Times 28 Apr. 1975: 34.

New Yorker 51 (5 May 1975): 115-117.

Newsweek 85 (19 May 1975): 90.

Penthouse 6 (Aug. 1975): 37-39.

Positif 171-172 (July-Aug. 1975): 68.

Revue du cinéma 301 (Dec. 1975): 117; 309-310 (Oct. 1976): 247-248.

Rolling Stone 189 (19 June 1975): 16.

Saturday Review 2 (31 May 1975): 44-46.

Time 105 (26 May 1975): 58-59.

Variety 19 Mar. 1975: 32.

Village Voice 5 May 1975: 81-82.

Vogue 165 (July 1975): 30.

Abel, Christian, et al. "Entretien: Monty Python." *Revue du cinéma* 351 (June 1980): 74-81.

Burns, E. Jane. "Nostalgia Isn't What It Used to Be: The Middle Ages in Literature and Film." In *Shadows of the Magic Lamp, Fantasy and Science Fiction in Film*, ed. George Slusser and Eric S. Rabkin. Carbondale: Southern Illinois University Press, 1985.

Garel, Alain. "A propos du Monty Python's Flying Circus." *Image et son* 304 (Mar. 1976): 21-26.

Gow, Gordon. "'he said with incredible arrogance. . . .'" *Films and Filming* 21 (Dec. 1974): 12-17.

Magill's Survey of Cinema: English Language Films, ed. Frank N. Magill. Series 2. 6 vols. Englewood Cliffs, N.J.: Salem, 1981. 4: 1633-1637.

Monty Python and the Holy Grail (Book). New York: Methuen, 1977.

Nash, Jay Robert, and Stanley Ralph Ross. *The Motion Picture Guide, 1927-1983*. 9 vols. Chicago: Cinebooks, 1985. 5: 2018.

Rubenstein, Lenny. "The Wonderous Return of the Wacky Monty Python's Flying Circus." *Cineaste* 7 (Fall 1975): 15-18.

•*Perceval le Gallois*
dir. Eric Rohmer, Gaumont-New Yorker Films, 1978 (New Yorker Films, 161 W. 61st Street, New York, NY 10023).

Reviews:

    Amis du film et de la television 272 (Jan. 1979): 18; 275 (Apr. 1979): 33.

    Cahiers du cinéma 299 (Apr. 1979): 41-46.

    Christian Science Monitor 16 Nov. 1978: 16.

    Cinema Nuovo 290-291 (Aug.-Oct. 1984): 61-62.

    Cinemateca Revista 39 (Nov. 1983): 79.

    Cinématographe 44 (Feb. 1979): 11-15.

    Continental Film Review 25 (Aug. 1978): 16-17.

    Ecran 76 (15 Jan. 1979): 71-72.

    Etudes 350 (Apr. 1979): 541-545.

    Film a Doba 25 (Feb. 1979): 110.

    Film en Televisie 294 (Nov. 1981): 33.

    Film Quarterly 33 (Winter 1979-1980): 49-52.

    Films in Review 76 (Jan. 1979): 53-54.

    Hollywood Reporter 12 Oct. 1978: 1.

    Image et son 334 (Dec. 1978): 109-112.

    Jeune cinéma 116 (Feb. 1979): 28-31.

    Nation 227 (11 Nov. 1978): 520.

    New Leader 61 (6 Nov. 1978): 19-20.

    New Republic 179 (21 Oct. 1978): 30-31.

    New York Times 6 Oct. 1978: n. p.

    Newsweek 92 (30 Oct. 1978): 95.

Penthouse 10 (Feb. 1979): 45-47.

Positif 216 (Mar. 1979): 74.

Segnocinema 13 (May 1984): 68.

Shakespeare on Film Newsletter 8 (Apr. 1984): 5, 9.

Take One 7 (Jan. 1979): 9-10.

Télérama 1517 (10-16 Feb. 1979): 86-89.

Time 114 (20 Nov. 1978): 104.

Variety 13 Sept. 1978: 36.

Village Voice 23 Oct. 1978: 23.

Adair, Gilbert. "Rohmer's Perceval." *Sight and Sound* 47 (Autumn 1978): 230-234.

Amiel, Mireille. "Des Arts, des armes et des lois...." *Cinéma* 242 (Feb. 1979): 8-10.

Angeli, Giovanna. *Eric Rohmer*. Milan: Moizzi Editore, 1979.

Botermans, J. "De lange weg van Eric Rohmer." *Mediafilm* 142 (Spring 1983): 2-11.

Burns, E. Jane. "Nostalgia Isn't What It Used to Be: The Middle Ages in Literature and Film." In *Shadows of the Magic Lamp, Fantasy and Science Fiction in Film*, ed. George Slusser and Eric S. Rabkin. Carbondale: Southern Illinois University Press, 1985.

Cormier, Raymond J. "Rohmer's Grail Story: Anatomy of a French Flop." *Yale French Review* 5 (Winter 1981): 391-396.

Crisp, C. G. *Eric Rohmer: Realist and Moralist*. Bloomington: Indiana University Press, 1988.

Delavaud, Gilles, and Jacques Montaville. "Entretien avec Eric Rohmer." *Education 2000* 18-20 (Mar. 1981): 85-90.

Detassis, Piera. "Perceval di Eric Rohmer." *Cineforum* 234 (May 1984): 37-44.

"Dossier film: *Perceval*." *Cinéma français* 21 (1978): 37-42.

Douin, Jean-Luc. "Entretien avec Eric Rohmer: 'Perceval,' C'est Buster Keaton au moyen âge." *Télérama* 1517 (10-16 Feb. 1979): 90-91.

"Eric Rohmer." *Cahiers du cinéma* 400 (Oct. 1987): suppl. 44-45.

"Eric Rohmer Talks about the Concept of Perceval." *Continental Film Review* 26 (June 1979): 16-17.

"Eric Rohmer's *Perceval le Gallois*." *L'Avant-scène cinéma* 221 (1 Feb. 1979): 9-64. [Screenplay.]

Fieschi, Jacques. "Une Innocence mortelle." *L'Avant-scène cinéma* 221 (1 Feb. 1979): 4-6.

Fischer, Lucy. "Roots: The Medieval Tale as Modernist Cinema." *Field of Vision* 9-10 (Winter-Spring 1980): 21-25, 33.

Huchet, Jean-Charles. "Mereceval." *Litterature* 40 (1980): 69-94.

Jourdat, Alain. "L'Espace comme support d'un récit romanesque." *Le Technicien du film* 272 (15 July-15 Sept. 1979): 8-11.

Larsen, Jan Kornum. "Virkelighed og vindmller." *Kosmorama* 28 (Aug. 1982): 104-115.

Magill's Survey of Cinema: Foreign Language Films, ed. Frank N. Magill. 8 vols. Englewood Cliffs, N.J.: Salem, 1985. 5: 2409-2413.

Magny, Joël, and Dominique Rabourdin. "Entretien avec Eric Rohmer." *Cinéma* 242 (Feb. 1979): 11-19.

_____. *Eric Rohmer*. Paris: Rivages, 1986.

_____. "Eric Rohmer or la quete du graal." *Cinéma* 242 (Feb. 1979): 20-32.

Mancini, Michele. *Eric Rohmer*. Florence: La Nuova Italia, 1983.

Marty, Joseph. "'Perceval le Gallois' d'Eric Rohmer, un itinéraire roman." *Les Cahiers de la cinémathèque* 42-43 (Summer 1985): 125-132.

_____. "'Perceval le Gallois': une symbolisme de l'alliance chrétienne." In *Éric Rohmer 2*, ed. Michel Estève. Paris: Minard, 1986.

Milne, Tom. "Rohmer's Seige Perilous." *Sight and Sound* 50 (Summer 1981): 192-195.

Rohmer, Eric. "Note sur la traduction et sur la mise en scène de 'Perceval.'" *L'Avant-scène cinéma* 221 (1 Feb. 1979): 6-7.

Roud, Richard, ed. *Cinema, A Critical Dictionary*. New York: Viking, 1980.

Sterritt, David, "Rohmer's Thoughts About Perceval. " *Christian Science Monitor* 27 Dec. 1978: 18.

Tesich-Savage, Nadja. "Rehearsing the Middle Ages." *Film Comment* 14 (Sept.-Oct. 1978): 50-56.

Williams, Linda. "Eric Rohmer and the Holy Grail." *Literature/Film Quarterly* 11 (Apr. 1983): 71-82.

•**The Legend of King Arthur**
dir. Rodney Bennett, BBC, Time-Life Television, and the Australian Broadcasting Commission (8-part series), 1979 (aired in the United States in 1988 on A&E Cable).

Reviews:

Broadcast 1029 (15 Oct. 1979): 13.

Daily Telegraph 8 Oct. 1979: 13.

Radio Times 225 (6-12 Oct. 1979): 22.

Television Today 11 Oct. 1979: 18.

Davies, Andrew. *The Legend of King Arthur*. London: Fontana/Armada, 1979.

Hattersley, Roger. "Pre-Raphaelite Avalon." *Listener* 202 (25 Oct. 1979): 554.

Press Release: Arts & Entertainment Cable Television, P. O. Box 729, Madison Square Station, New York, NY 10159.

•**Tristan and Isolt / Lovespell**
dir. Tom Donovan, Clar Productions, 1979 (V).

Alpert, Hollis. *Burton*. Toronto: Paper Jacks, 1987.

Tobin, Yann. "'Ce Soir, je ferai pleurer le public. . . .'" *Positif* 236 (Dec. 1984): 11-15.

The Video Sourcebook. 8th ed. Syossett, N.Y.: National Video Clearinghouse, 1986.

Willis, John. *Screen World*. Vol. 33. New York: Crown, 1982.

•**The Unidentified Flying Oddball / The Spaceman and King Arthur**
dir. Russ Mayberry, Disney, 1979 (V).

Reviews:

Boxoffice 115 (6 Aug. 1979): 20.

Ecran fantastique 11 (1979): 7.

Film Bulletin 48 (Sept. 1978): Review-D.

Films Illustrated 8 (July 1979): 412.

Independent Film Journal 82 (Sept. 1979): 14, 55.

Monthly Film Bulletin 46 (July 1979): 154-155.

Screen International 198 (14-21 July 1979): 18.

Variety 18 July 1979: 16.

Crume, Vic. *Unidentified Flying Oddball*. New York: Scholastic Book Services, 1979. [Novelization.]

Nash, Jay Robert, and Stanley Ralph Ross. *The Motion Picture Guide, 1927-1983*. 9 vols. Chicago: Cinebooks, 1985. 8: 3633.

Simon, Heather. *The Spaceman and King Arthur*. London: New English Library, 1979. [Novelization.]

Vaines, Colin. "King Arthur's Yankee Enters the Space Age." *Screen International* 150 (5-11 Aug. 1978): 10-11.

Willis, Donald C. *Horror and Science Fiction Films II*. Metuchen, N.J.: Scarecrow, 1982.

•*Parzival*
dir. Richard Blank, West Deutsche Rundfunk, 1980.

Müller, Ulrich. "Parzival 1980—auf der Bühne, im Fernsehen und im Film." In *Mittelalter-Rezeption II*, ed. Jürgen Kühnel et al. Göppingen: Kümmerle, 1982.

•*Excalibur*
dir. John Boorman, Orion, 1981 (V).

Reviews:

Amis du film et de la television 301-303 (July-Aug. 1981): 15.

Cahiers du cinéma 326 (July-Aug. 1981): 61-62.

Casablanca 7-8 (July-Aug. 1981): 79.

Celuloide 331 (Jan. 1982): 15-18.

Christian Century 98 (27 May 1981): 619; 98 (29 July 1981): 774-776.

Christian Science Monitor 23 Apr. 1981: 19.

Ciné Revue 20 (14 May 1981): 5.

Cinefantastique 11 (Fall 1981): 47.

Cinéma 270 (June 1981): 112-113.

Cinema Canada 75 (July 1981): 34.

Cinema Nuovo 31 (Feb. 1882): 49-50.

Cinema Papers 34 (Sept.-Oct. 1981): 399-401.

Contracampo 28 (Mar. 1982): 65.

Ecran fantastique 19 (1981): 66-67.

Film a Doba 30 (Jan. 1984): 43-45.

Filmcritica 32 (Aug. 1981): 349-351; 33 (Jan. 1982): 20-24.

Film en Televisie 290-291 (July-Aug. 1981): 14-15.

Filmfaust 24 (Oct.-Nov. 1981): 28.

Filmihullu 6 (1981): 35.

Film Journal 84 (6 Apr. 1981): 13-14.

Film og Kino 49. 4 (1981): 143-144.

Films 1 (June 1981): 26-30; 1 (July 1981): 36-37.

Films in Review 32 (July 1981): 377.

Hablemos de Cine 18 (May 1982): 91-92.

Hollywood Reporter 6 Apr. 1981: 2.

Jeune cinéma 136 (July-Aug. 1981): 41-44.

Kosmorama 27 (June 1981): 98.

Levende Billeder 7 (Oct. 1981): 63.

Los Angeles Times 5 Apr. 1981: Calendar 28; 17 June 1981: Calendar 1.

Listener 106 (9 July 1981): 61; 115 (27 Feb. 1986): 30.

Maclean's 27 Apr. 1981: 50.

Medien + Erziehung 26 .1 (1982): 19-22.

Monthly Film Bulletin 48 (June 1981): 112.

Motion Picture Product Digest 15 Apr. 1981: 87.

Mythlore 31 (Spring 1982): 29-30.

Nation 232 (16 May 1981): 612.

New Leader 64 (4 May 1981):17.

New Statesman 102 (3 July 1981): 22.

New York 14 (13 Apr. 1981): 50-52.

New York Post 10 Apr. 1981: 43.

New York Times 10 Apr. 1981: 3. 11; 10 May 1981: 2. 13.

New Yorker 57 (20 Apr. 1981): 146-151.

Newsday 10 Apr. 1981: 27.

Newsweek 97 (13 Apr. 1981): 82.

Positif 242 (May 1981): 16-17.

Prevue 44 (Feb.-Mar. 1981): 34-37.

Rolling Stone 14 May 1981: 36-37.

Screen International 300 (11-18 July 1981): 15.

Segnocinema 2 (Dec. 1981): 58.

Skoop 17 (Aug. 1981): 14-15; 17 (Sept.-Oct. 1981): 58.

Soho News 15 Apr. 1981: 55.

Starburst 35 (1981): 16-19.

24 images 10 (Sept. 1981): 71-72.

Time 117 (13 Apr. 1981): 96.

Variety 8 Apr. 1981: 18.

Village Voice 15 Apr. 1981: 51.

Washington Post 10 Apr. 1981: F 1, Weekend 17.

Women's Wear Daily 10 Apr. 1981: 8.

"The Art of *Excalibur*." *Starburst* 38 (1981): 20-21.

"Boorman and the Arthurian Legend." *Photoplay* 31 (Nov. 1980): 40-41.

Borie, Bertrand. "Entretien avec John Boorman." *Ecran fantastique* 19 (1981): 6-8.

_____. "Table ronde autour d'*Excalibur*." *Ecran fantastique* 20 (1981): 70-72.

Boyle, Sarah. "From Victim to Avenger: The Women in John Boorman's *Excalibur*." *Avalon to Camelot* 1 (Summer 1984): 42-43.

Brode, Douglas. *The Films of the Eighties*. New York: Citadel, 1990.

Burns, E. Jane. "Nostalgia Isn't What It Used to Be: The Middle Ages in Literature and Film." In *Shadows of the Magic Lamp, Fantasy and Science Fiction in Film*, ed. George Slusser and Eric S. Rabkin. Carbondale: Southern Illinois University Press, 1985.

Canby, Vincent. "Of a Hit, a Series and the Word." *New York Times* 10 May 1981: D 13.

Ciment, Michel. "Deux Entretiens avec John Boorman." *Positif* 242 (May 1981): 18-31.

_____. *John Boorman*, trans. Gilbert Adair. London: Faber, 1986.

Clegg, Cynthia. "The Problem of Realizing Romance in Film: John Boorman's *Excalibur*." In *Shadows of the Magic Lamp, Fantasy and Science Fiction in Film*, ed. George Slusser and Eric S. Rabkin. Carbondale: Southern Illinois University Press, 1985.

Decampo, M., and F. Vega. "John Boorman habla de 'Excalibur.'" *Casablanca* 7-8 (July-Aug. 1981): 52-53, 56-57.

de la Brétèque, François. "L'Épée dans le lac, 'Excalibur' de John Boorman ou les aléas de la puissance." *Les Cahiers de la cinémathèque* 42-43 (Summer 1985): 91-96.

_____. "Une 'Figure Obligé' du film de chevalrie: le Tournoi." *Les Cahiers de la cinémathèque* 42-43 (Summer 1985): 91-96.

"Dossier: *Excalibur*." *Positif* 247 (Oct. 1981): 29-43.

Dubost, Francis. "Merlin et le texte inaugural." *Les Cahiers de la cinémathèque* 42-43 (Summer 1985): 85-89.

Haller, Robert. "*Excalibur* and Innovation." *Field of Vision* 13 (Spring 1985): 2-3.

Holley, Linda Tarte. "Medievalism in Film." *Southeastern Medieval Association Newsletter* 9. 2 (1983-1984): 13-17.

"Interview with Alex Thompson." *American Cinematographer* 63 (May 1982): 452, 491-493, 504-506.

"John Boorman Talks About *Excalibur*." *Film Directions* 4. 15 (1981): 16-19.

Kennedy, Harlan. "The World of King Arthur According to John Boorman." *American Film* 6 (Mar. 1981): 30-37.

Maeder, Edward. *Hollywood and History, Costume Design in Film*. Los Angeles: Los Angeles County Museum of Art, 1987.

Magill's Cinema Annual, 1982, ed. Frank N. Magill. Englewood Cliffs, N.J.: Salem, 1982.

Magill's Survey of Cinema: English Language Films, ed. Frank N. Magill. 2nd series. 6 vols. Englewood Cliffs, N.J.: Salem, 1981. 2: 731-734.

Nash, Jay Robert, and Stanley Ralph Ross. *The Motion Picture Guide, 1927-1983*. 9 vols. Chicago: Cinebooks, 1985. 3: 788.

Open, Michael. "The Dynamic Principle of Fantasy." *Film Directions* 4. 15 (1981): 20-21.

Piccardi, Adriano. "*Excalibur* di John Boorman." *Cineforum* 21 (Oct. 1981): 39-46.

_____. *John Boorman*. Florence: La Nuova Italia, 1982.

Pietzsch, Ingeborg. "Gewalt für Jugend zugelassen?" *Film und Fernsehen* 11 (1986): 24.

Polinien, Gilles. "Le nouveau John Boorman." *Ecran fantastique* 18 (1981): 42-43.

Rooney, Phillip J. *The Quest Elements in the Films of John Boorman*. Ph.D. Dissertation: University of Nebraska-Lincoln, 1989. [*DAI* 50 (Nov. 1989): 1314A.]

A Bibliography on Arthurian Film

Shichtman, Martin B. "Hollywood's New Weston: The Grail Myth in Francis Ford Coppola's *Apocalypse Now* and John Boorman's *Excalibur*." *Post Script* 4 (Autumn 1984): 35-49.

Stanbrook, Alan. "Is God in Showbusiness too? The First Twenty-five Years of John Boorman, Our Most Anti-materialist Director." *Sight and Sound* 59 (Autumn 1990): 259-263.

Strick, Philip. "John Boorman's Merlin." *Sight and Sound* 49 (Summer 1980): 168-171.

Tessier, Max. "Entretien avec John Boorman (sur *Excalibur*)." *Revue du cinéma* 363 (July-Aug. 1981): 31-34.

_____. "*Excalibur*." *Revue du cinéma* 362 (June 1981): 19-23.

Vaines, Colin. "Magic Moments." *Screen International* 252 (2-9 Aug. 1980): 15.

Verniere, James. "The Technology of Style: An Interview with John Boorman." *Filmmakers Monthly* 14 (June 1981): 22-29.

Yakir, Dan. "The Sorcerer." *Film Comment* 17 (May-June 1981): 49-53.

●*Feuer und Schwert / Tristan und Isolde*
dir. Veith von Fürstenberg, Genée und von Fürstenberg Filmproduktion, 1981 (V).

Reviews:

Continental Film and Video 29 (Nov. 1981): 18.

Das Fernsehspiel im ZDF 4 (Mar.-May 1984): 43.

Film und Fernsehen 12. 7 (1984): 35.

Kino 4 (Aug. 1981): 33.

Month 14 (Nov. 1981): 388.

Variety 10 June 1981: 18.

Helt, Richard C., and Marie E. Helt. *West German Cinema Since 1945: A Reference Handbook*. Metuchen, N.J.: Scarecrow, 1987.

●*Knightriders*
dir. George Romero, United Film, 1981 (V).

Reviews:

Boxoffice 117 (4 May 1981): 82-84.

Christian Science Monitor 23 Apr. 1981: 19.

Cineaste 11.3 (1981): 31-33.

Ecran fantastique 19 (1981): 68.

Film Journal 84 (20 Apr. 1981): 13-14.

Filme 10 (July-Aug. 1981): 52.

Films and Filming 334 (July 1982): 38.

Los Angeles Times 9 Apr. 1981: Calendar 1.

Motion Picture Production Digest 20 May 1981: 96.

Nation 232 (16 May 1981): 613.

New Leader 67 (4 May 1981): 17-18.

New York 14 (27 Apr. 1981): 364-365.

New York Post 17 Apr. 1981: 31.

New York Times 17 Apr. 1981: 3. 8.

New Yorker 57 (18 May 1981): 147-151.

Newsday 17 Apr. 1981: 2.7.

Newsweek 97 (13 Apr. 1981): 82.

Rolling Stone 28 May 1981: 51-52.

Soho News 15 Apr. 1981: 55, 61.

Time 117 (27 Apr. 1981): 54-55.

Variety 8 Apr. 1981: 20.

Village Voice 15 May 1981: 51.

Burke-Block, Candace. "The Film Journal Interviews George Romero on *Knightriders*." *Film Journal* 84 (4 May 1981): 25.

Gagne, Paul R. *The Zombies That Ate Pittsburgh: The Films of George Romero*. New York: Dodd, Mead, 1987.

Heimel, Cynthia. "The Living Dead Ride Again." *New York* 21 July 1980: 46-48.

Martin, Bob. "*Knightriders*." *Fangoria* 12 (1981): 17-19, 66-67.

Nash, Jay Robert, and Stanley Ralph Ross. *The Motion Picture Guide, 1927-1983*. 9 vols. Chicago: Cinebooks, 1985. 4: 1557.

Seligson, Tom. "George Romero: Revealing the Monsters Within Us." *Twilight Zone* 1 (Aug. 1981): 12-17.

Weldon, Michael. *The Psychotronic Encyclopedia of Film*. New York: Ballantine, 1983.

Yakir, Dan. "Knight After Night with George Romero." *American Film* 6 (May 1981): 42-45, 69.

•Arthur the King
dir. Clive Donner, CBS, 1982 (aired Apr. 26, 1985).

Reviews:

>Courier-Journal (Louisville, Ky.) 25 Apr. 1985 (located in Newsbank, Review of the Arts, Film and Television Microform 11 [July 1984-June1985]; FTV 108: E13, fiche).
>
>New York Daily News 26 Apr. 1985: 74.
>
>New York Times 26 Apr. 1985: 3. 30.
>
>Marill, Alvin H. Movies Made for Television, 1964-1986. New York: Zoetrope, 1987.
>
>TV Guide 33 (20-26 Apr. 1985): A-144.

•Excalibur, the Raising of the Sword
dir. Dorian Cowland, Whaddon Boys Club Film Unit, 1982.

"Sword Play." Movie Maker 17 (Feb. 1983): 90-91.

•Parsifal
dir. Hans-Jürgen Syberberg, Gaumont-TMS Films, 1982 (V).

Reviews:

>L'Actualité 9 Feb. 1984: 89.
>
>L'Avant scène cinéma 291-292 (1-15 July 1982): 121; 360 (May 1987): 80.
>
>Cahiers du cinéma 338 (July-Aug. 1982): 51-55.
>
>Casablanca 19-20 (July-Aug. 1982): 56.
>
>Cinéma 283-284 (July-Aug. 1982): 95.
>
>Cinema Nuovo 32 (Aug.-Oct. 1983): 8-9.
>
>Cinématographe 79 (June 1982): 71-72.
>
>Ciné Revue 21 (20 May 1982): 44.
>
>Continental Film and Video Review 29 (Aug. 1982): 44-45; 30 (May 1983): 10-11.
>
>Ecran fantastique 25 (1982): 19-20.
>
>Film Journal 86 (18 Feb. 1983): 41.
>
>Films 3 (June 1983): 34.
>
>High Fidelity and Musical America 33 (June 1983): bet. 80 and 83 [18-20].
>
>Hollywood Reporter 11 Mar. 1983: 34.

Image et son 374 (July-Aug. 1982): 78-80.

Monthly Film Bulletin 50 (May 1983): 137-138.

New Republic 188 (14 Feb. 1983): 24-26.

New York 16 (31 Jan. 1983): 54-56.

New York Times 23 Jan. 1983: 1. 46; 11 Feb. 1984: 3. 8.

Newsweek 101 (31 Jan. 1983): 49.

Opera News 47 (12 Mar. 1983): 42-43.

Positif 259 (Sept. 1982): 65-66.

Séquences 115 (Jan. 1984): 40-42.

Time 121 (24 Jan. 1983): 84.

Time Out 657 (25-31 Mar. 1983): 12-13.

24 Images 19 (Winter 1983-1984): 13-14.

Variety 26 May 1982: 16; 9 Feb. 1983: 18.

Video Review 11 (Sept. 1990): 11.

Village Voice 22 Feb. 1983: 60; 3 Feb. 1987: 41-42.

Wagner News 22 (Apr.-May 1983): 11-15.

"Beim 'Parsifal' keine Konfrontationem." *Kino-Information* 8 (22 Apr. 1982): 5.

Bonnet, Jean-Claude, and Michel Celemenski. "Entretien avec Hans-Jürgen Syberberg." *Cinematographe* 78 (May 1982): 12-19.

Borie, Bertrand. "Entretien avec Hans-Jürgen Syberberg." *Ecran fantastique* 25 (1982): 20-21.

Dénes, Zoltai. "Opera és film." *Filmvilág* 29 (Jan. 1986): 2-5.

Ellero, Roberto, et al. "Conversazione con Hans-Jürgen Syberberg." *Cinema e cinema* 10 (Jan.-Mar. 1983): 66-69.

"A Golden Age of German Cinema." *Continental Film and Video Review* 29 (Sept. 1982): 40-42.

"Hans-Jürgen Syberberg on His New Film 'Parsifal.'" *Kino* 1 (Feb. 1982): 15.

Henahan, Donal. "The Wagner Enigma and Mystique Live On." *New York Times* 13 Feb. 1983: 2. 1, 25.

Holloway, Ronald. "Exhibition Formula for Syberberg's 'Parsifal' Follows 'Epic' Scenario." *Variety* 20 Oct. 1982: 33.

Larsen, Jan Kornum. "Tyskland—et Vintereventyr." *Kosmorama* 30 (Apr. 1984): 18-25.

A Bibliography on Arthurian Film

László, Földényi F. "Az üdvkeresés terhe." *Filmvilág* 29 (Jan. 1986): 13-16.

Lévi-Strauss, Claude. "Od Chrétiena de Troyesa do Richarda Wagnerja." *Ekran* 8. 6 (1983): 9-13.

Magill's Cinema Annual, 1983, ed. Frank N. Magill. Englewood Cliffs, N.J.: Salem, 1984.

Nash, Jay Robert, and Stanley Ralph Ross. *The Motion Picture Guide, 1927-1983*. 9 vols. Chicago: Cinebooks, 1985. 6: 2346.

Sainderichen, Guy-Patrick. "Voyage à Munich." *Cahiers du cinéma* 331 (Jan. 1982): 22-29.

Socci, Stefano. "*Parsifal*, film-opera dell'avvenire." *Filmcritica* 381-383 (Jan.-Feb. 1988): 7-13.

Stanbrook, Alan. "The Sight of Music." *Sight and Sound* 56 (Spring 1987): 132-135.

Syberberg, Hans-Jürgen. "Filmisches bei Richard Wagner." In *Richard Wagner: Mittler Zwischen Zeiten*, ed. Gerhard Heldt. Anif (Austria): Müller-Speiser, 1990.

_____. "'... nur der Kranke hält es aus.'" *Medium* 12 (Apr. 1982): 27-29.

_____. "'. . . ohne Neugier und Lust und Informationsredlichkeit.'" *Medium* 12(Sept.-Oct. 1982): 78-80.

_____. *Parsifal: Ein Filmessay*. Munich: Heyne, 1982.

_____. "'Vorführen braucht soviel Energie und Phantasie wie Machen.'" *Medium* 12 (Dec. 1982): 31-33.

_____. "'. . . wir sollen den anderen ins Gesicht spucken.'" *Medium* 12 (July 1982): 40-41.

Vollemanns, Kees, and Agnes Schreiner. "Hans-Jürgen Syberberg." *Skrien* 131 (Oct.-Nov. 1983): 4-8.

Vrdlovec, Zdenko. "Kaj zmore glas." *Ekran* 8. 6 (1983): 4-8.

•*Sword of the Valiant / The Legend of Gawain and the Green Knight* dir. Stephen Weeks, Cannon, 1983 (V).

Reviews:

Monthly Film Bulletin 52 (May 1985): 164-165.

Philadelphia Inquirer 3 Dec. 1984: 8-E.

Variety 5 Dec. 1984: 17.

Western Mail 27 July 1985: 19.

Jackson, Paul. "Please Don't Scratch the Walls." *Western Mail* 4 Dec. 1982: 7.

Munn, Michael. *Trevor Howard: The Man and His Films.* London: Robson, 1989.

●*The Morte d'Arthur*
dir. Gillian Lynne, BBC2, 1984.

Reviews:

Daily Express 7 May 1984: 19.

Daily Telegraph 7 May 1984: 13.

Guardian 7 May 1984: 12.

Listener 111 (3 May 1984): 31.

New Statesman 11 May 1984: 30-31.

Standard 27 Apr. 1984: 21.

Sunday Telegraph 13 May 1984: 15.

Sunday Times (London) 13 May 1984: 54.

Television Today 21 Apr. 1984: 19.

Times (London) 7 May 1984: 15.

Times Educational Supplement 11 May 1984: 25.

Times Literary Supplement 11 May 1984: 25; 18 May 1984: 552.

Totten, Eileen. "The Knight's Tale." *Radio Times* 5-11 May 1984: 8-9.

●*Novye Priklucheniia Janke pri Dvore Korola Artura (The New Adventures of a Connecticut Yankee in King Arthur's Court)*
dir. Viktor Gres, Dovzhenko Studios, 1987.

Cowie, Peter, ed. *Variety International Film Guide 1990.* Hollywood, Calif.: Samuel French, 1989.

The Motion Picture Guide: 1989 Annual (The Films of 1988). Evanston: Cinebooks, 1989.

"On the Spot Report." *Soviet Film* 6 (1987): 18-19.

●*I Skugga Hrafnsina / In the Shadow of the Raven / The Shadow of the Raven*
dir. Hrafn Gunnlaugsson, Sandrews, 1988.

Reviews:

Chaplin 219 (Dec. 1988): 308-309.

Hollywood Reporter 9 Oct. 1990: 11, 151.

San Francisco Chronicle 31 Aug. 1990: E 7.

San Francisco Examiner 31 Aug. 1990: C 7.

Variety 19 Oct. 1988: 249.

Cowie, Peter, ed. *Variety International Film Guide 1989*. New York: Zoetrope, 1988.

———. *Variety International Film Guide 1990*. Hollywood, Calif.: Samuel French, 1989.

The Motion Picture Guide: 1989 Annual (The Films of 1988). Evanston: Cinebooks, 1989.

●*A Connecticut Yankee in King Arthur's Court*
dir. Mel Damski, NBC, 1989.

Reviews:

Baltimore Sun 18 Dec. 1989 (located in Newsbank, Review of the Arts, Film and Television Microform 17 [Jan.-Apr. 1990]; FTV 3: C2, fiche).

Boston Herald 18 Dec. 1989 (located in Newsbank, Review of the Arts, Film and Television Microform 17 [Jan.-Apr.1990]; FTV 3: C1, fiche).

New York Post 18 Dec. 1989 (located in Newsbank, Review of the Arts, Film and Television Microform 17 [Jan.-Apr. 1990]; FTV 3: C3, fiche).

New York Times 18 Dec. 1989: 2. 4.

Variety 20 Dec. 1989: 48.

Knutzen, Eirik. "Michael Gross in a Royal Role." *Philadelphia Inquirer TV Week* 17-23 Dec. 1989: 4-5.

●*Indiana Jones and the Last Crusade*
dir. Steven Spielberg, Paramount, 1989 (V).

Reviews:

L'Actualité 14 Aug. 1989: 69.

America 160 (17-24 June 1989): 591.

American Spectator 22 (Aug. 1989): 73.

Boston Globe 24 May 1989: 53, 59.

Chatelaine 30 (Aug. 1989): 25.

Christian Science Monitor 9 June 1989: 15; 13 June 1989: 11.

City Limits 403 (22-29 June 1989): 19.

Commonweal 116 (14 July 1989): 403-404.

Cosmopolitan 207 (Aug. 1989): 73.

Film Comment 25 (July-Aug. 1989): 9-11.

Films and Filming 417 (July 1989): 40-41.

Hollywood Reporter 19 May 1989: 4, 13.

Insight 5 (5 June 1989): 57.

Maclean's 5 June 1989: 56.

Monthly Film Bulletin 56 (July 1989): 198-200.

Nation 248 (19 June 1989): 862.

National Catholic Reporter 25 Aug. 1989: 13.

New Republic 200 (19 June 1989): 28-29.

New Statesman and Society 2 (30 June 1989): 15.

New York 22 (5 June 1989): 58-59.

New York Daily News 24 May 1989: 37.

New York Native 29 May 1989: 25.

New York Post 24 May 1989: 31.

New York Press 9 June 1989: 13.

New York Times 24 May 1989: 3. 15; 14 Jan. 1990: 2. 32.

New Yorker 65 (12 June 1989): 103-105.

Newsday 24 May 1989: 2. 2; 1 June 1989: 2. 13.

Newsweek 113 (29 May 1989): 69.

People 31 (5 June 1989): 13.

Rolling Stone 15 June 1989: 31.

St. Anthony Messenger 97 (July 1989): 6.

Screen International 3-9 June 1989: 21.

Starburst 11 (July 1989): 24-25.

Time 133 (29 May 1989): 82-84.

Time Out 983 (21-28 June 1989): 34.

Variety 24 May 1989: 25; 31 May 1939: 27.

Video Review 10 (Mar. 1990): 51.

Village Voice 30 May 1989: 57.

Washington Post 24 May 1989: D 1; 26 May 1989: WW 41.

Briggs, Nicholas. "Licensed to Crusade." *Starburst* 130 (June 1989): 8-11.

_____. "Producing the Hero." *Starburst* 131 (July 1989): 17-19.

Canby, Vincent. "Spielberg's Elixir Shows Signs of Mature Magic." *New York Times* 16 June 1989: 2. 15-16.

Eisenberg, Adam. "Father, Son and the Holy Grail." *Cinéflex* 40 (Nov. 1989): 46-67.

"Great New Indy Jones Special Effects." *Popular Mechanics* 166 (July 1989): 18.

Griffin, Nancy. "Manchild in the Promised Land." *Premiere* 2 (June 1989): 86-94.

Heuring, David. "Effects Maestros Put Buckle in Indy's Swash." *American Cinematographer* 70 (Dec. 1989): 66-74.

_____. "Indiana Jones and the Last Crusade." *American Cinematographer* 70 (June 1989): 57-66.

Indiana Jones and the Last Crusade. [Hollywood, Calif.]: Paramount, 1989. [Production handbook.]

James, Caryn. "It's a New Age for Father-Son Relationships." *New York Times* 9 July 1989: 2. 11-12.

MacGregor, Ron. *Indiana Jones and the Last Crusade*. New York: Penguin, 1989. [Novelization.]

The Motion Picture Guide: 1990 Annual (The Films of 1989). Evanston: Cinebooks, 1990.

Royal, Susan. "*Indiana Jones and the Last Crusade*: An Interview with Harrison Ford." *American Premiere* 9 (June-July 1989): 12-19.

White, Armond. "Keeping Up with the Joneses." *Film Quarterly* 24 (July-Aug. 1989): 9-11.

Woodward, Richard B. "Meanwhile, Back at the Ranch." *New York Times* 21 May 1989: 2. 1, 16.

•*Isolde*
dir. Jytte Rex, Camera Film, 1989.

Review:

Variety 29 Mar. 1989: 17.

Appendix: An Alphabetical Filmography

Kevin J. Harty

The Adventures of Sir Galahad, dir. Spencer Bennett, Columbia, 1949.

Arthur the King, dir. Clive Donner, CBS, 1982.

The Black Knight, dir. Tay Garnett, Columbia, 1954.

Camelot, dir. Joshua Logan, Warner Brothers, 1967.

A Connecticut Yankee, dir. David Butler, Fox, 1931.

A Connecticut Yankee at King Arthur's Court, dir. Emmett J. Flynn, Fox, 1920.

A Connecticut Yankee in King Arthur's Court, dir. Tay Garnett, Paramount, 1949.

A Connecticut Yankee in King Arthur's Court, dir. Mel Damski, NBC, 1989.

L'Éternel Retour, dir. Jean Delannoy, Discina International, 1943.

The Eternal Return see *L'Éternel Retour*.

Excalibur, dir. John Boorman, Orion, 1981.

Excalibur, the Raising of the Sword, dir. Dorian Cowland, Whaddon Boys Club Film Unit, 1982.

Feuer und Schwert, dir. Veith von Fürstenberg, Genée und von Fürstenberg Filmproduktion, 1981.

Gawain and the Green Knight, dir. Stephen Weeks, United Artists, 1973.

I Skugga Hrafnsina, dir. Hrafn Gunnlaugsson, Sandrews, 1988.

In the Shadow of the Raven see *I Skugga Hrafnsina*.

Indiana Jones and the Last Crusade, dir. Steven Spielberg, Paramount, 1989.

Isolde, dir. Jytte Rex, Camera Film, 1989.

King Arthur and the Siege of the Saxons see *The Siege of the Saxons*.

King Arthur, or The Knights of the Round Table, dir. ?, New Agency, 1910.

King Arthur, the Young Warlord, dir. Sidney Hayers, Patrick Jackson, and Patrick Sasdy, Heritage Enterprises, 1975.

King Arthur Was a Gentleman, dir. Marcel Varnel, Gainsborough Films, 1942.

Knightriders, dir. George Romero, United Film, 1981.

Knights of the Round Table, dir. Richard Thorpe, MGM, 1953.

Knights of the Square Table, or The Grail, dir. Alan Crosland, Edison, 1917.

Lancelot and Guinevere see *The Sword of Lancelot*.

Lancelot du Lac, dir. Robert Bresson, Mara Films, 1974.

Launcelot and Elaine, dir. Charles Kent, Vitagraph, 1909.

The Legend of King Arthur, dir. Rodney Bennett, BBC, Time-Life Television, and the Australian Broadcasting Commission, 1979.

The Legend of Gawain and the Green Knight see *The Sword of the Valiant*.

Die Legende von Tristan und Isolde see *Feuer und Schwert*.

Love Eternal see *L'Éternel Retour*.

Lovespell see *Tristan and Isolt*.

Monty Python and the Holy Grail, dir. Terry Gilliam and Terry Jones, Python Pictures, 1975.

The Morte d'Arthur, dir. Gillian Lynne, BBC2, 1984.

The New Adventures of a Connecticut Yankee at King Arthur's Court see *Novye Prikluchenia Janke pri Dvore Korola Artura*.

Novye Prikluchenia Janke pri Dvore Korola Artura, dir. Viktor Gres, Dovzhenko Studios, 1987.

Parsifal, dir. Edwin J. Porter, Edison, 1904.

Parsifal, dir. Mario Caserini, Ambrosio, 1912.

Parsifal, dir. Daniel Mangrane, CineEspañol-Regents, 1953.

Parsifal, dir. Hans-Jürgen Syberberg, Gaumont-TMS Films, 1982.

Parzival, dir. Richard Blank, West Deutsche Rundfunk, 1980.

Perceval le Gallois, dir. Eric Rohmer, Gaumont-New Yorker Films, 1978.

Prince Valiant, dir. Henry Hathaway, Twentieth Century-Fox, 1954.

The Quest of the Holy Grail, dir. D. W. Griffith, uncompleted project, 1916.

The Shadow of the Raven see *I Skugga Hrafnsina*.

The Siege of the Saxons, dir. Nathan Juran, BLC-Columbia, 1963.

The Spaceman and King Arthur see *The Unidentified Flying Oddball*.

The Sword in the Stone, dir. Wolfgang Reitherman, Disney, 1963.

The Sword of Lancelot, dir. Cornel Wilde, Emblem, 1963.

Sword of the Valiant, dir. Stephen Weeks, Cannon, 1983.

To Parsifal, dir. Bruce Baillie, Canyon Cinema Co-op, 1963.

Tristan and Isolt, Tom Donovan, Clar Productions, 1979.

Tristan et Iseult, dir. Yvan Lagrange, Film du Soir, 1972.

Tristan et Yseult, dir. Albert Capellani, S.C.A.G.L.-Pathé, 1909.

Tristan et Yseut, dir. Maurice Mariaud, Nalpas, 1920.

Tristan und Isolde see *Feuer und Schwert*.

The Unidentified Flying Oddball, dir. Russ Mayberry, Disney, 1979.

INDEX

Abbey, Edwin Austin 6
Achmann, Werner 166-167
Addie, Robert 139, 195
The Adventures of Sir Galahad 9-10, 211
Antolek, Vladimir 46
Arthur the King 21, 237
Askey, Arthur 9
Augustine 160

Baden-Powell, Robert 6
Baillie, Bruce 12-13
Barton, John 21
Beardsley, Aubrey 183
Ben Hur 181
Bendix, William 108
Bergman, Ingrid 197-198
Bernard, Patrick 46
Béroul 132
Black Prince 197
The Black Knight xv, 10, 12, 29-39, 197-199, 214-215

Blank, Richard xvii, 19, 157-160, 166
Book of Kells 170
The Book of Merlyn 76
Boorman, John xvii, 20, 44-45, 63-64, 114, 121-133, 142, 146-155
Boorman, Katrina 138
Bresson, Robert xv-xvi, 16-17, 41-56
Bridges, Jeff xviii
Bruns, George 71
Buckley, Keith 139
Burton, Richard 19, 170
Butler, David 77
Byrne, Gabriel 138

Camelot (1967 film) xvi, xvii, 15, 29, 74-81, 100, 147-148, 155, 185-189, 197, 219-221
Camelot (musical) xvi, 15, 25, 74
Canning, Victor 135
Capellani, Albert 4

Carmina Burana 142
Carroll, Lewis 198
Caserini, Mario 4
Cassenti, Frank 42, 53
Caxton, William 33, 135
Chaplin, Charlie 7
Chapman, Graham 86, 90, 189
La Chanson de Roland 53
Le Chevalier à L'Épée 59
Chrétien de Troyes 3, 18, 29, 41-44, 49-53, 58, 62, 93, 100-101, 121, 124, 132, 137, 157, 190
Churchill, Winston 36, 112
Clay, Nicholas 126, 170
Cleese, John 189
Clemens, Samuel Langhorne see Mark Twain
Clever, Edith 161-162
Cocteau, Jean 8, 169-179
Condimas, Laura Duke 46
A Connecticut Yankee (1931 film) 7, 107-108, 207
A Connecticut Yankee at King Arthur's Court (1920 film) 6-7, 106-107, 206-207
A Connecticut Yankee in King Arthur's Court (1949 film) 8-10, 29, 108-110, 211-213
A Connecticut Yankee in King Arthur's Court (1989 film) xvii, 22, 94, 98-99, 103, 112-113, 199, 241
A Connecticut Yankee in King Arthur's Court (novel) xvii, 6, 7, 22, 29, 38, 93, 94, 98, 103, 105-113

The Connecticut Yankee in King Arthur's Court (1978 film) 118
Connery, Sean 21, 64
Le Conte du Graal 3, 18, 41, 43, 50-51, 53, 101, 157
Contes Moraux 50-51
Coppel, Alec 31, 35
Cowland, Dorian 21
Crosby, Bing 8-9, 29, 108-111
Crosland, Alan 21
Cuchulain 170
A Curious Dream 105

Dall, Evelyn 9
Damski, Mel 94
Dante 87
Dawn of the Dead 114
Deal, Babs 132
Delannoy, Jean 8, 42, 169-179
de la Tour, Bernard 42, 53
Dombasie, Arielle 47
Donner, Clive 21
Donovan, Tom 19, 169-179
Dugan, Dennis 97
Du Guesclin 42, 53

Edison, Thomas vii, xviii, 3-4, 6
Eliot, T. S. 12-13, 132, 137
L'Éternel Retour xviii, 8, 42, 169-179, 209-211

Cinema Arthuriana

The Eternal Return see *L'Éternel Retour*

Excalibur xvi-xvii, 20, 44-45, 63-64, 114, 121-142, 146-155, 191-195, 231- 235

Excalibur, the Raising of the Sword 21, 237

Fairbanks, Douglas 118

Fassbinder, Rainer Werner 162

Feuer und Schwert xviii, 19, 169-179, 235

The Fisher King xviii

Fleming, Rhonda 108, 111

Flynn, Emmett J. 6-7, 107

Foster, Hal 12, 183

Franklin, Benjamin 31

Franzreb, John 197

Freud, Sigmund 154

Gardner, Eva 11

Garnett, Tay xv, 8-9, 29-39, 108-110

Gawain and the Green Knight xvi, 16, 61-62, 222

Geoffrey of Monmouth 5-7, 58, 121, 145, 198

Gilliam, Terry xviii, 62, 86, 93

Goldberg, Rainer 166

The Grail: A Novel 132

Green, Nigel 61

Gres, Viktor 21, 118

Griffith, D. W. 6

Gross, Michael 22, 112

Gunnlaugsson, Hrafn 26

Hardwicke, Sir Cedric 108

Harris, Ed 116

Harris, Richard 74, 79, 187

Hathaway, Henry 12, 61

Haugland, Aage 166

Hayden, Sterling 61

Hayers, Sidney 17

Head, Murray 61-62

Henry V 18, 181, 195-196

Henry VIII 196

Herz, Joachim 166

Hitler: Ein Film aus Deutschland 161, 167

Howard, Trevor 21, 65

Hunbaut 59

Idle, Eric 189

I Skugga Hrafnsina 26, 240-241

Idylls of the King 5-6, 74, 121, 136-142, 145-146

In the Shadow of the Raven see *I Skugga Hrafnsina*

Indiana Jones and the Last Crusade 22, 241-243

Ingersoll, Amy 116

Invasion of the Body Snatchers xv, 38

Isolde 22-23, 243

Ivanhoe 114, 197

Jackson, Patrick 17
Jameson, Frederic 85-86, 87
Jannson, Kim 23
Joan of Arc 196, 198
Jones, Terry 17, 62, 93, 188-189, 196
Jordan, Armin 161-162
Juran, Nathan 14

Kent, Charles 5
The Kid 7, 107, 118
King Arthur and the Siege of the Saxons see *The Siege of the Saxons*
King Arthur, or The Knights of the Round Table 6, 205
King Arthur, the Young Warlord 17, 225
King Arthur Was a Gentleman 7-9, 209
Knightriders xvii, 20-21, 105, 114-117, 119, 132, 147-148, 235-236
Knights of the Round Table xv, xvii, 10-11, 30, 133, 146-147, 213- 214
Knights of the Square Table, or The Grail 6, 206
Krick, Karin 165
Kunkel, Wolfram 159
Kutter, Michael 165

Ladd, Alan 31, 33, 34
Lagrange, Yvan 15-16, 169-179
Lancelot (poem) 58

Lancelot and Guinevere see *The Sword of Lancelot*
Lancelot du Lac xv-xvi, 16-17, 41-56, 222-225
Laubethal, Sander Anne 198
Launcelot and Elaine (1909 film) 5-6, 205
Lawhead, Stephen R. 187, 198
Layamon 58, 145-146
The Legend of King Arthur 18, 190, 230
The Legend of Gawain and the Green Knight see *The Sword of the Valiant*
Die Legende von Tristan und Isolde see *Feuer und Schwert*
Leigh, Janet 61
Lerner, Alan Jay 74, 77, 100, 148, 155
Levignac, Sylvain 47
Lloyd, Robert 166
Loewe, Frederick 74, 100, 148, 155
Logan, Joshua 15, 185
The Lord of the Rings 141
Love Eternal see *L'Éternel Retour*
Lovespell see *Tristan and Isolt*
Lowell, James Russell 38
Loy, Myrna 7, 107-109
Luchini, Fabrice 43-44, 47
Ludwig II: Requiem für einen jungfraülichen König 161
Lunghi, Cherie 126, 139

Mabinogi 154

Madame Mim 15, 73, 75, 94- 95
Malamud, Bernard 22-24, 132
Malory, Sir Thomas xvii, 10, 14, 20, 21, 30, 33, 37, 44-45, 63, 113, 121-135, 150, 181
Mangrane, Daniel 25
Mantle, Burns 7, 107, 118
Marais, Jean 172, 177
Mariaud, Maurice 4
Martin 114, 118
Marx, Karl 36, 85-86, 162-163
Mayberry, Russ 94
Medina, Patricia 31
Mim see Madame Mim
Minton, Yvonne 166
Mirren, Helen 137, 152
Mohr, Wolfgang 159
Monty Python and the Holy Grail xvi, xvii, 17, 62-63, 83-94, 99-104, 147 188-189, 225-227
Mort Artu 16, 41, 43, 51, 53, 67
Morte Arthure 59
Morte Darthur xvii, 10, 14, 20, 21, 33, 44, 63, 113, 121-133, 135, 150, 181
The Morte d'Arthur (1984 BBC production) 21, 240
La Mule sans Frein 58-59
Mulgrew, Kate 170
My Fair Lady 25
My Night at Maud's 44
Myers, Harry 106

The Natural 22-24, 132

Neeson, Liam 63
Nero, Franco 15, 74, 76, 79
The New Adventures of a Connecticut Yankee at King Arthur's Court see *Novye Prikluchenia Janke pri Dvore Korola Artura.*
Night of the Living Dead 114
Novye Prikluchenia Janke pri Dvore Korola Artura 21-22, 118, 240

O'Keeffe, Miles 64-65
Olivier, Laurence 18, 195-196
The Once and Future King 14-15, 29, 71-72, 74, 115, 17, 145-148, 187
Orff, Carl 142
O'Sullivan, Maureen 7, 107

Palin, Michael 90
Pallenberg, Rospo 122
Parsifal (1904 film) vii, xviii, 3-5, 204-205
Parsifal (1912 film) 4, 205
Parsifal (1953 film) 25, 213
Parsifal (1982 film) xviii, 20, 157, 160-167, 237-239
Parzival (1980 film) xviii, 19, 157-160, 166, 231
Parzival (poem) see Wolfram von Eschenbach
Patterson, Lee 88
Peet, Bill 72

Perceval le Gallois xv-xvi, 17-18, 29, 41-56, 159, 188-190, 196, 227-229

Piers Plowman 92

Preser, Antonia 170

Porter, Edwin J. 3-5

Powys, John Cowper 132

Prince Valiant xv, 10, 61, 63, 183-184, 215-216

Pulliam, Keshia Knight 22, 98, 112, 199

Pyle, Howard 32, 183, 198

La Queste du Saint Graal 100, 121

The Quest of the Holy Grail 6, 206

Rackham, Arthur 136, 142, 183, 199

Rank, Otto 154

Rauf Coilyear 30

Redgrave, Vanessa 74, 76, 79

Reitherman, Wolfgang 93

Rex, Jytte 22-23

Richard III 181

Robert de Boron 3, 133, 157, 164

Rogers, Will 7, 107-109

Rohmer, Eric xv-xvi, 17-18, 29, 41-56, 159, 188-190, 196

Romero, George xvii, 20-21, 105, 114-117, 132, 147-148

Sasdy, Patrick 17

Savini, Tom 149

Schöne, Wolfgang 166

Schuchardt, Eva 159

Schygulla, Hanna 162

Scott, Sir Walter 7

The Seven Faces of Dr. Lao 22

The Shadow of the Raven see *I Skugga Hrafnsina*

The Siege of the Saxons 14, 217

Simon, Luc 46

Sir Gawain and the Carl of Carlisle 60

Sir Gawain and Green Knight 16, 21, 29, 60-61, 64, 145, 151-153

Society for Creative Anachronism 114

Solange, Madelaine 172, 177

The Spaceman and King Arthur see *The Unidentified Flying Oddball*

Spielberg, Steven 22

Sutcliff, Rosemary 135, 198

The Sword in the Stone xvi-xvii, 14-15, 71-74, 93-96, 103, 217-218

The Sword of Lancelot 13-15, 29, 218-219

Sword of the Valiant xvi, 16, 21, 29, 64-66, 239-240

Syberberg, Hans-Jürgen xviii, 20, 157, 160-167

Taylor, Robert 11, 114

Tennyson, Alfred Lord 5-6, 74, 121, 136-142, 145-146

Terry, Nigel 126, 137

Theby, Rosemary 106
Thorpe, Richard 146-147
Tolkien, J. R. R. 141
To Parsifal 12-13, 219
Treece, Henry 135
Tristan and Isolt (1979 film) xviii, 19, 169-179, 230
Tristan et Iseult (1972 film) xviii, 15-16, 169-179, 221
Tristan et Yseut (1920 film) 4, 207
Tristan et Yseult (1909 film) 4, 205
Tristan und Isolde (film) see *Feuer und Schwert*
Tristan und Isolde (opera) 124, 131
Truscott, John 185
Tschammer, Hans 166
Twain, Mark xvii, 6-10, 18, 22, 38, 93, 110-112

The Unidentified Flying Oddball xvii, 18, 93-94, 96, 103, 230-231

Varnel, Marcel 7-8
Vieth, Pia 23
The Vision of Sir Launfal 38
von Fürstenberg, Veith 19, 169-179

Wace 58, 145-146
Wagner, Richard vii, xviii, 3-4, 13, 20 131, 137, 141-142, 155, 157-167

Wagner, Robert 61, 124, 137
Wagner, Winifred 161, 166
Wallace, Jean 13
Waltz, Christopher 170
The Waste Land 12-13, 132
Wauthion, Claire 172
Weeks, Stephen 16, 21, 61-62, 64, 66
Weston, Jessie 20, 61, 63, 122-23, 132, 137
White, Sheila 97
White, T. H. xvi, 14-15, 25, 29, 71-72, 74, 93, 115-117, 132, 145-148, 187
Wilde, Cornel 13-15, 114
Wilder, James 6
Williams, Robin xviii
Williamson, Nicol 130, 137, 152
Winchester Manuscript 33
Winifred Wagner und die Geschicte des Hauses Wanfried von 1914-1975 161, 167
Wolfram von Eschenbach xviii, 19 132, 137, 157-160, 163
Wyeth, N. C. 183

Yvain 62, 64-65

Zanuck, Daryl 12
Zardoz 132